Introducing
PC-DOS and MS-DOS

W9-CYS-025

Introducing
PC-DOS and MS-DOS

A Guide for Beginning and Advanced Techniques

Thomas Sheldon

Nov. 25, 1985

Villa Park, IL.

Clifton J. Ve_____

MCGRAW-HILL BOOK COMPANY

New York   St. Louis   San Francisco   Auckland
Bogotá   Hamburg   Johannesburg   London
Madrid   Mexico   Montreal   New Delhi
Panama   Paris   São Paulo   Singapore
Sydney   Tokyo   Toronto

Library of Congress Cataloging in Publication Data

Sheldon, Thomas.
  Introducing PC-DOS and MS-DOS.

  Includes index.
  1. PC-DOS (Computer operating system)   2. MS-DOS
(Computer operating system)   I. Title.
QA76.6.S53   1985   011.64′2   84-28924
ISBN 0-07-056559-7

1234567890   DOC/DOC   898765

ISBN 0-07-056559-7

*The editors for this book were Stephen Guty and Nancy Young, the designer
was Naomi Auerbach, and the production supervisor was Thomas G. Kowalczyk.
It was set in Century Schoolbook by University Graphics, Inc.
Printed and bound by R. R. Donnelley & Sons Company.*

DEDICATION

*I dedicate this book to my wife, Alexandra, who saw me through
and kept asking how many words I had written each day.
I would like to thank Bill Alvernaz for having
similar objectives, and for reminding my wife to keep reminding me
about the number of words.
Last, but not least, I thank Gordon and Julia Held, who
unsuspectingly set this book in motion. Finer people would
be hard to find.*

Contents

Part 2   Advanced User's Guide   133

Introduction

Man is a tool using animal . . .
Without tools he is nothing,
with tools he is all.

These words, spoken by Thomas Carlyle, apply well to the subject of computers. The computer can be considered a tool, and like other tools it must have features that allow people to use it: hammers have handles, telephones have receivers and speakers, and computers have operating systems. Operating systems provide the link between human beings and the computer, giving them the means to turn a pile of metal, plastic, and silicon into one of the most powerful tools yet devised.

This book is about the IBM Personal Computer Disk Operating System, or PC-DOS as it is more commonly referred to, and is also about MS-DOS, the Microsoft version of PC-DOS that runs on most IBM compatible microcomputers. Throughout this book we will refer to both operating systems as simply DOS, and we will often refer to your computer as "the PC."

Who This Book Is For

The level or stage you are at with your computer doesn't matter as far as this book is concerned. You will find many things of interest and value throughout the book whether you are a beginner or an advanced user. If you are a beginner, you should start at the beginning of the tutorial and work your way through each chapter. If you've had your computer for a while and would like to know more about DOS, you can simply skim through the first few chapters and pick up at the level at which your expertise begins.

Part 2 of this book is for those who have been through the tutorial and for advanced users. We introduce many DOS routines and techniques that you can use to perform useful tasks such as data management and word processing. These routines may eliminate the need to buy prepackaged software. Part 2 is also filled with useful tips, techniques, and tricks that we have learned through many hours of using DOS and training other people on it. We pass them on to you here.

Because of the advanced nature of the second half of the book, we recommend that you proceed through the tutorial one chapter at a time if you are a new user. Each chapter is designed to build upon the others, and you will learn by working your way through each step and performing the example exercises. The examples in this book apply to normal day-to-day operations you will be performing with DOS.

We will build files that you will use every day such as the telephone list in Chap. 10 or the data management routines in Chaps. 26 and 27. We will also show you how to organize your system with help screens and menus that guide you when you're having trouble or when you need to see how a command is entered. Owners of fixed-disk systems will appreciate the chapters covering fixed-disk organization.

This book is more than a tutorial. As you progress through the chapters, you will be building a working environment and a collection of software "tools" that you can use every day. In the last chapter we will bring all the techniques and tools together by building a desktop workstation diskette.

What Is an Operating System?

PC-DOS is a set of programs supplied on a disk that are ready to run on your PC. When you place the DOS disk in the disk drive and turn the computer on, the operating system is automatically loaded into your computer's memory. From there, you can use any of the programs and utilities on the disk.

For the most part, DOS is invisible. It does most of its work inside the machine, acting as a foreman, directing the flow of work to be done, and controlling the way your computer acts. DOS could be considered the "personality" of your computer and is used to establish a working environment within the computer when it is loaded. After setting up this environment, the operating system waits for a command from you, the operator. At first, you may not consider DOS's personality to be so friendly, but after working with it for a while and learning its peculiarities, you will soon realize its powerful features and ease of use.

Operating systems in general share many features. Some of the most important ones are the management of files on diskettes and the acceptance of commands from the user. As commands are entered, it is the job of the operating system to interpret and execute them. Operating systems also provide a standard link that allows software developers to easily write programs that will run on your computer. These programs include prewritten applications such as word processors, electronic spreadsheets, data managements systems, and games. The operating system gives these programs a standard way of interacting internally with the computer and externally with devices such as printers, disk drives, keyboards, and video monitors.

DOS consists of a set of tools and utilities that exist as programs on the DOS disk. With these utilities you can get started with your computer right away without buying other software. Many of these utilities are devoted to the handling of diskette files, which can be compared to the paper files used in offices everywhere. You can write these files on the screen with the keyboard and save them on a disk for later use. You can read these files, search through them, sort them, and print them at any time with DOS. DOS also contains a set of tools that is used to prepare diskettes for use on your computer and another set that is used to handle devices attached to your computer, such as printers and plotters.

History

The different versions of DOS help illustrate its growth and expansion. PC-DOS was first introduced with the announcement of IBM's Personal Computer in 1981 and was known as PC-DOS version 1.0. This version was almost immediately updated to version 1.1.

In March of 1983, IBM announced its XT Personal Computer. This computer contained a 10 megabyte hard-disk storage unit and other hardware improvements over the original PC. At the same time IBM introduced IBM PC-DOS 2.0, an enhanced version of its PC operating system. This new operating system was designed for the IBM XT and was capable of supporting a hard-disk storage device. It also provided additional commands and support that are normally found on more advanced operating systems, such as the UNIX system.

In August of 1984, IBM announced DOS 3.0 and 3.1, operating systems designed to run on their new line of Advanced Technology (AT) machines. These newest operating systems are very similar to their predecessors (DOS 2.0 and 2.1) but have the ability to address higher amounts of memory and storage and provide the means to tie many IBM computers together in a network. Computers linked into networks can share files and communicate with one another over interconnected cables.

In this book we refer to versions 2.0 and 2.1 as DOS-2 and versions 3.0 and 3.1 as DOS-3.

Which Version Should You Have?

If you own versions 1.0 or 1.1, we recommend that you upgrade to one of the newer version of DOS. You may want to refer to some of the chapters in this book, such as the one on batch files, to see the capabilities of DOS-2 and DOS-3 that are not available in earlier versions.

Why switch? DOS-2 and DOS-3 contain many new features, an important one being their ability to store more information on diskettes than previous versions. The new DOSs also provide advanced batch processing features and have special files that allow you to easily control the start-up configuration of your system and add special hardware devices. Many features of more sophisticated operating systems such as UNIX have been implemented in the latest versions. These features include tree-structured filing, input/output redirection, filters, and piping.

DOS Documentation

DOS is extensively documented in the IBM PC-DOS manual and in other manuals, but it may not be immediately comprehensible to beginning users because these manuals are meant for reference. The operator's manual of a car does not tell you how to drive. It shows you the location of the oil stick and how to control the windshield wipers, but driving instructions are left to a qualified instructor. The instructor guides the student through real-life driving situations, thereby increasing the student's skills. We have written this book as a hands-on tutorial so that you can develop your DOS skills. Exercises are given throughout the book that are directly related to your day-to-day use of the computer.

You should be familiar with some aspects of your computer before starting this book. We will not discuss disk handling and printer paper loading; your computer operator's manual should cover these topics. We assume that the computer is already set up and ready to go.

You should browse through the introductory sections of your DOS manual before starting this book. You'll find an explanation of diskettes and how to handle them and an explanation of how to start your system. Some systems come with a diskette that will introduce you to the keyboard, providing an excellent way to get started.

Most DOS manuals supplied with systems are extensive and will serve as excellent reference tools in the future. You should, however, avoid certain sections as a beginner. The sections on DEBUG and LINK can be skipped, as well as the sections on drivers, interrupts, and control blocks. These chapters are meant for programmers. Owners of fixed-disk systems such as the IBM XT should refer to the chapters entitled "Fixed Disk" and "Directories" in their operator's guides.

How to Read This Book

Throughout this book, we will be working with practice diskettes, so you won't have to worry about making mistakes and ruining files. After the tutorial, you can erase the diskettes and use them for other tasks. Making mistakes on a computer is sometimes useful because under certain conditions the computer will tell you what you did wrong. It is better to discover how mistakes are made now instead of later when you are working with valuable data or under the pressure of deadlines.

Chapter 1 starts the tutorial. The first thing you will need to do before beginning an actual hands-on session is to prepare a working diskette. You will find this information in Chap. 2. Remember to follow the tutorial in sequence so that you can take full advantage of the way this book is structured.

Part

1

Tutorial

Equipment and Software Overview

Welcome to the world of IBM PC and Microsoft DOS (MS-DOS). DOS contains many utilities and tools that allow you to start performing useful tasks on your computer right away. You're probably anxious to get started, so in this chapter we'll have you turn the system on and begin the tutorial. We will also describe some important hardware and software concepts.

The first thing to do is locate the DOS disk. Whether you are using version 2.0, 2.1, 3.0, or 3.1 does not make any difference at this point. In this book we will refer to all versions of DOS 2.0 (including 2.0, 2.1, 2.15, etc.) as DOS-2 and all version of DOS 3.0 (including 3.0, 3.1, etc.) as DOS-3. Your IBM DOS manual comes with two diskettes, one of which is the DOS program disk; the other is the DOS supplemental programs disk. The supplemental programs disk is not needed here, so you can keep it stored in the DOS manual.

Pull out the DOS disk and place it in the main floppy drive. This is the drive on the left on all IBM PC and PC/XT systems and is the drive that is activated when you turn your computer on. If you own an IBM AT, the main floppy drive is the drive on top; if you own an IBM PC*jr* or a single-drive PC, this main drive is the only floppy drive you have.

This main drive is known as "drive A." If you own a system that has two floppy drives, the second drive is known as "drive B"; if you own a fixed-disk system such as the IBM XT or AT, the fixed disk is referred to as "drive C" in most cases. The floppy disk and fixed disk in your computer, as well as the keyboard, screen, and printer, are all referred to as "devices" by DOS, and each device is given a name so you can easily refer to it when telling DOS what to do. Refer to the section, "DOS Hardware

Devices," which is toward the end of this chapter, for a more complete description of the names given to each device. Referring to the devices on your system by name is a convenient way of telling DOS where to move or get information.

Starting the System

The DOS disk supplied with your DOS manual is ready to use. All you have to do is place the disk in the start-up drive, label side up, and turn the system on. This will be one of the few times you actually use the original DOS disk that was supplied with your DOS manual. In the next chapter you will see how to make a backup "working copy" of this disk for everyday use. After you flick the switch on, the system will go through a diagnostics procedure in which it checks its internal components and memory. Eventually, you will be prompted to enter the date and the time and will then see the DOS system prompt, which will be described later.

Starting a computer is often called "booting the system." "Booting" is a word that goes back to the early days of computing and now refers to the process of turning your computer on and starting the operating system. To start DOS, you must have a "bootable" disk in the start-up floppy drive—one which contains the DOS system files. If you attempt to start your system with a disk that is not bootable, a "Non-system disk" error message will appear on the screen. The original DOS disk supplied with your system is a bootable DOS disk that can be used to start your system. A blank disk that you pull from a new box of diskettes is not a bootable disk and will not start your computer properly. All new diskettes must be prepared to run on your computer, a procedure we will discuss later. In the next chapter, you'll create a bootable DOS disk from the original DOS disk and use it for the exercises in this book.

The DOS Command Level

If you see the DOS prompt A> on the screen followed by the blinking cursor, you'll know that you have successfully booted your system and are at the DOS command level. At this level, DOS is waiting for you to tell it what to do. In the next few chapters we will explain some of the commands that you can give to DOS at this level to have it perform various tasks.

The character displayed in the DOS prompt is important because it tells you which disk drive DOS is operating from. At this point your prompt should be A>, which means that DOS will perform all disk-related activities on drive A. The drive designated in the DOS prompt is referred to as the default drive, and all disk activities will default to this drive unless you specify another. You can make other drives the default drive by simply changing the default drive assignment. We will cover more on this subject under "Default Drive" later in the chapter.

DOS Commands and the Command Line

The right angle bracket (>) in the DOS prompt points to the DOS "command line" that contains the blinking cursor. The command line is where you type in the commands you want to issue to DOS. The characters and command, however, are not sent to DOS until you press the Return (Carriage Return or Enter) key. If you make a mistake while entering a command, you can use the Backspace key and other keys to make corrections to the characters on the line. In the next few chapters, we will show you various editing keys that can be used for making corrections or simplifying the entry of DOS commands and statements on the command line.

A command is a line of input typed on the command line that is sent to DOS for processing when you press the Return key. DOS knows about 37 major commands and understands a variety of combinations of them. By issuing a command, you can instruct DOS to perform a task such as displaying a list of files or preparing a diskette.

All commands must be typed on the command line, in a format that DOS will understand. If you misspell a command or enter characters or words that DOS does not recognize, DOS will reject the entry and display the message "Bad command or file name." This is known as a "syntax" error and refers to DOS's inability to understand the command you entered.

How Commands Are Shown in This Book

DOS commands, as well as file names (described below), will be shown in uppercase throughout this book. We use the terms "disk," "diskette," and "fixed disk" interchangeably.

In the examples throughout this book, commands you are to enter are shown in **BOLDFACE CAPITAL** letters. All messages and output displayed by the computer will be shown in normal type. A carriage return should be assumed at the end of all command lines. The listing that follows illustrates how examples will be shown in this book. We have typed DIR on the command line directly following the DOS A prompt. After the command has been executed, the DOS prompt will reappear. Occasionally, you'll see three dots indicating that a longer display of text was produced by the command than is shown. The underscore following the DOS prompt indicates the location of the blinking cursor.

```
A>DIR        (type DIR and press return)
  .
  .          (disk directory is displayed)
  .
A>_          (the DOS prompt returns)
```

At times, it may not seem apparent when to press the carriage return. If so, we will indicate a carriage return with <Return>. Comments will appear in parentheses as shown in the example above. Do not type these comments.

DOS Files

Files are an important concept to understand when working with DOS. A file is a collection of information initially created in memory and then stored with a file name on a diskette. There are basically two type of files—command files and text or data files. Command files contain program code that the computer reads and uses as instructions when doing a task. When you type the name of a command file on the command line and press Return, the code in the file is loaded into computer memory and the program is started.

Text and data files contain standard alphanumeric information that has been entered into the file by you or someone else while using a word processor, spreadsheet program, or data management application. Text and data files can also be created from DOS, as will be shown extensively throughout this book. To read these files you should use the applications program that created them, or an editor.

A single diskette has the capacity to hold a large number of files. Each file on the disk has its own special file name which distinguishes it from other files on the disk. Files tend to shrink and grow in their lifetime as you add and delete text. File size is measured in bytes—a single byte being the equivalent of one character. If a file listing indicates that a particular file contains 3000 bytes, the file contains 3000 characters.

Typical data and text files are shown in Fig. 1-1. A text file contains standard alphanumeric characters, whereas a spreadsheet file contains alphanumeric characters that may be coded in a way that only the spreadsheet program will understand.

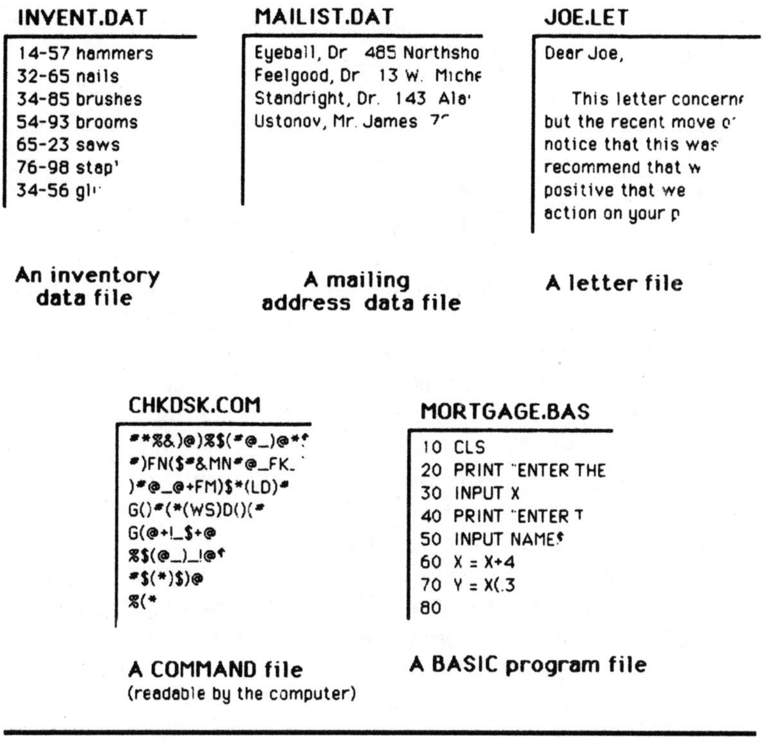

INVENT.DAT
14-57 hammers
32-65 nails
34-85 brushes
54-93 brooms
65-23 saws
76-98 stap'
34-56 gl·

An inventory
data file

MAILIST.DAT
Eyeball, Dr   485 Northsho
Feelgood, Dr   13 W. Miche
Standright, Dr. 143 Ala·
Ustonov, Mr. James 7⌐

A mailing
address data file

JOE.LET
Dear Joe,
This letter concerns
but the recent move o'
notice that this was
recommend that w
positive that we
action on your p

A letter file

CHKDSK.COM
**%&)@)%$(*@_)@*·
)FN($&MN*@_FK_ '
)*@_@+FM)$*(LD)*
G()*(*(WS)D()(*
G(@+l_$+@
%$(@_)_!@†
*$(*)$)@
%(*

A COMMAND file
(readable by the computer)

MORTGAGE.BAS
10 CLS
20 PRINT "ENTER THE
30 INPUT X
40 PRINT "ENTER T
50 INPUT NAME$
60 X = X+4
70 Y = X(.3
80

A BASIC program file

Figure 1-1

Files on a disk must be given unique names, not only to differentiate them from other files on the disk, but also to help you remember what is inside the file. Typical file names might be: MYDATA.DAT or MYLET-TER.TXT or JANBUDG.WKS. A file name consists of a "file name" and an "extension," separated by a period. The file name portion may not exceed eight characters or contain spaces. The extension portion of the file name cannot exceed three characters; it is used to group files into file types, such as text (TXT) files or command (COM) files. File names and extensions will always be shown in uppercase. Complete file names will be shown as FILE NAME.EXTENSION. This can be called file name dot extension.

In some cases an essential part of a file name is the drive specifier. This specifier must be placed before the file name so DOS knows where the file is located. For instance, a file on drive B is known to DOS as B:FILE NAME.EXT. This is called B colon file name dot extension, and the colon is used to separate the drive designator from the file name. Note that a file in the default drive (discussed next) does not need a file specifier because DOS will automatically look on this drive for a file if not told to look elsewhere.

Default Drive

The default drive is initially the disk from which you booted your system (you can later change it to another drive if you want). On floppy-drive systems this is the drive on the left, referred to as drive A. On fixed-disk systems such as the IBM XT, you can boot from the floppy drive or from the fixed disk. On these systems, the computer will look for a disk in the floppy drive first; if a disk with system files is not found there, the system will then boot from the fixed disk (assuming the fixed disk has been formatted properly and contains the system files). After booting from a fixed disk, you will usually see a C> prompt. If you booted your system as described in the first part of this chapter, the default drive should still be drive A.

You can change the default drive at any time by entering the drive specifier of the new default drive, followed by a colon. For instance, to change the default drive from drive A to drive B you would type B: and press the Return key. Now, all request for commands, disk reads, and disk writes will go to drive B.

Physical and Logical Drives

The disk drives on your system have specific names. When you want the computer to refer to a drive, you specify its name in a DOS command. This book and various other books may refer to these drives and the diskettes in them by other names. The following list shows what they may be called:

1. *Source and Target:*   When copying files from one disk to another, the "source" disk contains the file you want to copy and the "target" disk is the disk you want to copy the file to. You can place the source disk in one drive and the target in another to copy from one to another.

2. *Original and Backup:*   When you want to make a duplicate copy of a diskette, you refer to the initial disk as the "original" and the new copy as the "backup."

3. *Master and New (or Blank):*   An original disk, such as the DOS disk supplied with your DOS manual, is known as the "master" disk. The normal procedure is to make a backup of this original onto a "new" or "blank" disk and then store the master in a safe place.

4. *Logical Drive A and Logical Drive B:*   On single-drive systems, DOS sees the single drive as two logically separate disk drives so that you can easily copy files from one disk to another. DOS will prompt you to place an original in the floppy drive; it will then read its contents and copy those contents to a backup disk after asking you to place the backup in the drive. You will find this a labor-intensive task as you swap diskettes in and out of the single-disk drive.

5. *Program and Data Disks:*   Typically, you will have program diskettes and data diskettes. Owners of two-drive systems will usually keep the data diskette in drive B and the DOS or program disk in drive A.

DOS Hardware Devices

There are a number of hardware devices attached to your computer system (see Fig. 1-2). Typical hardware devices include the video display, keyboard, disk drives, and ports (used for plugging in external devices such as modems and printers). Each device and port is given a name by DOS. The disk drives, for instance, may be called A, B, and C; a printer may be called LPT1 or PRN; and the communications port may be called COM1 or COM2. There are also two standard devices that are known as the console devices, or CON.

The keyboard is the standard input device and the monitor is the standard output device. These are the devices that DOS uses by default when sending and receiving information unless you specify different devices. Text is normally entered at the keyboard and displayed on the screen, but you can direct this flow of information to other devices if you wish, as you will see later.

The keyboard (see Fig. 1-3) is the standard device used to enter information into your computer. Most of the keys on the keyboard are like those found on standard typewriter keyboards; however, there are several keys and key combinations that are specific to computers. On the left of the keyboard (or along the top) are the Function keys. The definition of these keys depends on the application program you are using. In DOS

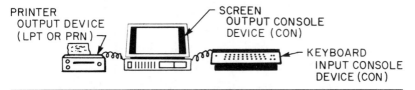

PRINTER
OUTPUT DEVICE
(LPT OR PRN)

SCREEN
OUTPUT CONSOLE
DEVICE (CON)

KEYBOARD
INPUT CONSOLE
DEVICE (CON)

Figure 1-2

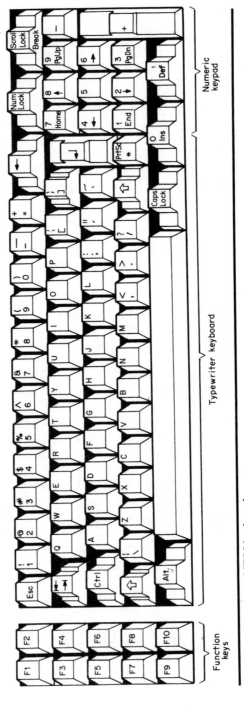

Figure 1-3 Top view of IBM keyboard.

TABLE 1-1   How Keys and Keystrokes
Are Shown in This Book

Form used	Key name
F1–F10	Function
Alt	Alternate
Shift	Shift
Ctrl	Control
Esc	Escape
Num Lock	Number Lock
Scroll Lock	Scroll Lock
Break	Break
PrtSc	Print Screen
Caps Lock	Caps Lock
Return	Carriage Return or Enter

these keys are used to fix typing mistakes or reissue a previous command. Keys that have special meaning and are not found on normal keyboards are the Control (Ctrl) key, the Alternate (Alt) key, and the Escape (Esc) key. These keys are always used in conjunction with another key to change its meaning, just as the Shift key on a normal keyboard is used to produce capital letters.

On the right side of the keyboard are the Number Lock (Num Lock) and Scroll Lock keys. Num Lock lets you shift between the numeric keypad and the Arrow keys. Scroll Lock is used to control the scroll of the display. On the lower right of the keyboard are the Insert (Ins) key and the Delete (Del) key, which are used for inserting or removing text within a document. Immediately to the left of the numeric keypad is the Carriage Return or Enter key, which is used to send a command to DOS.

Table 1-1 shows each of the keys or key combinations and how we will show them in this book. If the keys are to be entered at the keyboard as part of an exercise they will be shown between the arrow brackets (<>). For instance, when you are asked to press the Control key and the Break key at the same time in an exercise, it will be shown as **<Ctrl-Break>**. The keys are shown in the format that most closely resembles the way they appear on the keyboard. Keys pressed in combinations will be separated by a hyphen (-).

Some important key combinations used in this book:

Ctrl-Alt-Del (Control-Alternate-Delete)   Used to completely reset the computer to its power-up state. Pressing these keys in combination will perform what is known as a soft reboot.

Ctrl-Break (Control-Break)   Can be used to stop a running program or a scrolling display.

Ctrl-NumLock (Control-Number Lock)   Pauses scrolling display or program.

Alt-F1 (Alternate-Function)   Keys F1 through F10 are known as A1 through A10 when used with the Alt key.

Shift-F1 (Shift-Function)   Keys F1 through F10 are known as S1 through S10 when used with the Shift key.

Ctrl-F1 (Control-Function)   Keys F1 through F10 are known as C1 through C10 when used with the Ctrl key.

Storage Devices

Personal computers primarily use floppy disks and fixed disks for the storage of data. Your system may have one floppy drive, two floppy drives, or a floppy drive and a fixed disk. The normal default drive that DOS uses for most of its activities is known as drive A. A second floppy drive may be called drive B, and subsequent drives attached to the system take on successive letters of the alphabet as their names. If you own a fixed-disk system, the main drive will be the fixed disk, which DOS calls drive C (see Fig. 1-4).

Port Devices

The screen is not the only output device. DOS can send output to printers attached to ports called LPT1 (line printer 1), LPT2, or PRN (printer). DOS can also send output to communications ports that are attached to

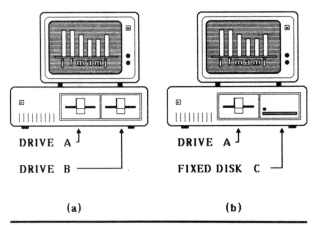

DRIVE A

DRIVE B

DRIVE A

FIXED DISK C

(a)   (b)

Figure 1-4   (a) IBM PC system (b) IBM XT fixed-disk system.

the phone lines. These ports are called COM1 (communications port 1), COM2, or AUX (auxiliary) by DOS. Both LPT and COM refer to ports attached to the back of your computer, but you should keep in mind that not all systems will have these ports (see Fig. 1-5).

Command Syntax

The commands given to the operating system must follow various rules of syntax. Webster's dictionary defines syntax as "the way in which words are put together to form phrases and sentences." The computer will not understand commands which do not abide by its rules of syntax. For instance, if you enter PRIN instead of PRINT, the computer will attempt to find the command file in memory or on disk. When it is not found, you will see a "File not found" error message.

Some commands have several "parameters." A parameter is an option, extra letter, word, or command typed on the command line along with the DOS command. It is usually separated from the main command by a space, slash, period, or colon. In the command formats that follow, optional parameters are shown in square brackets.

There are five types of DOS commands. The following discussion will describe each and show the syntax that must be used when typing in the commands. The first type directly affects the computer and takes the form:

command [options][parameters]

The command is always specified first. The option or parameter is specified next. A space is required between the options and the command

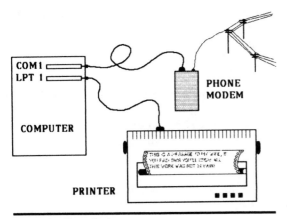

Figure 1-5 Port devices.

unless they are separated by a symbol such as a slash. Commands directly affecting the computer include the DATE and TIME commands in which the new date or time is specified as a parameter of the command on the command line.

The next type affects a particular drive. The syntax is:

    command [d:]

Here d: designates the drive to be affected. Once again, the command is always specified first. The drive designator is preceded by a space and is followed by a colon. Default drives need not be specified. The command will automatically affect the default drive if another drive is not specified. These commands are usually used to perform an action on a whole diskette. For instance, you can check the surface of a disk for flaws or available free memory by issuing the CHKDSK command followed by the drive you wish to check.

The third type of command is similar to the one above, except that you specify a file as well. This command takes the form:

    command [d:][file name]

Once again the command is typed first and is followed by the drive and the file to be affected. A common use for this type of command is to list and erase files.

The fourth type of command uses two parameters following the command name. The form is:

    command [d:][source file] [d:][destination file]

In this type of command, a source file is either copied to the destination or altered and then copied to the destination. Files may also be compared or renamed using this command. The destination file usually is made the source file after it has been altered. The original source file is not affected by this type of command.

The last type of command is for those who own fixed-disk systems or systems with high-capacity diskettes and will be using subdirectories. The format is very similar to that of the last command except for the addition of the name of the subdirectory, which is placed in the parameter position shown below by [path].

    command [d:][path][source file] [d:][path][destination file]

As you can see in the formats shown above, you can specify any drive in a DOS command. For instance, you can copy from drive A to B, or from

B to A, or from C to A, etc. Spaces, colons, and the proper positioning of parameters are important to the successful completion of a command. In the following example, we show the correct and incorrect way to execute various commands.

Incorrect	*Correct*
COPY A:MYFILEB:MYFILE (space needed before B:MYFILE)	COPY A:MYFILE B:MYFILE
RENAME B:NEWFILE (what is this being renamed to?)	RENAME B:NEWFILE B:OLDFILE
ERASE A JUNK (colon left out)	ERASE A:JUNK

In the correct version of the COPY command above, COPY is the command, A:MYFILE is the source file, and B:MYFILE is the destination.

In the correct version of the RENAME command, B:NEWFILE is the source and B:OLDFILE is the destination. (Notice that source and destination are both on the same disk.)

In the incorrect version of the ERASE command, DOS would attempt to erase a file called A. Since the colon was left out, DOS does not know that the A was meant to be a drive specifier. This command would produce an error message if a file called A was not found.

This concludes the introduction to DOS and the concepts you will need to proceed through the rest of this book. In the next chapter you'll start the hands on tutorial.

2

Preparing for the Lessons

In the last chapter you read through a review of the hardware and the software, so now it's time to prepare for the lessons and examples. Before starting the tutorial you'll need to prepare two blank diskettes, following the procedures outlined below. If you are using DOS-2, refer to the section, "Preparing Diskettes: DOS-2." If you are using DOS-3, refer to section "Preparing Diskettes: DOS-3." If you own a fixed-disk system such as the IBM PC/XT or PC/AT, refer to "Fixed Disk Systems" for information on how to prepare your fixed disk. If you own a fixed-disk system, but still want to prepare a set of floppy diskette, you can read the section that pertains to your version of DOS.

In the following sections, some of the procedures may seem unfamiliar. For now you can just follow along; we will explain them later. The most important thing is to prepare for the tutorial at this point. You can also refer to your DOS manual under "Getting a Diskette Ready to Be Used" or "Backing Up a Diskette" for more information.

Preparing Diskettes: DOS-2

Place the *original* DOS disk in the boot drive and turn the system on. If you've had the system on, reboot with Ctrl-Alt-Del. Answer the date and time prompts and then enter the commands shown in bold type. (Owners of single-drive systems will be asked to place the target disk in drive B. Since DOS considers the single drive as both A and B, the prompt will tell you to remove the source disk in the drive and replace it with the target disk.) Remember to type just what is shown in boldface type. You may have to occasionally swap diskettes in the floppy drives, depending on how much memory your system has. Owners of single-drive systems will see the following display:

```
A>DISKCOPY A: B:

Insert source diskette in drive A:

Strike any key when ready . . .
```

Owners of dual-drive systems will see the following display:

```
A>DISKCOPY A: B:

Insert source diskette in drive A:

Insert target diskette in drive B:

Strike any key when ready . . .
```

Follow the prompts until the copy is completed. You will know the copy has been made when the DOS prompt reappears on the command line. Once the new copy is made, pull out a label and mark it TUTORIAL before placing it on the disk. You can now put the original DOS disk in a safe place. The copy will be used from now on; therefore, place it in the default drive. You can now jump to the section entitled "Creating a Data Disk: The DOS FORMAT Command."

Preparing Diskettes: DOS-3

Owners of DOS-3 will need to use the SELECT command to prepare a DOS disk and to select the type of keyboard and country code that will be used. SELECT will automatically copy the contents of the original DOS disk to a new disk and set the keyboard and country code according to the following table:

Country	Country code	Keyboard code
United States	001	US
France	033	FR
Spain	034	SP
Italy	039	IT
United Kingdom	044	UK
Germany	049	GR

Enter the SELECT command in the following format in which xxx is the country code and yy is the keyboard code you will be using:

SELECT yyy xx

For instance, if you live in the United States, you would issue the following command at the DOS prompt:

```
A>SELECT 001 US
```

The following will be displayed if you own a single-drive system:

```
A>SELECT 001 US

Insert source diskette in drive A

Strike any key when ready . . .
```

Follow all the prompts, making sure to keep track of which diskette is the source and which is the target. If you own a dual-drive system, you will see the following display:

```
A>SELECT 001 US

Insert source diskette in drive A

Insert target diskette in drive B

Strike any key when ready . . .
```

When the SELECT routine has finished, you can store the original disk in a safe place and then continue reading below to create a data diskette.

Creating a Data Diskette: The DOS FORMAT Command

FORMAT is a DOS command used to initialize a new blank diskette for use with DOS. It checks the disk for flaws and prepares it to accept files. FORMAT sets up an area on the disk that will keep track of the file names of the files you store on the disk. Note the following:

1. FORMAT is only required the first time you use a diskette.
2. FORMAT erases any existing information on the disk. It can be used to prepare a disk for another use.
3. Using FORMAT is sometimes called "initalizing" a disk.
4. The DISKCOPY command used previously automatically formats diskettes.

To create the data disk, place the DOS disk in drive A and type the following command:

```
A>FORMAT B:/V

Insert new diskette for drive B:
and strike any key when ready _
```

DOS will ask you to put the disk in the appropriate drive, and you can strike a key when ready. If you have a two-drive system, place the disk to be formatted in the second disk drive. If you have a single-drive system, replace the DOS disk in drive A with the blank disk.

When the format routine is complete, DOS will ask for a volume label. Call this disk TUTORDATA and place a label on the outside of the disk with that name. Now that the disks have been prepared, you can skip the rest of this chapter and proceed to the next chapter to continue with the tutorial. Keep in mind that the FORMAT command is used to initialize all new diskettes. An uninitalized disk will not work in the computer. Refer to Chaps. 9 and 18 for more information on the FORMAT command.

Fixed-Disk System Setup

A fixed disk is a single storage unit that is capable of storing hundreds, even thousands of files. It may be referred to as either the hard disk, hard drive, or Winchester drive in this book and in many other. A 10-megabyte fixed disk such as the one on the IBM PC/XT can hold the equivalent of about 30 diskettes worth of information. Fixed disks contain solid spinning platters in a sealed, dirt-free environment. Although you cannot remove the platters, fixed disks have plenty of room for files. When the drive becomes full, you simply copy the unneeded files onto a floppy disk and delete those files from the fixed disk to create more room.

Owners of fixed-disk systems will need to prepare the drive for use. The shop from which you purchased your system should have done this, but if they didn't, refer to your DOS manual under "Preparing the Fixed Disk." The following brief description will help you prepare the drive. If your drive is already prepared, you can read the last section of this chapter and then move on to the next chapter.

To begin preparing the fixed disk, place the original DOS disk in the floppy drive and boot the system. The routines described here are the same for both DOS-2 and DOS-3. After entering the date and time, run the fixed disk partitioning program by typing:

```
A>FDISK
```

You can divide the fixed disk into several partitions in which each partition can have its own operating system and files. For instance, you can reserve half of the disk for DOS and the other half for the CP/M operating system. Refer to the FDISK section in your DOS manual for details. To set up a single partition, press Return in answer to all questions.

After the DOS partition has been created, the disk must be formatted. Enter the following command to format the drive and to copy the DOS system files to it.

```
A>FORMAT C:/S/V
```

This command assumes that your fixed disk is drive C; if not, replace the C with the drive designator of your drive. DOS asks for a volume label after completing the format. You can use your name, the name of your company, or any volume label you wish.

Make sure the original DOS disk is still in the floppy drive and copy the rest of the DOS command files to the fixed disk by typing:

```
A>COPY A:* . *C:
```

After the files have been copied, the drive is ready for use. To make drive C the default drive, type:

```
A>C:
C>_
```

You should make sure that your system will boot from the hard drive. To test this out, remove the disk from the floppy drive and reboot the system. You can either turn it off and then on or press the Ctrl-Alt-Del soft reboot key sequence. As the system boots, it will look for a disk in drive A, but when it doesn't find a disk there, it will default to drive C. The date and time request will appear and the DOS C prompt will appear after you enter the date and time.

How to Read This Book If You Own a Fixed Disk

Many of the examples we show in this book are designed for systems that use drive A as the default drive. The examples in the tutorial will show the DOS prompt as an A prompt. You simply need to substitute C (or the appropriate drive designator) in each of the examples. When a reference is made to drive B, you can still use drive C unless we specify that the action should take place on the floppy drive (which is logical drive A and B).

3

Hands-on DOS

Starting the Computer with DOS

You are ready to start the tutorial, so place the copy of the DOS disk you made in the last chapter in the boot drive and turn the computer on. If you start with a non-DOS disk in the drive or with a disk that is not formatted, a message will appear asking you to insert a system disk.

Owners of fixed-disk systems can boot from the fixed disk or the floppy drive, however, most of the time you will want to start from the fixed disk. If DOS does not find a system disk in the floppy drive, it will jump over to the fixed disk and boot from there.

IBM PC computers load BASIC if DOS is not present. All IBM systems contain a version of BASIC known as Cassette BASIC that is built into the computer. If DOS is not found when the system starts, Cassette BASIC will be loaded (except on the IBM XT, which will look for DOS on the fixed disk). This feature dates back to the days when IBM sold systems without disk drives. Users of those early systems could only operate their computer in BASIC.

Exploring DOS

If you have successfully loaded DOS and entered the date and time, you will see a display similar to the one below. The start-up display message you see on your screen will depend on the type of computer and version of DOS that you have.

```
Personal Computer DOS
Version 3.xx
A>
```

If you own a hard-disk system and booted from drive C, the prompt will read C> instead of A>. The DOS prompt appears on the command line; it is waiting for you to enter a command. The prompt indicates which drive is the current default drive and always appears as the last line of text on the screen unless DOS is processing a command. If DOS is processing a command, a message informing you of DOS's last activity may appear as the last line of the screen. You can enter a command when DOS is processing another, but the new command will not be processed until DOS finishes with its current task. DOS stores these commands in an area called the "type-ahead buffer." You can enter up to 15 characters into this buffer before DOS "beeps" to show that it's full.

Telling DOS What to Do

DOS has a "vocabulary" of about 37 major commands. Everything else it understands is either a variation on the major commands or new commands contained in the software programs you buy off the shelf. DOS is ready to accept a command if the prompt is visible and the blinking cursor is directly to the right of it. The drive designator in the prompt identifies the drive that will be affected by any commands you enter. When typing in commands, remember to follow the rules of command syntax that are described in Chapter 1.

In the following discussion you will use the DIR (directory) command to explore DOS. DOS recognizes DIR as one of its built-in commands and interprets it as a command to list the files on a disk (see Fig. 3-1). If you were to type DER, DOS would display "Bad command or file name." You can tell DOS to list the files on the disk in drive B by placing B: as a parameter after the DIR command. The command would take the form: DIR B:. If you were to accidentally type DIRB:, DOS would again display

```
┌─────────────────────────┐
│   TABLE OF CONTENTS      │
│ ·· ─────────────── ··    │
│  COMMAND   COM           │
│  ANSI      SYS           │
│  FORMAT    COM           │
│  CHKDSK    COM           │
│  SYS       COM           │
│  DISKCOPY  COM           │
│  DISKCOMP  COM           │
│  COMP      COM           │
│  EDLIN     COM           │
│  MODE      COM           │
└─────────────────────────┘
```

Figure 3-1 The DIR (Directory) command list; the table of contents of a disk.

an error message because it requires a space between DIR and B: to recognize it as a DOS command. If there was a program called DIRB: on the disk in the drive, DOS would run that program. DOS will always attempt to find any command you enter, even if it's a mistake or not a real command.

Let's try the DIR command. Type it next to the system prompt and then press the Return key. A list of the files on the disk in the default drive will scroll by on the screen. Remember that in this book long listings are shown with dots to indicate that material has been left out of the screen. Notice that the red light on the default disk drive comes on, indicating that the files on the screen are a listing from this drive.

```
Personal Computer DOS
Version 2.xx

A>DIR

.
.
.
SORT     EXE      1408   10-20-83   12:00p
FIND     EXE      5888   10-20-83   12:00p
MORE     COM       384   10-20-83   12:00p
BASIC    COM     16256   10-20-83   12:00p
BASICA   COM     26112   10-20-83   12:00P
        23 File(s)      28672 bytes free

A>_
```

Try typing **DIR**. You can mix upper and lowercase characters, though there is usually no reason to do this. DOS will convert lowercase letters to uppercase. Now type DIRECTORY.

```
A>DIRECTORY
Bad command or file name

A>_
```

The computer doesn't understand this long version of DIR. This demonstrates that DIR is not necessarily an abbreviation for directory. Notice that the disk drive light still came on, indicating that DOS was looking

Figure 3-2   You can stop a scrolling display by pressing Ctrl-S or Ctrl-Num Lock.

for a command or program called DIRECTORY on the disk. When you typed the line and pressed Return, DOS went through several steps in an attempt to execute the command. It first looked in the computer's internal memory for the command and when it was not found there, it looked externally on the disk in the drive. When it failed to find a command called DIRECTORY, DOS then displayed the error message.

Type **DIR** at the system prompt and take a look at the files on the DOS disk. The name of each file on the disk is displayed on the screen, one after the other. The size of each file, its date, and the time of its creation are also listed with each name. This listing is known as the diskette directory and is equivalant to a table of contents for the disk.

If the screen scrolls by too fast, you can temporarily stop it by pressing Ctrl-S. This is accomplished by holding down the Ctrl (Control) key while pressing S. The scroll will pause until you press another key, such as the Space Bar. You may also press the Ctrl-Num Lock key sequence on the IBM PC and on some compatibles, but you will find it much easier to press Ctrl-S (see Fig. 3-2).

The Command Line and the Command Processor

When you typed the DIR command, you typed it on the command line, and when you pressed the Return key, the command was sent to DOS for processing. These two steps will be referred to as "entering" a command from now on. The command line is like a blank template—you can type characters, backspace to make corrections, and then send the command to DOS by pressing the Return key. The command goes to a special area of DOS known as the DOS command processor.

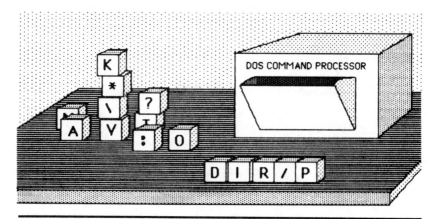

Figure 3-3 You can build commands on the command line before sending them to the DOS command processor.

Using Switches with Commands

Another way to "suspend" the diskette directory listing is by using a "switch." A switch is an extra part of a command that tells the system to do something special with that command (see Fig. 3-3). In the case of the DIR command, a switch can temporarily turn off the scrolling of the directory listing so you can view it. The DIR command has two switches, /P and /W. By typing the command shown on the next screen, you will see how the /P switch works. A screen full of text will be displayed on your monitor together with message "Strike a key when ready." You can press any key (the Space Bar for instance) to resume the listing.

```
A>DIR /P
   .
   .
   .
BASIC    COM    16256  10-20-83  12:00p
BASICA   COM    26112  10-20-83  12:00p
Strike a key when ready . . .
```

The /P switch stands for page and causes DOS to display a page of file names at a time until it runs out of names. The /W switch stands for wide and causes DOS to displays a list of files in wide format. The following display is similar to the list you may see when using /W. Differences in the file listing depend on the version and distributor of your DOS.

```
A>DIR /W

    Volume in drive A is TUTORIAL
    Directory of  A:\

COMMAND  COM    ANSI     SYS    FORMAT   COM . . .
DISKCOPY COM    DISKCOMP COM    COMP     COM . . .
    .
    .
    .
MORE     COM    BASIC    COM    BASIC    COM
        23 File(s)      28672 bytes free

A>_
```

The /W switch will display the files across the screen but leave out the directory information, such as the file size, date, and time of creation. This mode is useful for listing as many files as possible at one time. The /W command can be combined with the /P command to list a disk such as a fixed disk that has many files. From now on we will refer to switches and additional characters, words, or commands typed on the command line with another command as a parameter of that command.

Printing the Directory List

Pressing Ctrl-P will turn the print "echo" feature on. This mode will cause all commands and messages displayed on the screen to be printed on the printer (LPT device) as well. You can use this mode to document your sessions on the computer. To turn the echo off, press Ctrl-P again. On IBM systems and on most compatibles you can also press the Ctrl-PrtSc key combination to turn print echo on and off.

Listing Selected Files: Using Global File Name Characters

You can list a single file by specifying its name as a parameter of the DIR command. This feature is a handy way of finding out if a particular file exists on the disk. You can also use this format to display the directory information about a single file, such as its size and creation date. To display the file information for the file SORT.EXE, you can type:

```
A>DIR SORT.EXE

Sort    EXE    1408    10-20-83    12:00p

A>
```

When you used the DIR command earlier in the tutorial, it produced a list of every file on the disk. You can list selected files by using special characters as parameters with the DIR command. These special characters are known as global parameters or "wild-card" characters. With global characters, you can tell DOS, "Show me all files with file names that start with the letter S" or "Show all files that have a file extension of EXE." Wild-card characters are convenient for listing specific groups of files.

The asterisk character is the first wild card we will discuss. With it you can specify a range of file names or a range of extensions in the parameter of the DIR command. Type the following command to display all files with the EXE extension.

```
A>DIR *.EXE
    Volume in drive A is TUTORIAL
    Directory of   A:\

SORT    EXE    1408    10-20-83    12:00p
FIND    EXE    5888    10-20-83    12:00p
        2 File(s)        28672 bytes free

A>_
```

Your system may display more files—once again, this depends on your version of DOS and its distributor. The asterisk in the above command tells DOS that any group of characters may occupy its position. By specifying EXE as the extension, you tell DOS to list only files having this extension. Note that DIR *.* has the effect of listing all files on the disk because any file name will work and any extension will work.

Another wild-card character is the question mark (?). This character is used in place of a single character and tells DOS that any character may occupy its position. For instance, the following command will list all files that have DISKCO in the first six positions of the file name. The last two positions may be occupied by any character.

```
A>DIR DISKCO??.*

DISKCOPY COM     2576   10-20-83   12:00p
DISKCOMP COM     2188   10-20-83   12:00p
        2 File(s)        28672 bytes free

A>_
```

Here, two similar file names are displayed. The asterisk used in place of an extension tells DOS that any extension will work. The ? is useful for listing groups of files that have dates, numbers, or characters in similar positions in the file name.

The DOS Editing Keys

DOS remembers the last command you entered and lets you use it over again without having to retype it. Pressing the F3 key will reissue the last command you entered. When you type in a command and press the Return key, a copy of the command is sent to a temporary storage location called the "template." When you press F3, this template is copied to the command line, but the command is not executed until you press the Return key.

Try pressing the **F3** key now. The last command you typed in is now displayed on the command line. You can execute this command again by pressing the Return key or you can cancel it by backspacing over it or pressing the Esc key.

Suppose you want a listing of the files on several diskettes. You insert the first disk and type DIR /W, which produces a file list for the current disk in the drive. You can now insert another disk in the drive and press F3 to reissue the DIR /W command. You can keep doing this as long as you have diskettes to list.

In the following example you will use another DOS editing key, the F1 key. The F1 editing key will be used to build a new command from one already in the template. Type the command shown on the next screen and press the Return key. This will place the command in the template, replacing any previous command that may have been there. You will see a listing of drive A in the process.

A>DIR /W   (place DIR /W in the template by pressing
              Return)

DIR /W is now in the template and can be used to build the next command. To see a listing of files on the disk in drive B, the designator B: must be inserted before the /W in the command. If you own a hard disk and are working from drive C (the prompt is C>), substitute A for B in the examples below. Be sure your data disk is in drive B. Press the F1 key four times to copy the first part of the template to the command line.

A>DIR   (press **F1** four times)

Now you press the Ins key. This will open the template and allow you to insert characters. Type in B:, then press the F1 key to copy the rest of the template to the command line. (Figure 3-4 illustrates how this command works.)

A>DIR B:/W   (type in **B:**, and then press **F1** until the
                 remainder of the template is copied)

As you can see, the template has saved you a few keystrokes. If you have a disk in drive B, you can issue this command to see a list of files for that disk.

Another way to save time and keystrokes is to use the F2 editing key. The F2 key will copy characters from the template out to a specified character. F2 eliminates the need to repeatedly press the F1 key when copying from the template. Using the template created in the last example, press

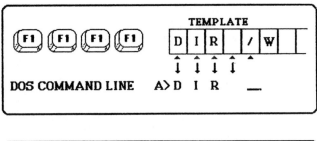

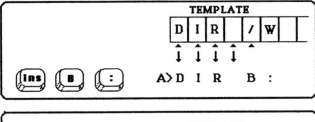

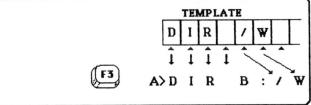

Figure 3-4

F2 and then press the slash (/) key. The template will be copied out to the /. Now add P to the end of the command line, press Return, and the directory listing will be "paged."

```
A>DIR B:/        (copy the template out to the slash by
                  pressing F2 and /)
A>DIR B:/P       (now type a P to replace the W and press
                  Return)

press
Return)
```

To further illustrate the use of the template and editing keys, a typing mistake will be corrected. Type in the following command as if you had typed it with the mistake.

TABLE 3-1   DOS Editing Keys

Key	Explanation
⸱F1	Copies one character at a time from the template.
F2	Copies up to a specified character. Press the F2 key and then press the key you want to copy the template to.
F3	Copies the entire template to the screen.
F4	Copies all characters from a specified character to the end of the line. F3 will display the line.
F5	Moves the cursor down one line to allow you to edit or retype the currently displayed line. This key is useful for correcting typing mistakes.
Esc	This key lets you start all over when entering a command and leaves the template unchanged.
Ins	Opens up a portion of the template for insertion of characters. Moves existing characters to the right.
Del	Deletes character to the right in the template.

```
A>DER /W        (do not press Return)
```

It is easy to fix this line with the editing keys. The F5 key replaces the contents of the template with the line just typed and allows you to place new characters in the template without pressing the Return key. The command is not sent to DOS for processing, but instead allows you to further edit the line. Pressing F5 will allow you to fix the mistake because it places the new text in the template, replacing the old text.

Press the F5 key to save the line. Notice that you are still working "within" the same DOS prompt. The line has not been sent to the command processor. You may now use the other DOS editing keys to fix the line. Press F1 to copy the first character.

```
A>DER /W        (press F5)
   D            (press F1 to copy the first character)

A>DER /W
   DIR /W       (type an I and press F3 to copy the rest of
                the template)
```

The right Arrow key performs the same function as the F1 key and may be in a more convenient place on the keyboard. Try using the Arrow key instead of the F1 key.

This ends the first lesson. The examples shown here were designed to let you interact with the command processor and to familiarize you with the keyboard. The following lessons will increase your experience with DOS and prepare you for the advanced lessons.

4

Working with DOS Commands and Files

By now you have seen the files on the DOS disk several times and have some experience with entering DOS commands. In working through these exercises, you have been interacting with the DOS command processor. The command processor is visible to you as the DOS prompt. When you see this prompt followed by a blinking cursor, you know that the command processor is waiting for you to enter a command. In this chapter we will continue the exploration of the DOS commands and our interaction with DOS.

Changing the System Prompt

The DOS prompt can be changed to make drive B the default drive. Type the following on the command line:

A>B: (make B the default drive)

You can now list the files on drive B by typing DIR. Drive B does not have to be specified in the command line because the default drive is now drive B; now you will have to specify A in the DIR command to get a listing of the files on drive A. For example:

```
B>DIR            (list files on B)
 .
 .
 .
B>DIR A:         (list files on A)
 .
 .
 .
B>_
```

To return the default status back to drive A, type:

```
B>A:        (return default status to A)
A>_
```

Using the Prompt Command

There is a DOS command called PROMPT that you can use to change
the DOS system prompt. With it, you can place messages or other symbols
on the command line to replace the normal DOS prompt. Type the following and watch what happens.

```
A>PROMPT WHAT'S UP DOC?$g

WHAT'S UP DOC?>
```

Now change the prompt to display the time:

```
WHAT'S UP DOC?>PROMPT $t$g

0:11:51.17> <Return>

0:11:52.05> <Return>
```

TABLE 4-1   DOS Prompts

Symbol	Prompt produced
$$	A $, familiar to UNIX users
$t	The time
$d	The date
$p	The current directory
$v	The version number of your DOS
$n	The default drive
$g	The > character
$l	The < character
$b	The " " character
$q	The = character
$h	A backspace and erasure of the previous character
$e	The Escape character
$-	The CR-LF sequence (go to beginning of new line)

Next, change the prompt to display a message:

```
0:12:00.12>PROMPT WAITING $n$g

WAITING A>_
```

The examples above show several ways to change the prompt. In the first example, the prompt was changed to display a message. The $g adds the familiar greater-than (>) sign to the end of the prompt message. The only problem with this prompt is that you may not know what drive you are working with. The next example shown above uses the $t (time) and $g option as the prompt. The current time will now be displayed whenever the prompt reappears on the screen. Pressing Return several times will show you elapsed time. You may want to use this to time the excution of commands.

The last prompt shown above is the most practical because it tells you what DOS is doing. A full list of DOS prompts is shown in Table 4-1. Feel free to experiment with these until you find a prompt you like. To return to the normal prompt, type PROMPT by itself.

```
WAITING A>PROMPT

A>_
```

Internal and External Commands

When you enter a command, DOS follows a path to find the instructions for that command. It first looks in the memory of the computer. If the command is not found in memory, DOS then looks externally on the disk drives. If it is not found on the default disk drive, DOS will then display an error message.

A command stored in memory is known as an internal command, and a command file stored on disk is known as an external command. Some commands, such as the DIR command, are used so often that they are always resident in internal memory. Other commands that are not used as often are kept on the disk. Although internal commands have the advantage of immediate execution, they take up room in memory; therefore, many commands are stored on disk (see Fig. 4-1).

Look at the files on the DOS disk. With the DOS disk in drive A, type **DIR /W,** which produces a file list similar to the one below.

COMMAND	.COM	ANSI	.SYS
ATTRIB	.EXE	DISKCOPY	.COM
EDLIN	.COM	MODE	.COM
RESTORE	.COM	PRINT	.COM
TREE	.COM	GRAPHICS	.COM
MORE	.COM	BASIC	.COM
SYS	.COM	SELECT	.COM
SHARE	.EXE	CHKDSK	.COM
DISKCOMP	.COM	COMP	.COM
VDISK	.SYS	BACKUP	.COM
RECOVER	.COM	ASSIGN	.COM
SORT	.EXE	FIND	.EXE
BASICA	.COM	FORMAT	.COM
GRAFTABL	.COM	FORMAT	.COM

The majority of the files on the DOS disk are COM (command) files. Command files usually have the extension of COM, although some have the extension EXE. One of the most important files in the list above is COMMAND.COM. This file is essential to the operation of DOS. It contains the internal commands like DIR and PROMPT that you will use often when working with DOS.

The list above shows the command files DISKCOPY.COM and SELECT.COM, one of which you used in Chap. 2 to create a copy of the DOS disk. When you typed DISKCOPY or SELECT, the computer loaded the program into memory and began the disk copy procedures.

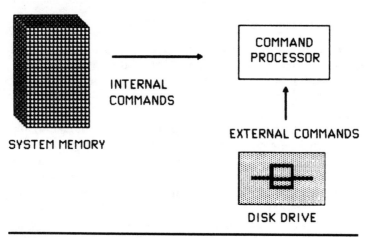

Figure 4-1

When it was through and you answered No to the "more copies" question, DOS discarded the program from memory. If you wanted to use the command again in the same session, DOS would have to reload the program. DISKCOPY and SELECT are classified as external commands.

Table 4-2 describes each of the files on the DOS disk (see also Fig. 4-2). Each of these files are considered external commands that DOS must load into memory when you request them.

Checking the Disk

Most of the DOS commands will be discussed in more detail later. For now, you can try a few of the commands to get a feel for their use. One of the most useful is CHKDSK.COM (check disk). This command is a utility used to check the status of a diskette. It performs the following:

- Reports on the available disk space left for files
- Reports problems on the surface of the disk
- Reports on the number of files and the space used by the files on the disk
- Displays total system memory and available memory

To check a disk, type the following:

```
A>CHKDSK
Volume in drive A has no label

179712 bytes total disk space
 22528 bytes in 2 hidden files
132608 bytes in 29 user files
 24064 bytes available on disk

131072 bytes total memory
102720 bytes free
```

To check the status of the data disk in drive B, type:

```
A>CHKDSK B:
Volume TUTORDATA created Apr 1, 1984 12:30a

     362496 bytes total disk space
          0 bytes in 1 hidden files
     362496 bytes available on disk

     131072 bytes total memory
     106480 bytes free

A>_
```

You may want to issue this command before starting any computing session. It will tell you how much room is left on the disk. CHKDSK also checks for bad files and will attempt to fix them if possible. Later, a special boot disk will be created that executes the CHKDSK command automatically every time the system is started with that disk in the drive.

Creating a File

The best way to learn about files is to create one. In this section the COPY command will be used to create a file. This may seem a little odd at first since the name COPY implies that it's used to copy files from one place to another. This is exactly what you will do with the command, but in the example shown here the contents of the file will come directly from the keyboard and be copied into the file. If you type COPY CON followed by a file name, all input received from the CON (console), or keyboard, will be copied into the designated file. If the file you specify in the file name parameter exists, DOS will write over the existing file, erasing it. If the file doesn't exist, DOS will create it.

TABLE 4-2   Files on the DOS Diskette

File name	Description
ANSI.SYS	Configures the system for different keyboard and screen parameters
ASSIGN.COM	Sends requests to alternate drives
ATTRIB.EXE[1]	Alters the read/write attitute of files
BACKUP.COM	Copies files from a fixed disk to a diskette
BASIC.COM BASICA.COM	Files that make up the BASIC interpreter
BASICA.EXE	(N/A on IBM systems)
CHKDSK.COM	Reports disk status
COMMAND.COM	DOS command processor
COMP.COM	Compares files
DEBUG.COM	Debugs programs
DISKCOMP.COM	Compares entire diskettes
DISKCOPY.COM	Copies entire diskettes
EDLIN.COM	Line editor
EXE2BIN.EXE	Converts .EXE files to .COM files
FDISK.COM	Partitions a disk
FORMAT.COM	Formats disks
GRAFTABL.COM[1]	Loads additional graphics characters
GRAPHICS.COM	Prints graphics from the screen
KEYxx.COM[1]	Loads a specified keyboard program
LABEL.COM[1]	Adds, changes, or deletes volume labels
LINK.EXE	Linker utility
MODE.COM	Sets mode of various devices
MORE.COM	Pages screen display
PRINT.COM	Print spooler or queue
RECOVER.COM	Recovers data on disk
RESTORE.COM	Copies files from diskettes to fixed disk
SELECT.COM[1]	Selects keyboard and country format
SHARE.EXE[1]	Installs file-sharing support
SORT.EXE	Sorts text file
SYS.COM	Transfers DOS system files to another disk
TREE.COM	Displays directory paths
VDISK.SYS[1]	Virtual disk device file

[1]DOS-3 only.

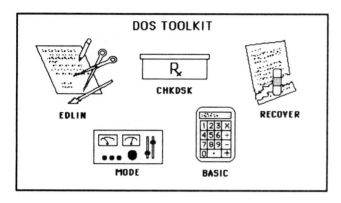

Figure 4-2 You can think of the commands on the DOS
disk as a set of tools.

Since most of the files used as examples in this book are short, you can use the COPY command to create many of them. It is much easier to create these files "on the fly" with COPY, instead of loading a word processor or editor. In the following example, a file will be created called SAMPLE.TXT. The file will then be manipulated in several ways.

Before starting, you should use the DIR command to see if a file called SAMPLE.TXT is already on your disk. If you already have such a file, then use another file name for the examples below. This is just a precautionary step to prevent you from writing over a file that might already be on the disk. The COPY CON command, although efficient for creating short files, will erase existing files with the same name. If you've been following along with this tutorial, your disk should only contain the DOS files we copied to it. Checking file names before creating new files is a good habit to get into and will protect valuable data from accidental erasure.

Enter the following at the keyboard to check for SAMPLE.TXT:

```
A>DIR SAMPLE.TXT
```

If the file does not exist, you will see the "File not found" message.

To start creating the new file, enter the COPY command below, making sure you follow the rules of syntax.

```
A>COPY CON:SAMPLE.TXT
```

When you press Return, the cursor jumps down to the next line and waits. You have essentially opened a file and can enter text into it by typing on the blinking cursor (see Figs. 4-3 and 4-4). Think of the screen as a blank piece of paper in a typewriter. Type the following text into the file:

```
A>COPY CON:SAMPLE.TXT
RED         LINE 1 OF THE FILE
BLUE        LINE 2
GREEN       LINE 3
BLACK       LINE 4
WHITE       LINE 5
<F6>  <Return>
A_
```

After the last entry, close the file and write it to the disk by pressing the F6 key (or Ctrl-Z) and the Return key. The symbol ^Z (Ctrl-Z) is a marker that tells DOS where the end of the file is. Most DOS machines have ^Z assigned to the F6 Function key. If your system doesn't, you can get the same results by pressing Ctrl-Z. This will place the ^Z end-of-file

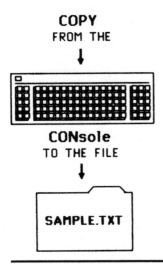

Figure 4-3 With the COPY CON command, you can enter data directly into a file.

market at the end of the file. Using the paper-in-the-typewriter analogy, closing a file is like pulling the piece of paper out of the typewriter and placing it in a folder in a file cabinet. The file cabinet in this case is the disk.

Displaying a File

You have created what is known as an ASCII text file. ASCII files contain standard text characters and can be displayed on the screen in a readable form. Refer to App. A for a list and explanation of ASCII characters. To view the file, use the DOS TYPE command as shown below. TYPE will open a file and display its contents on the screen so that you can read it.

```
A>TYPE SAMPLE.TXT
RED     LINE 1 OF THE FILE
BLUE    LINE 2
GREEN LINE 3
BLACK LINE 4
WHITE LINE 5
```

TYPE is an excellent command for looking inside files. You should know that not all files will be readable. For instance, try using TYPE on a COM file such as CHKDSK.COM.

Figure 4-4 When you enter COPY CON:SAMPLE.TXT, the screen becomes a writing tablet.

```
A>TYPE CHKDSK.COM
   .
   . (garbage)
   .
A>_
```

What you will see is an unrecognizable list of characters scrolling by, accompanied by an occasional beep. Some computer people refer to this type of display as garbage. In reality, it is not. Although the displayed characters may not be readable by you, they make sense to the computer. A COM file is a file containing machine instruction for the computer and therefore is unrecognizable to most people. On the other hand, a text file contains characters entered by a user that are readable by other users. Think of a text file as a note or letter typed on a typewriter. Any text file can be displayed on the screen in a readable form with the TYPE command as long as it follows the ASCII coding scheme. ASCII is a standard way of coding the alphabet that is recognized by a wide range of computers. For more information on ASCII, refer to App. A.

You can place any of the ASCII codes listed in App. A in your files. To do this, hold down the Alt key and enter the ASCII code for the character on the numeric keypad. This code is listed in the appendix next to the character. The numbers must be entered on the numeric keypad, not with the numbers keys along the top of the keyboard. You must hold down the Alt key while entering the numbers. Some printers will recognize these characters and print them exactly as you type them on the screen. The IBM Graphics Printer will print the full 256 character set shown in App. A.

Recovering from Error Messages

Occasionally as you work on your PC you will see the message "Abort, Retry, Ignore?" This is a message from DOS telling you that it is having problems with the last command you gave it. You are given three ways to recover from the problem. The first option, abort, stops the command and returns control to DOS. The second option, retry, can be used to resume the command after you have shut a disk-drive door or removed a write-protect tab from a disk. The third option, ignore, can be used to get DOS to try to read a file over again. If part of the file is corrupted, the message will be displayed, but you can tell DOS to retry and read the next part of the file by pressing I.

You can simulate a problem that will cause DOS to display the "Abort, Retry, Ignore?" message. Open the door on drive B and type **DIR B:**. DOS will attempt to read a disk in drive B, but because the door is open, it will display the message. To recover, close the drive door and press **R** to retry access to the disk.

You created your first file in this chapter using the COPY CON command. In the next few chapters you will see how the file can be manipulated in various way with DOS commands. If you're leaving the computer at this point, you can simply turn it off. It's a good idea to get in the habit of removing the diskettes from the drive and returning them to their sleeves before you shut the system down.

Chapter

5

Handling Files

There are many ways to manipulate a file once it has been created. In this chapter you will make copies of the file SAMPLE.TXT that was created in Chap. 4 and will use several DOS commands to sort and locate text in it.

Making a Duplicate of a File

To duplicate a file in a paper filing system you would pull out an empty folder and place a photocopy of the original in the new folder. You would then rename the copy of the file with a name that was different from the original. Once a copy of the original has been made, you can alter the copy or send it to another location.

DOS files can also be copied in much the same way by using the DOS COPY command to copy a "source" file to a "destination" file. The source file is the original, and the destination file is the file that the original is being copied to. The command below will make a copy of the SAMPLE.TXT file and name the copy SAMPLE2.TXT:

```
A>COPY SAMPLE.TXT SAMPLE2.TXT

A>_
```

DOS automatically creates a new file called SAMPLE2.TXT during the copy process (see Fig. 5-1). To see that this new file is indeed on the disk,

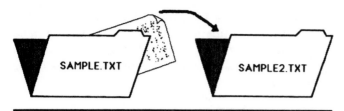

Figure 5-1 The command COPY SAMPLE.TXT
SAMPLE2.TXT copies the contents of SAMPLE.TXT to
the new file SAMPLE2.TXT.

type in the DIR command using the wild-card characters to list all files
that have SAMPLE as part of the name. The command below will accomplish this.

```
A>DIR SAMPLE?.TXT
SAMPLE     TXT      32    3————84   12:33a
SAMPLE2    TXT      32    3————84   12:33a
           2 File(s)      182272 bytes free

A>_
```

The two SAMPLE text files have the same contents; therefore, you can
now use the second for alterations. You can even copy text from another
file into this new file—something we will cover in a moment.

Copying Files to Another Disk

If you wanted to send a copy of a paper document to another person, say
a coworker, you could photocopy the original and send the duplicate copy.
With DOS, you can use the COPY command to make a duplicate of a disk
file, sending the duplicate to another disk, for instance. The following
command will copy the file SAMPLE.TXT from the disk in drive A to
the data disk in drive B. If you own a fixed disk and have SAMPLE.TXT
on the C drive, you can copy the file to drive A or B instead.

```
A>COPY A:SAMPLE.TXT B:SAMPLE.TXT

A>_
```

The full command is shown above for clarity. The source file SAM-PLE.TXT is on drive A and the destination file SAMPLE.TXT is now on drive B. In the command above, we typed more than is actually needed to make the copy (see Fig. 5-2). Instead, we could have typed the following to accomplish the same task:

A>COPY SAMPLE.TXT B:

In this command, COPY will assume that the new file in drive B will have the same name as the source file in drive A. Remember that COPY does not move the original file to drive B; it makes a copy of the file on the disk in B drive. You could change the name of the file as it is copied to drive B by specifying a new file name in the destination parameter of the COPY command (see Fig. 5-3). Type the following:

A>COPY SAMPLE.TXT B:NEWNAME.TXT

A>_

In the example above, the file NEWNAME.TXT now on drive B is a duplicate of the SAMPLE.TXT file on drive A. Only the name was

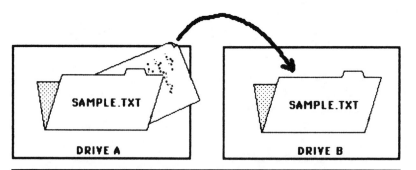

Figure 5-2 The commands COPY A:SAMPLE.TXT B:SAMPLE.TXT and COPY SAMPLE.TXT B: both copy the file SAMPLE.TXT from the disk in drive A to the disk in drive B, retaining the same file name.

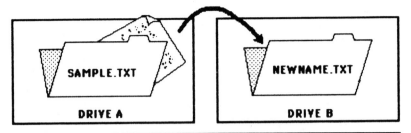

Figure 5-3 COPY SAMPLE.TXT B:NEWNAME.TXT
copies the contents of SAMPLE.TXT to NEW-
NAME.TXT, a file that is created during the copy, on drive
B.

changed during the copy process. Also, notice that the drive designator
for the source file was not specified. If you do not specify a drive designator for a file, DOS will assume it is on the default drive.

You can, of course, copy files in the reverse direction by specifying the
drive desginator before the name of each file. For example, the following
command would copy NEWNAME.TXT from drive B to drive A.

```
A:>COPY B:NEWNAME.TXT A:

A:>_
```

Comparing Files

Occasionally, you will want to make sure that the contents of a copied file
are exactly the same as its original. The COMP command can be used to
make a comparison between two files. The following command compares
SAMPLE.TXT on drive A with NEWNAME.TXT on drive B:

```
A:>COMP A:SAMPLE.TXT B:NEWNAME.TXT

A:SAMPLE.TXT and B:NEWNAME.TXT

Files compare ok

Compare more files (Y/N)? N

A:>_
```

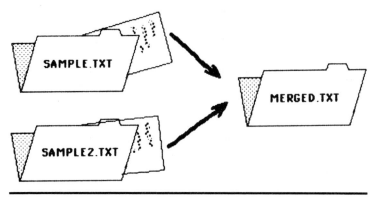

Figure   5-4 COPY   SAMPLE.TXT+SAMPLE2.TXT
MERGED.TXT combines the two files together into a single file called MERGED.TXT.

Merging Files

Next, you'll combine the two sample files into a single file called MERGED.TXT, a process known as "file merging." There are several reasons why you would want to merge files together:

- You can combine several files together so they can be printed as one complete document. This is helpful if you want to work with small sections of a document, one at a time, and then combine them for printing.

- Files created by several different applications programs can be combined into one complete document. For instance, you could combine a table of data created with a spreadsheet program such as VisiCalc with a report file that was created with a word processor.

- You can also create text files containing standard sentences or paragraphs and combine them in various documents that you print on a regular basis. These files are known as "boilerplates" and can be combined with the COPY command.

To combine the two SAMPLE files you can use the COPY command and the plus sign (+). The plus sign tells DOS to concatenate two files together, and it is place between the names of the files to be combined. The command shown below will combine the files into a new file called MERGED.TXT (see Fig. 5-4). Don't forget to include the spaces as shown. Note that there are no spaces surrounding the plus sign but that there is one before the destination file. Also note that the name of each file being copied to MERGED.TXT is listed on the screen as it is copied. This is an important feature that we will discuss later.

```
A>COPY SAMPLE.TXT+SAMPLE2.TXT MERGED.TXT
SAMPLE.TXT
SAMPLE2.TXT
           1 File(s) copied
```

In the example above COPY is the command, SAMPLE.TXT and SAMPLE2.TXT are the source files, and MERGED.TXT is the destination file. Displaying the file MERGED.TXT will show that the two files have been joined together into one file.

```
A>TYPE MERGED.TXT
RED           LINE 1 OF FILE
GREEN         LINE 2
BLUE          LINE 3
BLACK         LINE 4
WHITE         LINE 5
RED           LINE 1 OF FILE
BLUE          LINE 2
GREEN         LINE 3
BLACK         LINE 4
WHITE         LINE 5

A>_
```

Sorting Files

If you've ever been faced with the task of sorting a list of names into alphabetical order, you will appreciate the SORT command, a new feature in DOS-2. To sort a file you must use the redirection feature of DOS, which "points" the file to be sorted into the SORT command. The example below will illustrate how this works.

```
A>SORT < MERGED.TXT.
BLACK         LINE 4
BLACK         LINE 4
BLUE          LINE 3
BLUE          LINE 3
GREEN         LINE 2
GREEN         LINE 2
RED           LINE 1 OF FILE
RED           LINE 1 OF FILE
WHITE         LINE 5
WHITE         LINE 5

A>_
```

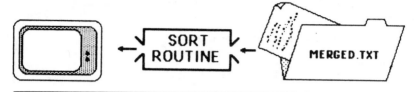

Figure 5-5 The sorted output from the file MERGED.TXT is sent to the screen with the command SORT< MERGED.TXT.

A sorted list of files is displayed on the screen (see Fig. 5-5). DOS's redirection feature allows you to direct the flow of standard input and ouput in your system. In the command above, the contents of the file SORTMERG.TXT are directed or pointed into the SORT routine, and a sorted list, known as the "output," is displayed on the screen. DOS's redirection feature can also be used to redirect this screen output to a location other than the standard console device (the screen). You can save the sorted list as a new file on the disk by using redirection once again to direct the output of the SORT command into a file. The command below directs the file MERGED.TXT into the SORT command and directs the sorted output to the file SORTMERG.TXT (see Fig. 5-6).

```
A> SORT < MERGED.TXT >SORTMERG.TXT

A>_
```

You can view the sorted file with the TYPE commmand:

```
A>TYPE SORTMERG.TXT
BLACK      LINE 4
BLACK      LINE 4
BLUE       LINE 3
BLUE       LINE 3
GREEN      LINE 2
GREEN      LINE 2
RED        LINE 1 OF FILE
RED        LINE 1 OF FILE
WHITE      LINE 5
WHITE      LINE 5

A>_
```

Redirection as used above may seem confusing and you may wonder why the following wasn't typed:

MERGED.TXT > SORT > SORTMERG.TXT

This seems more logical because the flow of the command is from left to right. The command will not work, however, because DOS requires that a command be the first parameter on a line. In the line above, MERGED.TXT is not a command but SORT is; therefore, SORT must be placed in the first position on the command line. Redirection is an advanced feature of DOS-2 and is not included in previous releases of DOS. Redirection will be covered in more detail throughout this book.

Printing Files

A file may be sent to the printer by specifying the device name of the printer in the COPY command. The printer attached to your system is known to DOS by the device names we discussed in Chap. 1. Here is an example of a COPY command in which the file SORTMERG.TXT is copied to the printing device LPT1:

```
A>COPY SORTMERG.TXT LPT1

A>_
```

In this example, SORTMERG.TXT is the source file and LPT1 (the printer) is the destination. There is another way of printing files to the printer in which you use a combination of the TYPE command and the redirection feature of DOS-2. The example below only demonstrates

Figure 5-6 The sorted output from MERGED.TXT is placed in the file SORTMERG.TXT with the command SORT<MERGED.TXT>SORTMERG.TXT.

how redirection can be used. The print command shown above, however, is preferred because it requires fewer keystrokes and makes more sense.

```
A>TYPE SORTMERG.TXT > LPT1

A>_
```

Using the TYPE command to send material to the printer is interesting because TYPE normally directs its output to the screen. In this example the normal output destination has been overridden by redirecting the screen output to the printer.

The screen has the reserved device name of CON and is normally the default output device. In other words, DOS usually displays it messages and listings on the screen. For example, the following two commands both display the contents of MERGED.TXT on the screen:

```
TYPE MERGED.TXT
TYPE MERGED.TXT > CON
```

Finding Keywords in Files

Throughout the course of your work on the computer, you will create many files and eventually will forget the contents of most of the files. Suppose you're trying to locate a file that contains a particular word or sentence, but you're not sure which file it is in. The FIND command can help you locate the right file. In the following example, the file SORT-MERG.TXT will be searched for the word RED. The word you are looking for in a file is known as the "keyword" or "search word." Note that the FIND routine will only find words exactly matching the keywords you enter. Keywords entered in uppercase will only find uppercase words and not words containing mixed uppercase and lowercase. Type the following to find the keyword RED in the SORTMERG.TXT file:

```
A>FIND "RED" SORTMERG.TXT

---------- SORTMERG.TXT
RED         LINE 1 OF FILE
RED         LINE 1 OF FILE

A>_
```

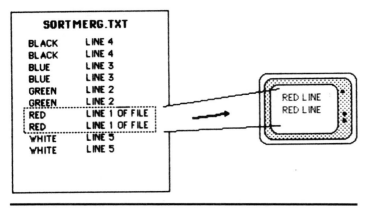

Figure 5-7 The FIND command can be used to locate words or strings in a document. Here, the command FIND "RED" SORTMERG.TXT was used to locate lines containing the keyword RED in the file SORTMERG.TXT and display them on the screen.

Each line containing the keyword RED is displayed. You now know that the file contains the text you were looking for and since the FIND command displays the whole line that the keyword is on, you can see the context of the line surrounding the word (see Fig. 5-7). In this example, we had an idea that the file SORTMERG.TXT contained the keyword so we specified it as the file to be searched. In future chapters you'll see how to search through whole groups of files or all the files on a diskette to find files containing specific keywords.

In the FIND command above, the lines containing the keywords were displayed on the screen. You can direct this screen output into another file by using the redirection facilities of DOS. In the following example, the output of the FIND command is directed to the file RED.DAT. (Don't forget to use the DOS editing keys. You can press the F3 key to reissue the FIND command typed above and add the rest of the command shown below.)

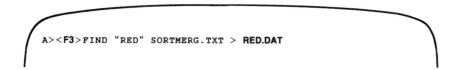

```
A><F3>FIND "RED" SORTMERG.TXT > RED.DAT
```

When you enter the command, nothing is displayed on the screen because the output normally displayed on the screen is directed to the file RED.DAT. You can use the TYPE command to see the contents of the file:

```
A>TYPE RED.DAT

---------- SORTMERG.TXT
RED        LINE 1 OF FILE
RED        LINE 1 OF FILE

A>_
```

Erasing Files

Files that are no longer needed take up room on a diskette. To make space on a disk for other files you can use the ERASE command to remove old files. If you think you might need the file sometime in the future, you can copy the file to another disk (a disk called ARCHIVE FILES, for instance) before erasing it from the original disk. In the following example, the file RED.DAT is removed from the tutorial disk:

```
A>ERASE RED.DAT

A>_
```

Protecting a File

If you have DOS-3, you can protect a file from accidental erasure or alteration by another user. The ATTRIB (attribute) command allows you to change the read/write status of a file. By specifying +R you set a file's attribute to read-only and by typing −R you remove the read-only attribute. Assume that you wanted to protect the file SORTMERG.TXT from accidental erasure or alteration. You would type the following:

```
A>ATTRIB +R SORTMERG.TXT

A>_
```

To return the file to a read/write status, type:

```
A>ATTRIB −R SORTMERG.TXT

A>_
```

Printing the File List

There is one last feature you should know about the DOS COPY and redirection features before moving to the next chapter. In Chap. 2, we used Ctrl-P to get a printout of the directory. Another way to print the directory listing is to use the DOS input/output redirection features. The following command is a convenient way to print a list of files on a disk.

```
A>DIR > PRN

A>_
```

In this chapter, you have built files and moved them around with the COPY command. You also altered their contents with the SORT command. In the next chapter, we will discuss files and file storage and create a special boot disk that is customized for the rest of this tutorial.

6

Files and File Names

Files come in all types and sizes. How you organize and group these files is determined by their content. Since the name of a file is usually a clue to its contents, you can use this name to help organize your diskettes. In this chapter we will discuss file types, file names, and file organization (see Fig. 6-1).

A file name consists of a name that may not exceed eight characters and an extension that may not exceed three characters. A period normally separates the file name from the extension; however, a file does not have to have an extension. The following file names are legal:

SCHEDULE	A file containing daily appointments
FORMLET	A standard letter
LIST1	A mailing list
LIST2	A different mailing list
MYFILE.TXT	A text file
YOURFILE.TXT	Another text file
9-10-83.DAT	A dated data file

There are several things you should be aware of when using or creating files:

- Make sure that a file does not already exist before you create a new one. A file copied to a disk will copy over a file that has the same name, erasing the original file.

- Try to create file names which make sense to you and other people who might be using the system. File names like FILE1.TXT and FILE2.TXT don't really give a clue to their contents. On the other

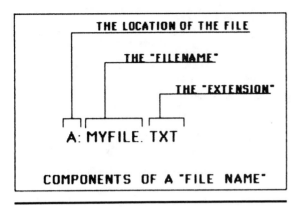

THE LOCATION OF THE FILE

THE "FILENAME"

THE "EXTENSION"

A: MYFILE. TXT

COMPONENTS OF A "FILE NAME"

Figure 6-1

hand, CHAP1.TXT and CHAP2.TXT have meaning. You may want to use the file extension to separate your files from those of another person by placing your initials in the extension.

- File names cannot contain spaces, commas, or quotation marks. If you need a space, use the underscore.

- Files may contain either programs or data. A program file contains code used by the computer to perform a task, and a data file contains characters, usually in the ASCII format (see App. A), in the form of notes, spreadsheets, reports, and other documents.

- A file name on a drive other than the default drive must also contain a drive specifier. For example: B:MYFILE.TXT

- A file name or an extension can be represented by the global wild card characters such as ? or *.

Table 6-1 is a list of file name extensions that have become common over the years, some of which are specific to DOS. Using these extensions will help keep your files organized in groups.

Organizing Files

In Chap. 5 you created several files with the extension of TXT. These files now form a group because they have a common extension. Files grouped in this way can be listed, printed, and even erased together. In this section we will show how wild-card characters can be used to your advantage

TABLE 6-1   Common DOS File Name Extensions

Extension	Meaning	Explanation
BAK	Backup	A backup of a file; created automatically by some programs when you create a new version of a file
BAT	Batch	A user-created command file (text format)
COM[1]	Command	A DOS command file
DAT	Data	A file containing data
DTA	Data	Another abbreviation for data
DOC	Document	A file documenting some other file or command file
EXE[1]	Execute	An executable program file, similar to the COM file
HLP	Help	A file containing help instructions
LET	Letter	A letter
LIB[1]	Library	A program library file
MSG	Message	A file containing a message
SYS[1]	System	A configuration or device driver file
TMP	Temporary	A temporary hold file
TXT	Text	An ASCII text file
$$$[1]		A defective or incorrectly stored file

[1]Used or created by DOS

when you are working with files (see Fig. 6-2). In the example below, the TXT files are listed using the asterisk wild-card character:

```
A>DIR *.TXT
SAMPLE     TXT
SAMPLE2    TXT
MERGED     TXT
SORTMERG   TXT
```

The asterisk has been used in the DIR command to separate the TXT files from the rest of the files in the directory. The following command will print the contents of all files with the extension TXT:

```
A>COPY *.TXT PRN
```

Remember that the syntax of a command is important, especially when using COPY. In the command above, COPY is the command, *.TXT represents all the source files, and PRN (printer) is the destination. Each parameter in the command must be separated by a space.

In the last chapter the file SAMPLE.TXT was copied to the data disk in drive B by using a single COPY command, but many times you will want to copy a whole group of files to another disk. The next screen shows how to copy a group of files on drive A that have a similar extension to the disk in drive B. The disk in drive A should have four files with the extensions of TXT. To copy each of the TXT files to the disk in drive B you can enter the COPY command four times, once for each file, or you can use a wild-card character to copy all the files at once as in the command below.

```
A>COPY A:*.TXT B:
```

Here, COPY is the command, A:*.TXT represents the source files, and drive B is the destination. This command clearly demonstrates the advantage of using similar file names or extensions; we were able to move several files with a single command and a minimum of keystrokes.

File Naming Strategies

It's a good idea to develop a file naming strategy. This section contains tips and suggestions to help you develop a systematic way of naming your

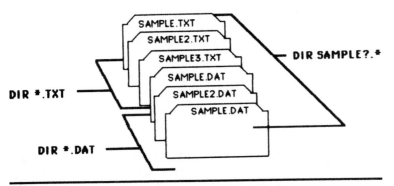

Figure 6-2 Files grouped by name can be separated using wild-card characters and DOS commands.

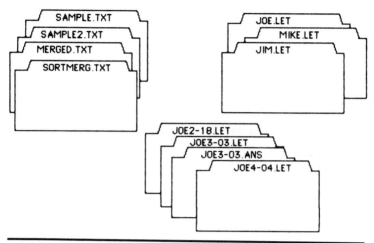

Figure 6-3 Files can be grouped by file names.

files. Table 6-1 lists the most common file name extensions, but you should keep in mind that some applications will tag files with their own extensions. BASIC, for example, tags all its program files with the extension BAS. Lotus 1-2-3 uses the extension WKS and dBASE II uses the extension DBF.

Most of the files you will be using can be grouped into several types. Files created by a database program can have an extension of DAT (data), and files created by your word processor can be tagged TXT, DOC, or LET. Once you have decided on an extension for a group of files, you can use the file name itself to separate files within the group (see Fig. 6-3). For example, assume that you are sending a series of letters to a person named Joe. The following file name could be used:

JOE2-18.LET	A letter sent to Joe on February 18th
JOE3-03.LET	A letter sent to Joe on March 3rd
JOE3-03.ANS	A summary of a reply to the March 3rd letter

If these files were on the disk in drive A and you wanted to copy them to the disk in drive B, all you would have to type is:

COPY JOE∗.∗ B:

In this command, you are using an asterisk in the file name to specify that any character may follow the first three characters. The asterisk in the extension denotes that any extension will do. The ? wild-card character may also be used in file names when copying or performing other

DOS commands. To display all files for the month of March, you could type:

DIR ???3*.*

Here, files with 3 in the fourth position of the file name will be displayed on the screen. The command may look complicated, but it is simple when broken down. The question marks are used to specify that any character will do in the first, second, and third position of the file name. They also help place the 3 in the fourth position.

The file name extension can also be used to separate files created by different people. You can use your initials as the extension for all your files, and other people using the system can use their initials as the extensions for their files.

DOS Device Names

As discussed in Chap. 1, DOS gives names to the devices attached to your system. By using these names, you can tell DOS where to direct the flow of information throughout the system. Table 6-2 gives a complete list of the device names and the device descriptions. These names are reserved by DOS and cannot be used in file names.

Removing Old Files

Before ending this chapter, we'll describe one last command—the ERASE command. ERASE deletes files or groups of files from a disk. You can erase one file at a time or use the wild-card characters to erase selective files. A word of caution: Be careful when using wild-card characters with the ERASE command because you could accidentally erase files that you did not want to erase. For example, assume that you have three Lotus 1-2-3 spreadsheet files on a DOS disk that are called COMPANY1.WKS, COMPANY2.WKS, and COMPANY3.WKS. To erase all three files at once, you could type:

ERASE COM*.*

If you look at your DOS directory listing, you will notice that there are DOS system files that also contain COM as the first three characters of their file names. These files are COMMAND.COM and COMP.COM, and they would have been erased if you had issued the above command.

To prevent erasure problems, list the files first with the DIR command, using the same form of wild-card characters you will be using with your

TABLE 6-2   MS-DOS Standard I/O Device Names

Name	Device	Explanation
CON:	Keyboard	CON stands for console; the keyboard is the input console.
CON:	Monitor	The monitor is the output console.
A:	Floppy drive A	The normal default drive on floppy-disk systems.
B:	Floppy drive B[1]	The second drive on floppy-disk systems.
C:	Fixed disk[1]	The fixed disk on fixed-disk systems.
COM1:	Serial port No. 1	Communications port No. 1; also may be called AUX:.
COM2:	Serial port No. 2	Communications port No. 2.
LPT1:	Parallel printer port No. 1	
PRN:	Another name for parallel port No. 1	
LPT2:	Parallel printer port No. 2	
LPT3:	Parallel printer port No. 3	
NUL:	Null device	A testing device.

[1]Floppy drives take on successive names as more are attached to the system. On an IBM XT, the fixed disk is drive C and the floppy disk is drive A, although a second floppy drive could be added which would become drive B.

ERASE command. For instance, the DIR command shown below will list the same files that will be deleted by an ERASE command that uses the same parameter (COM*.*). You can inspect the listing produced by the command to see if there are any files that might be accidentally erased when you issue ERASE.

DIR COM∗.∗

You should now have a good idea of how files are named and the strategies you can use when naming them. In the next chapter you will see how to create separate directories on a diskette to hold groups of files.

Working with Tree-Structured Directories

DOS 2.0 introduced an important file organization tool that is available for your use. This is the tree-structured or hierarchical filing system (see Fig. 7-1). Under this system, you can divide a disk into a main directory and several subdirectories. Although designed for hard-disk systems which store hundreds of files, hierarchical filing can be used on floppy-disk systems as well. This is especially true if you have DOS-3 and are using the new high-capacity floppy-disk drives that store up to 1.2 megabytes of information on one disk. This chapter is meant to introduce you to the concept of tree-structured filing systems and will lead to a full discussion of this subject in Chap. 20.

Every disk formatted by DOS contains a directory called ROOT that is used to hold a list of files stored on the disk. You can create a separate directory that is subordinate to this main directory and use it to hold files that you want to keep separate from those in the ROOT. Think of this new directory as a separate "room" or storage area on the disk. You can store files in this room and keep them separate from other files.

One use for a subdirectory is to store unneeded files out of the way until they are needed again. This will keep the ROOT directory free of unneeded files that would clutter it. Another use for subdirectories is to store the files of one program separately from the files of another program. Subdirectories are also useful if several people are using the system since each person's files can be stored in a separate directory. Hard-disk systems may have two or three people using the same system; therefore, subdirectories allow each user to maintain his or her own set of files.

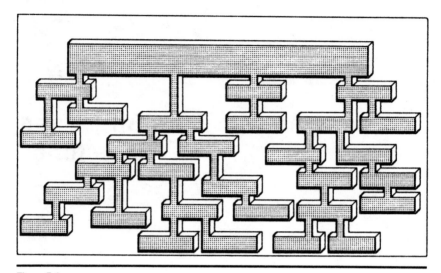

Figure 7-1

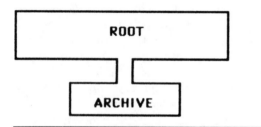

Figure 7-2 The new ARCHIVE directory is a subdirectory of the ROOT directory.

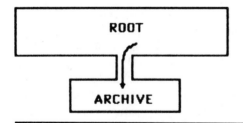

Figure 7-3 Use the command CHDIR ARCHIVE to move to the ARCHIVE directory.

Creating a Subdirectory

The following command will create a subdirectory called ARCHIVE on the disk in drive A. If you are working with a hard disk, your prompt will be C> and the subdirectory will be created on the hard disk. MKDIR stands for make directory and is followed by the name of the new subdirectory in the command below:

```
A>MKDIR ARCHIVE
```

Note that the MKDIR command can be abbreviated to MD and that we will sometimes show this way.

You now have two directories on the disk, the ROOT directory and the ARCHIVE directory. Figure 7-2 shows how the new ARCHIVE directory looks in the tree structure of the disk.

Changing Directories

Go into the ARCHIVE directory and run the DIR command by first entering the following command to change directories (see Fig. 7-3):

```
A>CHDIR ARCHIVE
```

Now, type the DIR command to list the ARCHIVE directory.

```
A>DIR

Volume in drive A is TUTORIAL
Directory of A:\ARCHIVE
.    <DIR>   4-01-84 12:02a
..   <DIR>   4-01-84 12:02a

A>_
```

There are no files in the list; the dot and the double dot refer to the branch of the tree this subdirectory is on, and they will be discussed later. Notice that the listing also shows the name of the directory being listed.

Setting the Directory Prompt

Now that you are using directories and subdirectories, how do you keep track of which directory you are in? If you recall, the PROMPT command that was discussed in Chap. 3 allows you to change the way the DOS prompt appears on the screen, and it has a switch that causes the prompt to display the current directory. The following PROMPT command will change the prompt:

```
A>PROMPT $p$g
A:\ARCHIVE>
```

If you refer to the list of prompts in Chap. 4 (Table 4-1), you will notice that the string $p displays the current directory. The new prompt indicates that the current directory is the subdirectory ARCHIVE. Notice the backslash (\) character, which is the symbol for the ROOT directory. Go back to the ROOT directory and see what the prompt for that directory looks like. Type the CHDIR command using the backslash character as a parameter to return to the ROOT directory (see Fig. 7-4).

```
A:\ARCHIVE>CHDIR \
A:\>
```

Since the backslash designates the ROOT directory, it can be used in the CHDIR command to tell DOS that you want to transfer to that directory. The prompt now indicates the ROOT directory.

Copying Files Between Directories

So far, the ARCHIVE directory is empty. To copy files to the directory, use the COPY command just as you did to copy files to other diskettes.

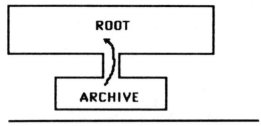

Figure 7-4 Type CHDIR / to return to the ROOT directory.

The name of the subdirectory to receive the files is used in the destination parameter of the COPY command in place of a drive specifier. In the example we show here, you will copy the TXT files (created in previous chapters) from the ROOT directory to the ARCHIVE directory and then erase the old files in the ROOT directory. This will help unclutter the file listing of the ROOT directory. First, type the following command:

```
A: \>COPY *.TXT A:\ARCHIVE
SAMPLE.TXT
SAMPLE2.TXT
MERGED.TXT
SORTMERG.TXT
          4 File(s) copied
```

In the copy command above the source files are designated by *.TXT and the destination is A:\ARCHIVE, the ARCHIVE subdirectory. Each file is copied to the ARCHIVE subdirectory one at a time. Notice the format used to specify ARCHIVE as the destination parameter. You typed the backslash before the name to tell DOS that ARCHIVE branched from the ROOT directory. This is referred to as the "path" to the directory (see Fig. 7-5).

Now, erase the old files on the ROOT directory, assuming that the only TXT files you have there are those created during this tutorial. Don't do this next step if you have TXT files in the ROOT that you want to save.

```
A: \>ERASE *.TXT
```

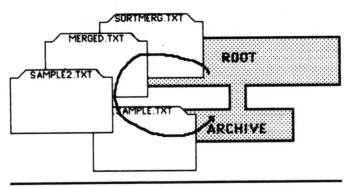

Figure 7-5 The four .TXT files are copied to the ARCHIVE
directory with the command COPY *.TXT A:\ARCHIVE.

Now, go back to the ARCHIVE directory and list the files by typing the
following commands:

```
A:\>CD ARCHIVE (CD is the same as CHDIR)

A:\ARCHIVE>DIR

Volume in drive A is TUTORIAL
Directory of A:\ARCHIVE

.               <DIR>     4-01-84   12:05a
..              <DIR>     4-01-84   12:05a
SAMPLE   TXT       32     4-01-84   12:05a
SAMPLE2  TXT       32     4-01-84   12:05a
MERGED   TXT       65     4-01-84   12:05a
SORTMERG TXT       65     4-01-84   12:05a
```

When working with subdirectories, you will need to add additional
parameters to your commands if you are working between directories.
These parameters tell DOS the specific directory you want to work with.
For instance, in the example above you first moved to the ARCHIVE
directory before issuing the DIR command. You could have listed the files
in ARCHIVE from the ROOT directory by specifying a path to it. Type
the following to try this out:

```
A:\ARCHIVE>CHDIR \

A:\>DIR \ARCHIVE
```

Here, \ARCHIVE tells DOS the path to the ARCHIVE subdirectory; the backslash refers to the ROOT directory, and it is followed by the name of the subdirectory that branches from it.

Entering Commands from a Subdirectory

As you can see, the commands used to copy files between directories and to list files in other directories are similar to the commands used when working with another disk drive. The commands, however, contain the path to the subdirectory instead of the drive specifier. If you own a fixed-disk system, you will be using directories to organize your filing system instead of diskettes, so you can think of the directories as separate diskettes that are similar to those used by owners of floppy-disk systems.

Remember the CHKDSK (check disk) command used to check the surface and file status of a diskette? It should still be a file on the disk you have in the default drive. To make sure, type the DIR command shown below from the ROOT directory.

```
A:\>DIR CHKDSK.COM

CHKDSK    COM      6400    10-20-83    12:00p

A:\>_
```

You can see that the CHKDSK external command is on the disk; therefore, you should be able to type the command name and have it executed by DOS. Before doing so, move to the ARCHIVE directory and then execute the command.

```
A:\>CD ARCHIVE

A:\ARCHIVE>CHKDSK
Bad command or file name

A:\>_
```

If the command is on the disk, why did you get the error message from DOS? The reason is simple. When you switched to the ARCHIVE directory, DOS forgot about the files in the ROOT directory of the disk and began keeping track of the files in the ARCHIVE directory instead. You were able to issue the DIR command previously because DIR is an internal command—one that DOS can find in the computer's memory. The CHKDSK command, on the other hand, is an external command that DOS tries to find on the disk in the default drive.

The PATH command can solve this problem and will let you issue commands from other directories. This command tells DOS to follow an alternate path when trying to find a command before issuing the "Bad command" message. If you type the PATH command below, DOS will know to look in the ROOT directory (remember, the backslash stands for the ROOT directory) for the command, *after* looking in the current directory. It is important to note that DOS will always look in the current directory first, before looking elsewhere along the specified path.

```
A:\ARCHIVE>PATH \

A:\ARCHIVE>CHKDSK
    .
    .
    .
A:\ARCHIVE>_
```

In this chapter, the ARCHIVE subdirectory was created and the SAMPLE text files were copied to it. The files were then erased in the ROOT directory. The command PROMPT pg was issued to set the DOS prompt to display the current directory. The PATH command was then set so that DOS looked in other directories, as well as in the current directory, for commands.

In the next few chapters, you will do more work with the ARCHIVE directory so that you can gain experience with tree-structured filing. Eventually, you will create a sophisticated filing system using directories and subdirectories.

Introducing Batch Files

What Are Batch Files?

Batch files are normal text files like the SAMPLE file you created earlier; however, they contain a command or series of commands that are executed when you type the name of the batch file on the DOS command line. Batch files must have the extension BAT so DOS will recognize them as batch files. In the next example you will create a batch file that will display a wide listing of the ROOT directory and a wide listing of the ARCHIVE directory that was created in the last chapter.

Normally, if you wanted to display these two directories, you would type the following commands:

```
DIR A:/ W
DIR A:\ARCHIVE/W
```

The first command is the familiar DIR command with the /W option used to list the files in wide format. The second command is similar to the first, except that a directory listing is requested for the ARCHIVE subdirectory.

If you needed to see the ROOT and ARCHIVE directories often, it would be tedious to have to retype the DIR commands shown above each time. Instead you can place the two commands in a batch file and then execute them by "running" the batch file. DOS will read each line in the batch file and execute it as if it were a command entered on the command line. Since the batch file is saved on disk, you can run it any time you want. In this book, we will call each command in a batch file an "event" because each command is carried out from start to finish before another begins (see Fig. 8-1).

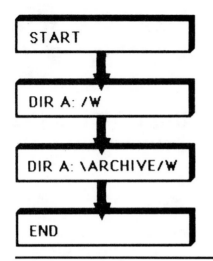

Figure 8-1 A batch file executes one instruction after another, in order.

To create the batch file, get into the ROOT directory so that the batch
file will be stored there after is is written. Since batch files can be called
from any directory, it's best to store them in the ROOT. This is an important feature of batch files which we will discuss later in the book.

```
A:\ARCHIVE>CD \

A:\>_
```

Creating a Batch File

To create your first batch file, type the commands shown below. This
batch file will be called DIR-ALL.BAT, and it can be created with the
COPY CON command. Note that if you have problems when entering the
file, you can start over by pressing Ctrl-Break. This will return you to the
DOS prompt. To begin again, press F3 to reissue the COPY command.
Don't forget to press F6 (or Ctrl-Z) and Return at the end of the file. This
will write the batch file to the disk and return you to the DOS prompt.

```
A:\>COPY CON:DIR-ALL.BAT
DIR A:/W
DIR A:\ARCHIVE/W
<F6>Z        <Return>
        1 File(s) copied

A:\>_
```

Running a Batch File

To execute the batch file, simply type its name at the DOS prompt. You will see the following displayed as the batch command executes its instructions.

```
A:\>DIR-ALL

A:\>DIR A:/W                              (the first event)

  Volume in drive A is TUTORIAL
  Directory of A:\

COMMAND.COM   . . .
  .
  .
  .

A:\>DIR A:\ARCHIVE/W                       (the second event)

  Volume in drive A is TUTORIAL
  Directory of A:\ARCHIVE

  .           ..            SAMPLE    TXT    SAMPLE2    TXT
MERGED TXT SORTMERG TXT
        5 File(s)    24576 bytes free

A:\>
```

This batch file is useful because it displays every file on the disk, including those in the ARCHIVE directory. If you add more directories later, you will need to update this file to include a DIR command for the new directory. In Chap. 11 we'll show you how to create a batch file by using the EDLIN line editor.

Batch files are useful because they provide instant access to commands used often. Once the keystrokes are placed in a file, you will never have to type them again. This will also eliminate the problem of keystroke errors. Batch files can also contain single commands that are too long or cumbersome to retype over and over again, and you can create temporary batch files that execute a series of commands while you are off on a coffee break.

Batch files can also be created for the benefit of inexperienced users such as a new secretary. The following command could be entered into a batch file that is used for starting a program. It asks the operator for the date and time and then starts a program. When the operator exits the program, the log-off message following the REM statement is displayed on the screen. REM stands for remark and is a batch file command that displays messages.

```
DATE
TIME
(command to start program)
REM BYE FOR NOW—YOU CAN TURN THE COMPUTER OFF.
```

To stop a running batch file you can press Ctrl-Break, which causes DOS to display the message "Terminate batch job (Y/N)." If you press Y, the batch file will end and you will be returned to DOS. If you press N, the current command will be stopped and the batch file will continue with the next command in the file.

Other Examples of Batch Files

If you own a dot-matrix printer like the IBM Graphics Printer, you can use a command called MODE to turn on the printer's compressed print mode. The compressed mode prints 132 smaller-than-normal characters across standard-sized paper. This mode is used for printing spreadsheets or other documents that are wider than the standard 80-character line width.

To set the 132-column mode on the printer, you would normally issue the command MODE LPT1:132 and then begin printing your file. After printing, you would type MODE LPT1:80 to set the printer back to its normal setting. You can automate these commands with a batch file and, in the process, get a chance to see an interesting batch-file feature called "replaceable parameters" (see Fig. 8-2). A replaceable parameter is a special feature of batch files that allows you to insert file names, numbers, or

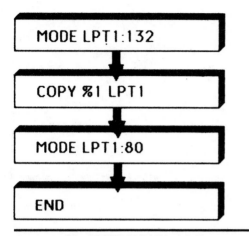

MODE LPT1:132

COPY %1 LPT1

MODE LPT1:80

END

Figure 8-2   The PRNT132.BAT batch file executes three events.

other information into a batch file. In the following batch file, the variable %1 can be replaced with the name of the file you wish to print by specifying that file name on the command line when executing the batch file. Replaceable parameters allow you to use a single batch file for many tasks.

You can use COPY CON to build the file by typing:

```
A:\>COPY CON:PRNT132.BAT
MODE LPT1:132
COPY %1 LPT1
MODE LPT1:80
<F6>   <Return>

A:\>_
```

To use the new file, which is named PRNT132.BAT, you'll need a file to print. The file MERGED.TXT, now stored in the ARCHIVE directory, is a good condidate, so you'll have to transfer to that directory. An important and useful feature of batch files is that you can execute them while in another directory as long as the PATH command has been set to tell DOS where the batch file is stored. Enter the following commands to see how the batch file works. (PATH is reissued here for those who turned their system off since the last session.)

```
A:\>CHDIR ARCHIVE

A:\ARCHIVE>PATH \

A:\ARCHIVE>PRNT132 MERGED.TXT

A:\ARCHIVE>MODE LPT1:132

LPT1: set for 132

A:\ARCHIVE>COPY MERGED.TXT LPT1        (DOS displays
        1 File(s) copied                these messages)

A:\ARCHIVE>MODE LPT1:80

LPT1: set for 80

A:\ARCHIVE>_
```

The first command in the batch file sets the printer to 132-column mode. The next command uses a feature called replaceable parameters to take the file name you typed on the command line (MERGED.TXT) and insert it into the position of %1. Because this batch file uses a replaceable parameter, it can be used to print any file in compressed mode. You simply indicate which file to print as a parameter of the batch file. After printing the file, the printer is reset to 80-column mode.

Each parameter on the command line can be used in a batch file as a replaceable parameter. The position of the parameters on the command line determines its parameter number. The first item on the command line is %0 and is always the batch file name. The second parameter is %1, the third is %2, and so on. Using replaceable parameters in batch files makes the file useful in a variety of different ways because you can specify different parameters every time you use it.

A Special Batch File: AUTOEXEC.BAT

When you first boot your computer, DOS will look for a file called AUTO-EXEC.BAT on the disk in the boot drive. If it exists, DOS will automatically execute the commands in the batch file. This provides you with a way of automatically starting programs, displaying special start-up messages, and executing commands or other batch files. Figure 8-3 illustrates this start-up chain of events.

For instance, suppose you are creating a disk for WordStar. Normally,

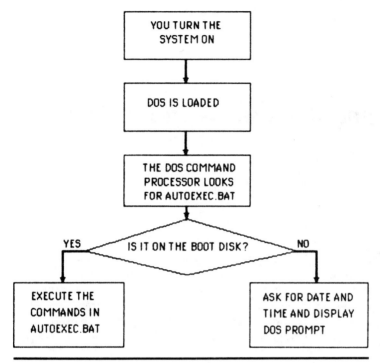

Figure 8-3 The normal system start-up sequence.

to start WordStar you would boot the system and then enter the command WS, which is the command that executes WordStar. You can put this command in the AUTOEXEC.BAT file so that WS will be executed every time you boot with the special disk. You can place messages in the AUTOEXEC file that display welcome messages or instruction for novice users. In the next chapter you'll create a new working disk and an AUTO-EXEC.BAT file that will be placed on the disk.

9

Creating Another Working Disk

In this chapter, you'll create a new version of the DOS disk which will contain improvements over the copy made in Chap. 2. This new disk will have an increased disk capacity and an AUTOEXEC.BAT file that will give you an opening message and set certain system parameters when booted. If you own a fixed disk, you can follow along with the exercises in this chapter even though you don't normally operate with floppy diskettes.

If you are starting this chapter after turning the system off, make sure you have the copy of the DOS disk in drive A before rebooting. (If you own a fixed-disk system, you can boot from the fixed disk.) After booting, issue the PROMPT command shown here to help keep track of the current directory. By the end of this chapter you will have created a boot disk that will set the prompt automatically every time you turn your system on.

```
A>PROMPT $p$g
A:\>
```

Disadvantages of DISKCOPY

Previously, you used the DOS command DISKCOPY to create a working diskette. This command is the easiest and fastest way to create a copy of another diskette; however, there is one problem with it. It creates an exact duplicate or clone of the source diskette. Many programs, including DOS, are supplied on single-sided diskettes. When you use DISKCOPY, you create another single-sided diskette, even though your system may handle double-sided diskettes. You are essentially wasting half of the disk. The reason IBM supplies software on single-sided diskettes is because many of the original buyers still have single-sided drives in their system.

Some software is supplied on two diskettes, each with data stored on one side only. If you have dual-sided drives, you can copy the contents of both of these diskettes to a single diskette that has been formatted for two sides. In the following discussion you will format a double-sided disk and then copy the DOS files to the disk one by one. Although this procedure may take longer than DISKCOPY, it allows you to get maximum use from your diskettes by creating a double-sided disk. Since the DOS files will use only half of the disk, you will have plenty of room left over for other files.

You can run the CHKDSK (check disk) command to determine the capacity of the DOS disk in the default drive by typing the command below:

```
A:\>CHKDSK

    179712 bytes total disk space
     22528 bytes in 3 hidden files
       512 bytes in 1 directories
    132096 bytes in 30 user files
     24576 bytes available on disk
```

Notice that the disk has a total disk space of about 180K, 24K of which is available for other files. Half of the disk space is being wasted because this disk was formatted to look like the original DOS disk from which it was copied with the DISKCOPY command. Formatting the disk with the FORMAT command will allow you to increase the capacity of this disk to about 360K (using DOS-2).

Formatting a New Disk

The DISKCOPY command automatically formats a disk as part of its routine, but as we discussed previously, the formatting routine of DISK-COPY is not ideal. You will need to format the new disk manually, using the FORMAT command, and then copy the DOS files to it one by one, using the COPY command.

When formatting diskettes, you must be careful to specify the correct drive designator of the disk to be formatted. Formatting erases all existing files and data on a disk as part of its routine. Owners of fixed-disk systems should be especially cautious when formatting a disk. It is possible to format and erase an entire fixed disk if you are not careful to specify which drive contains the disk to be formatted. If you do not specify a drive and the current default drive is the fixed disk, DOS will it.

The FORMAT command shown below assumes that you have a two-drive system and have a blank disk in drive B. Owners of single-drive systems should use the same command. DOS will ask you to place the disk to be formatted in drive B (logically drive A on single-drive systems). Owners of fixed disks can use the same command because DOS sees drive A as logical drive B.

```
A:\>FORMAT B:/S/V
Insert new diskette for drive B:
and strike any key when ready_
```

The /S tells DOS to copy the system files to the disk being formatted and the /V switch tells DOS to ask the operator for a volume label after formatting. The system files are special DOS files that are loaded into your computer at boot time and used to control the underlying processes of DOS. Without these files, DOS could not operate and an attempt to boot from a disk that does not contain these files will cause a "non-system disk" error. The system files are called "hidden" files because they reside on the DOS disk in a protected state. You cannot alter the files, and they do not appear in a directory listing. When you specify the /S option in the FORMAT command, the system files are copied to the disk, making it a bootable disk.

To start the formatting routine press any key, for example, the Space Bar. You will see the message "Formatting . . . " appear on the screen.

```
A:\>FORMAT B:/S/V
Insert new diskette for drive B:
and strike any key when ready

Formatting . . .
```

The lights on the disk drive will light up and the disk will spin for about 45 seconds. When finished, DOS will display the following message and ask for a volume name:

```
A:\>FORMAT B:/S/V
Insert new diskette for drive B:
and strike any key when ready

Formatting . . . Format complete
System transferred

Volume label (11 characters, ENTER for none)?_
```

DOS is waiting for a volume label; call this disk TUTORIAL II. Enter the name at the prompt and press Return. If there are any defective sectors or if the disk is bad, a corresponding message will appear on the display; otherwise DOS will display the status of the disk.

```
A:\>FORMAT B:/S/V
Insert new diskette for drive B:
and strike any key when ready

Formatting . . . Format complete
System transferred

Volume label (11 characters, ENTER for none)? TUTORIAL II
    362496 bytes total disk space
     40960 bytes used by system
    321536 bytes available on disk

Format another (Y/N)?_
```

You may choose to format more diskettes while the FORMAT program is still loaded in memory. If you have a box of diskettes, you can format the whole box now. Keep in mind that the system will be transferred to each diskette because you originally requested the /S option with the FORMAT command.

What Does FORMAT Do?

What happens when a disk is being formatted? Mechanically, the read/ write heads in the disk drive move across the surface of the disk in the same way that a needle on a record player moves from the outer edge to the inner edge of a record. You may hear the clicking of the stepper motor as it shifts the head from outer tracks toward the inner tracks. On double-sided disk drives, there are 40 tracks from outer to inner edges (80 tracks on high-capacity disks formatted under DOS-3). As the heads move toward the center of the disk, each track is checked for integrity and is divided into sectors. DOS will store files or parts of files in these sectors (see Fig. 9-1).

The outer tracks of the disk become the disk directory—an area where DOS will store information about the files on the rest of the disk. The system files and volume label are also stored in the outer tracks. If you want to save space on the disk for files, format the disk without the /S option so that space is not taken by the system files. The inner tracks of the disk hold the data, text, and program files you copy to it.

Copying the DOS Files to the New Disk

You can now copy the DOS files from the original tutorial disk to the new disk by typing the following command at the DOS prompt. Notice that the asterisk wild-card character is used in both the file name and exten-sion position of the source parameter. This tells DOS to copy all files on the disk in the default drive to the destination disk which has been spec-ified as B.

```
A : \>COPY A:*.* B:
```

The name of each file is displayed as it is copied to the disk in drive B. The whole copy process should take a minute or so. When finished, a count of the number of files that were copied is displayed.

Copying to Subdirectories

Remember the ARCHIVE subdirectory that you created in Chap. 8? It contains files that were not copied to the disk in drive B with the COPY

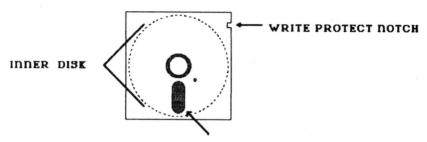

DISKETTE TERMS:

VOLUME A SINGLE DISKETTE IS CONSIDERED ONE VOLUME

FILES INFORMATION IS STORED ON DISKETTES IN UNITS CALLED FILES. FILES OCCUPY PHYSICAL TRACKS ON THE DISK.

RECORDS INFORMATION IN FILES IS FURTHER BROKEN DOWN INTO RECORDS WHICH OCCUPY SECTORS ON A DISK.

The surface of a disk is broken into 40 tracks and 8 or 9 sectors (depending on the version number). Files are stored on one or more tracks of the disk, depending on file size.

TRACKS exaggerated

SECTOR

A typical file is broken into records. Each record stored on a disk occupies one or more of the disks sectors. A mailing list file, for instance, might hold each name and cooresponding information in a record on sectors of a disk. A collection of these records make up a file and the name of the file is held in a special location known as the diskette directory. This directory acts as the table of contents for the disk, telling DOS how large files are and where on the disk they are located. Fortunately, DOS handles all of this — all you have to do is remember the file names and their contents.

Figure 9-1 About diskettes.

command above because the COPY command, even when using *.*, only copies files in the current directory. You could copy the files in the ARCHIVE directory to the disk in drive B by typing COPY \ARCHIVE B:. This would place the copied files in the ROOT directory of the B disk. Instead, copy them to a similar ARCHIVE directory on drive B. To do this you first must create the directory.Type the following at the prompt:

```
A:\>MKDIR B:\ARCHIVE
```

There are two ways to copy the files in A:\ARCHIVE to B:\ARCHIVE. You could change directories (CHDIR) on both diskettes so that you are in the ARCHIVE directories of both. To do this, you could type the following set of commands:

```
CD ARCHIVE        (move to ARCHIVE on A)
CD B:\ARCHIVE     (move to ARCHIVE on B)
COPY A:*.* B:     (copy the files)
```

The other method is to stay in the ROOT directory on both diskettes and issue the following command:

```
COPY A:\ARCHIVE\*.* B:\ARCHIVE
```

This tells DOS the path that it should follow when copying files. Either method will give you the same results. The first method may seem easier, but more typing is involved. The second method requires an understanding of the syntax required to copy the files. The *.* indicates that you want to copy all files in A:\ARCHIVE. This syntax will be discussed more thoroughly in Chap. 20.

Let's use the second method. Type the following on the command line:

```
A:\>COPY A:\ARCHIVE\*.* B:\ARCHIVE
B:\ARCHIVE
A:\ARCHIVE\SAMPLE.TXT
A:\ARCHIVE\SAMPLE.TXT
A:\ARCHIVE\MERGED.TXT
A:\ARCHIVE\SORTMERG.TXT
        4 File(s) copied

A:\>
```

In this example, COPY is the command, A:\ARCHIVE*.* is the source of the files, and the subdirectory B:\ARCHIVE is the destination of the files (see Fig. 9-2). Look closely at the names of the files as they are displayed during the copy. Each file is shown with its full file name indi-

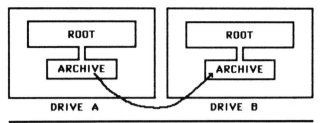

Figure 9-2 Once a directory named ARCHIVE has been
created on the disk in drive B, the files from the ARCHIVE
directory on drive A can be copied to it with the command:
COPY A:\ARCHIVE*.*B:\ARCHIVE.

cating the directory in which it "lives." You may now understand why you
specified the *.* after the directory name in the copy command. It occupies the position of the file names.

Customizing the Disk

The original tutorial disk is now duplicated and is optimized to take
advantage of the full disk space if you have a double-sided drive. The disk
can now be customized to take advantage of various DOS features. In this
section, an AUTOEXEC.BAT file will be created on the new diskette that
will set certain DOS parameters and display a message when the system
boots. In the beginning of this chapter you set the DOS prompt to display
the current directory by typing PROMPT pg. This will be the first command in our AUTOEXEC batch file. The second command will be the
PATH command as shown below:

    PATH \

The backslash represents the ROOT directory. This will direct DOS to
look first in the current directory and then in the ROOT directory when
searching for a command file.

Building an AUTOEXEC.BAT File

You can use the COPY CON command to build an AUTOEXEC.BAT file
by entering the following set of commands. Be sure to press F6 (or Ctrl-
Z) and Return when done; this writes the file to disk. Remember that if
you make a mistake, you can break out by using Ctrl-Break and then reissue the COPY command by pressing F3. In Chap. 16 we will discuss ways
to fix files after they have been created.

```
A: \>COPY CON:AUTOEXEC.BAT
PROMPT $p$g
PATH \
DATE
TIME
. TYPE DIR-ALL TO SEE THE CONTENTS OF THE ENTIRE DISK <F6> <Return>
```

We have included the DATE and the TIME commands in our AUTO-EXEC file, but you may wish to leave them out. We recommend DATE because it will tag all files with a specific date that you can use later when searching or listing files. The last line begins with the period which causes the message following it to be displayed on the screen. This message simply reminds you of the DIR-ALL command used for listing the contents of the disk. Note that if you are using a non-U.S. keyboard, you should include the KEYBxx command in your AUTOEXEC.BAT file to tell DOS which keyboard you will be using.

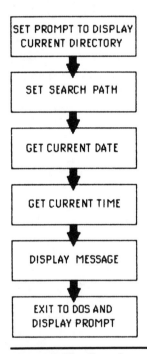

Figure 9-3 The flow of events with the new AUTOEXEC.BAT start-up file.

To see how this file works, reboot your system using Ctrl-Alt-Del (soft reboot). The computer will go through its normal boot procedures and in addition will run the AUTOEXEC.BAT file. PROMPT and PATH will be executed and the message will be displayed on the screen (see Fig. 9-3).

In this chapter, you have created a diskette by formatting and customizing it. The FORMAT example used above is common and will be used often as you work with your computer. In later chapters, we will expand on the concept of the boot message by building menus and help screens that are displayed when you start the system.

Chapter

10

DOS File Commands

Now that you've created a few files and have worked with the operating system, you're ready to further explore the DOS commands and use the sample files created in the previous chapters. These files should be located in the ARCHIVE subdirectory, so most of the work in this chapter will be done in that directory. This will keep the ROOT directory from becoming cluttered with the files you'll use for the tutorial and will also prevent you from accidentally erasing or altering important DOS files.

You can issue DOS commands from the ARCHIVE subdirectory even though the commands are in the ROOT directory because the path has been set by the AUTOEXEC.BAT file created in Chap. 9, assuming you booted with the new diskette.

Renaming Files

Occasionally, you'll want to change the name of a file so that you can reuse the name. You might also change the name so that the file can become part of a group of files that can be manipulated with global commands. To rename any file, use the RENAME command. For instance, you can rename the DIR-ALL.BAT batch file to DIRALL.BAT, eliminating the hyphen and making it easier to type. To do so, enter the following command while in the ROOT directory.

```
A : \>RENAME DIR-ALL.BAT DIRALL.BAT
```

The RENAME command is useful when you need to reuse an existing file name but want to keep the old file. For instance, assume that you wanted to create a new AUTOEXEC.BAT file but also wanted to save the old version for later use. To rename the existing file, you would type the following command:

RENAME AUTOEXEC.BAT AUTOEXEC.BAK

Renaming with Wild-Card Characters

Wild-card characters can be used with RENAME to rename a whole group of file names at one time. Use the RENAME command to change all TXT files to TMP files in the ARCHIVE subdirectory. First, move to the ARCHIVE subdirectory by typing the CHDIR (change directory) command:

```
A:\>CHDIR ARCHIVE

A:\ARCHIVE>
```

Once in the ARCHIVE subdirectory, issue the following command to change the names of all files with the extension of TXT so they have an extension of TMP:

```
A:\ARCHIVE>RENAME *.TXT *.TMP
```

RENAME does not alter the contents of any files. It only changes the names of the files (see Fig. 10-1).

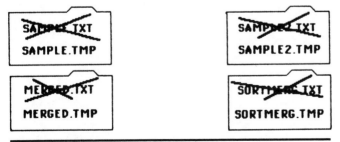

Figure 10-1   RENAME *.TXT *.TMP causes each of the .TXT files to be renamed with the extension .TMP.

Copying with Wild-Card Characters

The DOS COPY command has more combinations than any other command in DOS. In using wild-card characters, you can copy whole groups of files, make duplicates of those that have new names, or join them with other files (concatenation). The following command will make a copy of each of the TMP files in the ARCHIVE subdirectory, giving each copy a new name with the extension of TXT. Unlike the RENAME command, which gave an existing file a new name only, this command makes duplicates of the files and gives each a new name (see Fig. 10-2). Type the following:

```
A:\ARCHIVE>COPY *.TMP *.TXT
SAMPLE.TMP
SAMPLE2.TMP
MERGED.TMP
SORTMERG.TMP
        4 File(s) copied

A:\ARCHIVE>_
```

Now type **DIR** to see a list of the files in the ARCHIVE subdirectory. As you can see, you now have four TMP files and four TXT files. The next COPY command uses the asterisk wild-card character to join or concatenate all the files that have the extensions specified and put them in a new file with the same file name as the first file but with the new extension of BAK. The plus sign concatenates the files. Try the following command:

```
A:\ARCHIVE>COPY *.TMP+*.TXT *.BAK
SAMPLE.TMP
SAMPLE.TXT
SAMPLE2.TMP
SAMPLE2.TXT
MERGED.TMP
MERGED.TXT
SORTMERG.TMP
SORTMERG.TXT
        4 File(s) copied

A:\ARCHIVE>_
```

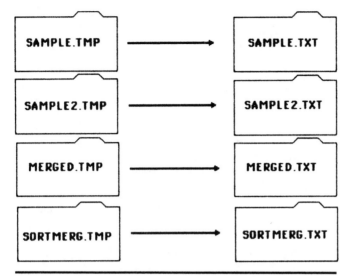

Figure 10-2 Copy *.TMP *.TXT copies all .TMP files, renaming each with the same file name, but with a .TXT extension.

All files that end in either TMP or TXT are joined together in a file having the same first name but an extension of BAK. The original files are left intact.

Saving the Screen Output of a Command

The following exercise will help illustrate several features of DOS. Type the following at the DOS prompt by pressing the F3 key to reissue the previous command and then enter the remainder shown below.

```
A:\ARCHIVE>  <F3>
A:\ARCHIVE>COPY  *.TMP+*.TXT *.BAK I SORT > DISPLAY.DAT
```

In this command, the screen output from the COPY command is directed to a file called DISPLAY.DAT. This file will serve as a record of the files combined with the COPY command and represents an excellent use of the redirection facilities of DOS.

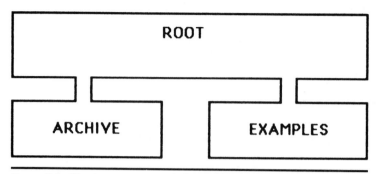

Figure 10-3 The tree structure of the disk with the new EXAMPLES subdirectory.

The F3 key can be used to reissue long commands like the COPY command above. Although most commands are not this long, you will appreciate the editing keys when faced with a similar task.

ERASE

The ERASE command is used for purging files from the disk, so you should be careful when using it, especially with wild-card characters. For instance, if you typed ERASE *.*, all the files in the current directory would be deleted. Remember, if you are erasing a range of files using wild-card characters, it's a good idea to list the files first using DIR and the same wild-card character parameter.

Duplicating and Removing a Directory

Occasionally, you will want to remove a subdirectory or want to change the name of a subdirectory. You cannot actually change a name of a subdirectory as you can a file, but you can create a new one and copy the files from the old directory to the newly named one.

In this exercise you will create a new directory and then copy the files from the ARCHIVE subdirectory to it. Finally you will remove the ARCHIVE subdirectory to make room on the disk. A subdirectory cannot be removed from a disk until the files have been removed or erased inside the directory. Therefore, the first thing to do is to create the new directory and copy the files in ARCHIVE to it. Type in the following command:

```
A:\ARCHIVE>MD \EXAMPLES

A:\ARCHIVE>_
```

It doesn't matter which directory you are in when creating the EXAM-PLES subdirectory as long as you tell DOS where the subdirectory will branch from. In this case it will branch from ROOT as represented by the backslash. Figure 10-3 shows the directory structure of the disk with the new EXAMPLES directory attached.

Now copy the files from the ARCHIVE subdirectory to the EXAM-PLES subdirectory using the command shown next (see Fig. 10-4). Since you are in the ARCHIVE subdirectory, you do not have to specify where the source files are. DOS assumes you want to copy all files in the current directory. The destination is the \EXAMPLES subdirectory.

```
A:\ARCHIVE>COPY *.* \EXAMPLE
SAMPLE.TMP
       .
       .
       .
SORTMERG.TXT
       15 File(s) copied

A:\ARCHIVE>
```

Make sure that the files are in the EXAMPLES subdirectory before erasing them from the current ARCHIVE subdirectory by typing the DIR command shown next. Note that the path has been specified to the EXAMPLES subdirectory.

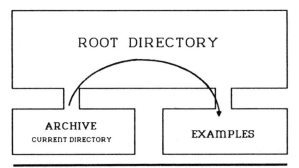

Figure 10-4   To copy all of the files in the ARCHIVE directory to the EXAMPLES directory, issue the command COPY *.*\EXAMPLES from the ARCHIVE directory.

```
A:\ARCHIVE>DIR \EXAMPLES

Volume in drive A is TUTORIAL II
Directory of A:\EXAMPLES
.
.
.
A:\ARCHIVE>_
```

The heading specifies that the files are a listing of the \EXAMPLES subdirectory.

Erasing a Group of Files

Now that the files have been safely copied to a new directory, you can erase the files in the ARCHIVE subdirectory and then remove the subdirectory.

```
A:\ARCHIVE>ERASE *.*
Are you sure (Y/N)? Y

A:\ARCHIVE>_
```

Now that the files in the ARCHIVE subdirectory have been erased, move to the ROOT directory.

```
A:\ARCHIVE>CHDIR \        (backslash is the ROOT directory)

A:\>_
```

Type the following to list the directories:

```
A:\>DIRALL
```

If you recall, you renamed DIRALL.BAT to DIRALL.BAT. DIRALL is the batch command created earlier to display the contents of the ROOT and ARCHIVE directories. As you can see from the listing, the ARCHIVE subdirectory is now empty. ARCHIVE is still shown in the directory listing of the ROOT. Even though this subdirectory is empty, it is using about 1K of disk space. To free up the 1K of disk space, type the following series of commands.

```
A: \>DIR /W
A: \>RMDIR ARCHIVE      (remove directory)

A: \>DIR /W
```

Notice the difference in bytes free after removing the ARCHIVE subdirectory. You have freed 1024 bytes. This is the amount of space required just to have a subdirectory on the disk; it does not include the files that go in it.

Subdirectories and Floppy Disks, Are They Compatible?

If you have a hard-disk system, the previous discussions about subdirectories has been relevant to your system. Are subdirectories really useful with floppy diskettes? If you own a floppy-based system and have been following along, you may have noticed that the drives seem to work harder when accessing subdirectories or transferring files to and from subdirectories. They *are* working harder, and the time it takes to carry out some commands is much longer. Most of the reasons for using subdirectories are only good if you have a hard-disk system. Floppy disks can benefit from one or two directories as a temporary storage area or archive, but an elaborate directory structure is not recommended.

If you are using DOS-3 and have high-capacity floppy diskettes, subdirectories are recommended as a means of dividing several software programs on one disk. Since a single high-capacity floppy can hold up to 1.2 megabytes of information, there is enough room on the disk to store hundreds of files. These files can be organized by dividing them into subdirectories.

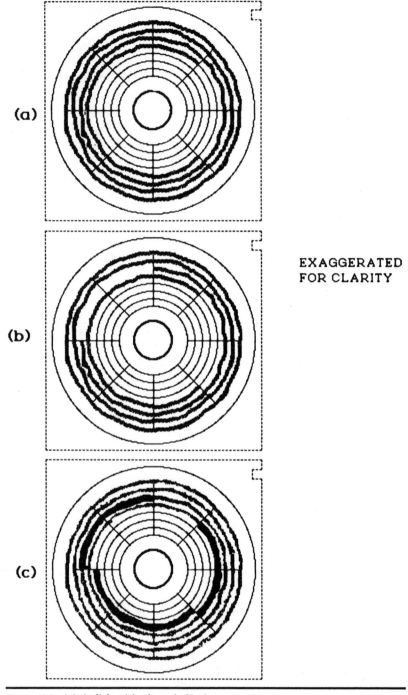

EXAGGERATED
FOR CLARITY

Figure 10-5 (*a*) A disk with about half of its sectors filled. (*b*) A disk with an erased file and open sectors. (*c*) A new file stored in a fragmented condition on the disk. The file fills the two opened sectors.

Optimizing a Disk with Copy

As you progressed through this tutorial, you stored and erased files from the disk. You created an entire directory and then erased everything in it. Think about what this has done to the disk. As you store files, they are placed on concentric tracks that progress toward the center of the disk. These tracks are broken into sectors in which DOS stores blocks of data. Each new file stored on the disk is placed in the next available sector or sectors.

When a file is erased, sectors are freed on the disk that can be used by new files. If the freed sectors are located in the middle of used sectors, there is a possibility that a new file will be stored in a fragmented condition. This will occur when the next file stored on the disk is larger than the sectors freed by the erased file and must be broken into nonadjoining sectors. Figure 10-5 illustrates how available sectors are filled as needed. DOS attempts to place as much of the new file as it can in the open spot and then places the rest of the file in the next available sector, which may be somewhere else on the disk.

If DOS fragements a file by storing it in available sectors on the disk, it has to work harder to read the file the next time it is needed. Fortunately, DOS knows where each sector of the file is located, but the performance of the disk is reduced. To correct a badly fragmented disk, you can copy the entire disk to a newly formatted disk using the COPY command. As each file is copied, it is stored in adjoining sectors on the new disk.

DISKCOPY

The DISKCOPY command copies a whole disk faster than the COPY command because it moves large blocks of data at a time instead of single files. We mentioned that DISKCOPY is not recommended for making backups of program diskettes because it duplicates the single-sided format of the original disk. The BACKUP command, however, is the best way to back up data diskettes or program diskettes that have been formatted to the more efficient double-sided format.

Note that the DISKCOPY command is not useful for cleaning up a fragmented disk, as described in the last section, because it makes an exact duplicate of the source disk. The fragmented files will be copied to the destination disk in exactly the same condition.

This chapter has covered commands used to move, copy, or concatenate files. In the next section, you will get a chance to alter the contents of an existing file by using the EDLIN editor that is supplied with DOS.

11

Working with Editors

What Is Text Editing

An editor will let you alter existing files or create and save a new file on disk. Previously, you used the COPY CON command to enter a simple, short file. One of the disadvantages of using COPY CON, however, is that it does not allow you to edit previous lines in the file. Once you press Return at the end of the line, you cannot go back and make changes to that line. When you use an editor, any line can be altered, deleted, moved, or inserted during an editing session.

EDLIN is a line editor that is supplied with most versions of DOS; you will use it extensively throughout this book. When using EDLIN, you can only work with one line of the file at a time. To work on a line you type in its number, followed by a single-character EDLIN editing command. Files created with EDLIN are stored on a disk in standard ASCII text format (see App. A). This is a way of storing files that has become common among many different type of computers and which allows these different computers to share files. ASCII text files may also be read without modification, as you have seen in previous chapters, when you use TYPE to display a file on the screen.

In this chapter, you will use EDLIN to edit the AUTOEXEC.BAT and DIRALL.BAT files that were created in the previous chapters. You will add a command to the AUTOEXEC file and change the name of the directory that DIRALL lists.

Fixing AUTOEXEC.BAT

Currently, AUTOEXEC.BAT sets the system prompt, sets the path, asks for the time and date, and then displays a message. Let's add the command CHKDSK to the file. By including CHKDSK in the AUTOEXEC batch file, the disk will be checked for errors every time you boot the system. The command also displays the current status of the disk and lists how much disk space is available, helping you determine if a new disk should be created. To edit the file, type:

```
A:\>EDLIN AUTOEXEC.BAT
```

The EDLIN command must include a file name. When you press return, DOS will load the editor and open the file you specified for editing. You will know you are in EDLIN when the asterisk prompt appears. The asterisk prompt is the EDLIN command line and is much like the DOS command line. To list the contents of the AUTOEXEC.BAT file, type an L on the EDLIN command line.

```
A:\>EDLIN AUTOEXEC.BAT
*L
        1:*PROMPT $p$g
        2: PATH  \
        3: DATE
        4: TIME
        5: . TYPE DIR-ALL TO SEE THE CONTENTS OF THE ENTIRE DISK
    *_
```

You should see a list similar to the one above with each line of the file preceded by a number. To insert the CHKDSK command directly after the TIME command and before the message in line 5, type 5I at the asterisk and press Return. EDLIN's INSERT command is simply I, preceded by the line number that is above the insertion point. Type in the CHKDSK command and press Return. Line 6 will appear because you are still in the insert mode. To break out of the insert mode press Ctrl-Break.

```
A:\>EDLIN AUTOEXEC.BAT
*L
        1:*PROMPT $p$g
        2: PATH  \
        3: DATE
        4: TIME
        5: . TYPE DIR-ALL TO SEE THE CONTENTS OF THE ENTIRE DISK
    *5I
        5:*CHKDSK
        6:<Ctrl-BREAK>
    *
```

If you type **L** now, you will see that the message previously in line 5 has been moved down because you inserted a new line in its position.

```
*L
     1:*PROMPT $p$g
     2: PATH \
     3: DATE
     4: TIME
     5: CHKDSK
     6: . TYPE DIR-ALL TO SEE THE CONTENTS OF THE ENTIRE DISK
   *_
```

You may recall that you changed the name of the DIR-ALL batch file to DIRALL in Chap. 10 because it was easier to type that way. You now need to change the message on line 6 so that a correct message will be displayed. With EDLIN, you don't have to retype the entire line to make this change, but instead can use the DOS editing keys to alter the line. EDLIN lets you see the editing template described in Chap. 3 as a line of text above an empty line. The editing keys will copy characters from the upper line to the lower line, making it easy to make alterations. If you type 6 and press Return, you should see a display similar to the one below.

```
*6
     6:*. TYPE DIR-ALL TO SEE THE CONTENTS OF THE ENTIRE DISK
     6:*_
```

The hyphen in DIR-ALL needs to be removed; press the **F1** key until you are directly under it. As you press F1, the characters from the template are copied to the new line. Press the **Del** (delete) key once to remove the hyphen, then press **F3** to copy the template out to the end of the line, and press the **Return** key when done.

```
*6
     6:*.TYPE DIR-ALL TO SEE THE CONTENTS OF THE ENTIRE DISK
     6:*.TYPE DIRALL TO SEE THE CONTENTS OF THE ENTIRE DISK
   *_
```

You can type **L** to list the file and make sure it's okay. To write the altered file to the disk, press **E** for END EDIT.

```
*E
End of input file

A:\>_
```

The AUTOEXEC.BAT file is now fixed. If you run a DIR of the disk, you will notice that EDLIN automatically saved the old version of the file under the name AUTOEXEC.BAK.

Fixing the DIRALL.BAT File

Before ending this chapter and rebooting with the new AUTOEXEC.BAT file, you need to change the DIRALL.BAT file so that it produces a directory listing of the EXAMPLES subdirectory instead of the deleted ARCHIVE directory. Enter the following at the DOS prompt to make this change:

```
A:\>EDLIN DIRALL.BAT
End of input file
*
```

Type an L (LIST) at the asterisk. There are two lines to this file, and the second line must be changed. Type a 2 at the asterisk and press Return:

```
*L
    1:*DIR A:/W
    2: DIR A:\ARCHIVE/W
*2
    2:*DIR A:\ARCHIVE/W
    2:*
```

Copy the template out to the backslash, using the **F1** editing key. Then type in **EXAMPLES/W** and press **Return.** At the asterisk, press E (END EDIT) to write the new file to disk.

```
*2
      2:*DIR  A:\ARCHIVE/W
      2:*DIR  A:\EXAMPLES/W
 *E

A:\>_
```

Both files are now fixed, and you have had your first experience with the editor. EDLIN is a simple, yet powerful editing tool that loads quickly and is ideal for editing short files like the batch files you will be creating in future chapters. For larger, multipage files, you may prefer to use a more powerful editor or a word processor such as WordStar, but for the small files, EDLIN is best.

12

I/O Redirection, Pipes, and Filters

I/O Redirection

What is I/O (input/output) redirection and what is it used for? You have already seen in Chap. 5 how a file can be "directed" into the SORT routine. The arrow symbols used in I/O redirection point to devices or files that you want to send or receive data. Remember that the DOS devices are each given a name such CON (console) and LPT1 (printer). Normally CON is the default data input device (the keyboard) to the computer and the output device (the screen). With DOS-2, and the later versions you can direct output to any device and use any text file as input.

Think about this for a minute. You can put data in a text file and then direct that file as input to a program. Many of the DOS commands will accept data in this way. For instance, the DATE command is used for changing the system date and is normally executed at boot time. You can put a date in a file and then direct the file contents to the DATE command. This may seem a little odd at first. The date changes daily; you would have to update the date file every day. But you may not care about the exact date and wish only to target a particular week or month. Since directory listing can be sorted on the date column, it is advantageous to use the date to group files. Note that if you don't specify a date when you boot, DOS will tag all files with 1-01-1980. In the following command, the file DATE.TXT contains the starting date for a particular week.

Use the COPY CON command to create a file that contains a date:

```
A:>COPY CON:DATE.TXT
04-04-84
<F6> <Return>

A:>  DATE < DATE.TXT
```

The date will now come from the DATE.TXT file every time you boot. When you need a new date simply create a new date file.

In Chap. 32, we will discuss a method of directing the contents of a data file into a BASIC program using the I/O redirection facilities.

When you are using I/O redirection with devices, you will notice many similarities between it and the COPY command. For example, you can direct a file to the LPT port by using the following command:

TYPE MYFILE.TXT > LPT1:

TYPE normally lists a file on the screen, but here it has been redirected to the printer port (see Fig. 12-1). Any output that normally goes to the screen can be directed to another device or into a file.

Many DOS commands display messages and prompts as they run. By directing the screen output from a command into a file, you can record the activities of the command as it executes. For instance, when you concatenate a large group of files into a single file, it would be useful to have a listing of the files that were combined when the COPY took place. Since

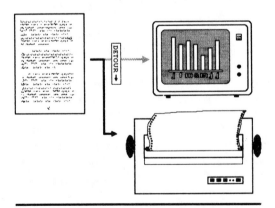

Figure 12-1 I/O redirection detours the standard output to another device.

TABLE 11-1   Standard I/O Redirection Symbols

Symbol	Explanation
>	Causes output to be directed to the device or file name to the right of the arrow. If a file name is specified, the file will be created if it does not already exist.
>>	Causes output to be appended to the end of an existing file. (This may not work with DOS 2.1 and later versions.)
<	Causes a program file or command file to receive input from the specified file.

the COPY command displays each file on the screen as it is copied, you can direct this listing into a file that will serve as a record of the file concatenation. The following command directs the output to a file called RECORD.DAT:

COPY *.TXT B:TEXTMERG.DAT > RECORD.DAT

You can append data or text to a file using the redirection features. The command below will cause characters typed at the keyboard to be sorted and added to the end of a file called SAMPLE.DAT. The double arrows tell DOS to add the data to the end of an existing file. (Note: This command may not work with DOS 2.1 and later versions.)

SORT < CON >> SAMPLE.DAT

Table 11-1 lists standard I/O redirection symbols.

Piping

Piping allows you to put several commands on one line and then direct the output of one command as input to the second command (see Fig. 12-2). The symbol used to pipe commands together is **|**, which can normally

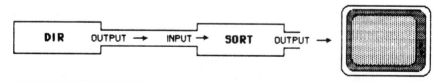

Figure 12-2 Piping directs the flow of data from one command to another.

be found above the Backslash key on the left side of the keyboard. The following command directs the file listing normally displayed on the screen by the DIR command to the SORT utility. The sorted directory is then displayed on the screen.

    DIR ! SORT

When programs share data, you can start more than one program at a time by using the piping feature. The piping symbol ! connects each command on the command line, executing one after the other sequentially from left to right. The following example will run the DIR command first. The listing produced by DIR is passed to a command called FIND, which is a DOS "filter" (discussed next), that filters out lines containing the string COM. These lines are then passed to the SORT utility, which puts them in alphabetical order and stores them in a file called COM-LIST.DAT. You can type this command on your computer to see how it works.

    DIR ! FIND "COM" ! SORT > COMLIST.DAT

Filters

Filters copy text or data from one place, change or rearrange it, and then output it to a different place. DOS-2 has three filters: FIND, SORT, and MORE. These filters are often used with the piping and redirection features. FIND allows you to specify a string to search for in the input and also allows you to output only those lines that contain the string. SORT allows you to sort a file in alphabetical order, and MORE allows you to "page" a file, displaying 24 lines of the file to the screen at a time.

In the example above you passed the directory listing to the FIND filter, through which only lines in the listing containing COM were passed on to the SORT filter (see Fig. 12-3).

The I/O redirection, piping, and filter features of DOS have been handed down from the UNIX operating system. Unix was developed at Bell Labs and is a sophisticated multiuser operating system designed to run on mainframe computers. In UNIX, there are many more "tools" and filters that can be used on a command line. For instance, a file can be passed through a spelling checker, then through a filter that lists each unique word. This list can then be piped into a filter that sorts the list.

FIND "RED"

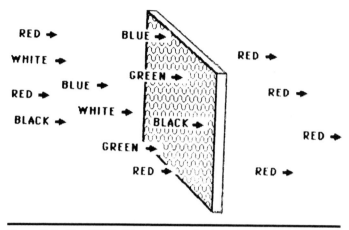

Figure 12-3 The FIND filter passes only those items that match a keyword.

Features and Restrictions of FIND and SORT

The two commands FIND and SORT have certain restrictions. The FIND command will only find text that exactly matches what has been specified. For instance, New York will not find NEW YORK. This is a limiting feature of the FIND command. To get around this limitation, create files in uppercase if you plan to search for text in them later. When FIND locates a match, it will display the whole line that the match was found on. In future chapters, you will see how FIND can be used more effectively in batch files.

The SORT command under DOS-2 sees upper- and lowercase letters differently. SORT uses the ASCII code when sorting characters. If you look at the list of ASCII characters in App. A, you will see that the capital letters A through Z are numbered 65 through 90 and the lowercase letters a through z are numbered 97 through 122. Since SORT uses these number values as its sort criteria, the letter Z would normally come before an a in a sorted listing. If you are using DOS-3, lowercase letters a through z are equated to uppercase A through Z and European characters (ASCII 128 through 175) are collated with the ASCII characters A through Z.

SORT normally uses the character in the first column as its sort character unless you specify another column. You can specify which column

SORT will use by adding /+nn, where nn is the number of the column, to the end of the command.

Sorting the File Directory

Previously, you used the piping feature to direct the listing from the DIR command into the SORT filter to produce a sorted listing of the disk. The command looked like this:

DIR I SORT

In the above command the sorted list would be displayed on the screen. To send the list to the printer use the DOS redirection symbol > (greater than).

A: \>DIR I SORT > PRN

The output from SORT can also be directed to a file. In the command below the file DIRLIST.DAT will receive the sorted directory listing.

A: \>DIR I SORT > DIRLIST.DAT

Paging Through a File

If you use TYPE to display the file DIRLIST.DAT on the screen, you will see a sorted list of the files that are in the ROOT directory. Since the file DIRLIST.DAT is longer that 24 lines (assuming you have been following along with this book), it scrolled off the screen before it could be read. You can page a file on the screen using the MORE filter. The following command redirects the output of the TYPE command into the MORE filter. MORE will then display 24 lines at a time, pausing with the message "— More —." Pressing any key will display more lines.

```
A: \>MORE < DIRLIST.DAT

  .
  .
  .
FDISK     COM    6369   10-20-83   12:00p
FIND      EXE    5888   10-20-83   12:00p
FORMAT    COM    6912   10-20-83   12:00p
— More —
```

Sorting the Directory by Date

The directory listing can be sorted by the date that is tagged to each file
when it is created. This is a good reason for entering the date when you
start a computer session. Since you can specify the column that SORT
should use when sorting, you can tell it to sort a directory listing by its
dates.

```
A: \>DIR I SORT /+24
```

Listing Specific Files with FIND

You can display a directory of specific files using the FIND command. The
following command will display all the lines from the directory listing that
contain the string MERG. You must be sure that MERG is in capital
letters.

```
A: \>DIR I FIND "MERG"
MERGED    TXT     65   4-01-84   12:07a
SORTMERG  TXT     64   4-01-84   12:07a

A: \>_
```

Using FIND in this way is similar to listing a directory with wild-card
characters, except that FIND is not limited by the positioning of the

string in each line. Here is another example in which you list all lines containing the string DIR.

```
A: \>DIR I FIND 'DIR'
DIRALL    BAT        28    04-15-84   12:00p
ARCHIVE          <DIR>     04-15-84   12:00p
DIRLIST   DAT      1534    04-15-84   12:00p

A: \>_
```

Excluding Files from a Listing

You can filter the directory listing, excluding any lines that contain a specific string. In the command below the FIND filter displays all the lines from the DIR listing, excluding those that contain COM.

```
A: >DIR I FIND /V 'COM'
```

Working with a Phone Number File

The following exercise is presented to help you get familiar with the commands that have been discussed in this chapter and to provide a useful utility you can use in your day-to-day operations on the computer. The file shown below, or one like it, can be created with COPY CON and edited with EDLIN. The file included here is for demonstration purposes only; you can create your own phone list now and substitute it in the following examples. In Chap. 26 we will expand on the phone list management concept introduced here.

Be sure to enter the names and other information in uppercase to increase the ability of the FIND command to locate phone numbers.

```
A:\>COPY CON:PHONE.NUM
1ST WORLD           983-3583      BANK
3RD WORLD           934-3857      BANK
BOB                 205/456-8734  BROTHER
DR. EYEBALL         485-3859      EYE DOCTOR
DR. FEELGOOD        987-2039      FAMILY DOCTOR
DR. STANDRITE       485-3434      CHIROPRACTOR
JOE                 837-3848      FRIEND
MR. ROOTER          769-3847      PLUMBER
SALLY               562-2346      AGENT 47
<F6>   <RETURN>
A:\>_
```

Sorting the Numbers

Once the file is entered, you can sort it alphabetically using the SORT command. After it is sorted, you can use TYPE to display the file on the screen.

```
A:\>SORT < PHONE.NUM > PHONE.NUM

A:\>TYPE PHONE.NUM

1ST WORLD           983-3583      BANK
3RD WORLD           934-3857      BANK
BOB                 205/456-8734  BROTHER
DR. EYEBALL         485-3859      EYE DOCTOR
DR. FEELGOOD        987-2039      FAMILY DOCTOR
DR. STANDRITE       485-3434      CHIROPRACTOR
JOE                 837-3848      FRIEND
MR. ROOTER          769-3847      PLUMBER
SALLY               562-2346      AGENT 47
```

Finding Numbers

Now, suppose you want to see Bob's phone number. Type the following, making sure that BOB is in uppercase:

```
A: \>FIND "BOB" PHONE.NUM

------------ PHONE.NUM
BOB                 205/456-8734    BROTHER

A: \>_
```

To find your doctor's phone number, you would type:

```
A: \>FIND "DOCTOR" PHONE.NUM

------------ PHONE.NUM
DR. EYEBALL         485-3859    EYE DOCTOR
DR. FEELGOOD        987-2039    FAMILY DOCTOR

A: \>_
```

Each occurrence of DOCTOR is found in the phone list and displayed on the screen.

Printing the List

To print the list, use the DOS I/O redirection feature, but before printing the list, sort it. The following command sorts the list by the characters in the thirty-third column (the description column) and directs the sorted output to the printer.

```
A: \>SORT/+33 < PHONE.NUM > PRN
```

Adding Names, Deleting Names, and Changing Numbers

You can use EDLIN to add names to the phone list, after which you should resort the list. Enter the commands shown in boldface.

```
A:\>EDLIN PHONE.NUM
End of input file
*L
        1: *1ST WORLD        983-3583        BANK
        2: 3RD WORLD         934-3857        BANK
        3: BOB               205/456-8734    BROTHER
        4: DR. EYEBALL       485-3859        EYE DOCTOR
        5: DR. FEELGOOD      987-2039        FAMILY DOCTOR
        6: DR. STANDRITE     485-3434        CHIROPRACTOR
        7: JOE               837-3848        FRIEND
        8: MR. ROOTER        769-3847        PLUMBER
        9: SALLY             562-2346        AGENT 47
           *10I
       10: *JACK            876-9876         BROKER
       11: *_  <Ctrl-BREAK>
           *E
```

To sort the new list type:

```
A:\>SORT < PHONE.NUM > PHONE.NUM
```

To print the new list type:

```
A:\>COPY PHONE.NUM PRN
```

You can use EDLIN to delete lines in the phone number list. There is usually no reason to sort the file after deleting a line. EDLIN can also be used to change a phone number.

A Batch File to Find a Name

A batch file can be created that will make the process of finding a name in the phone file easier. The batch file will accept a parameter on the command line and use this parameter in the file as the string to be searched for. The file is shown on the next page.

```
A: \>COPY CON:FND.BAT
FIND "%1" PHONE.NUM
<F6> <Return>

A: \>_
```

We called this file FND so that it would not interefere with FIND.COM, the DOS FIND command. To see how the batch file works, type the following:

```
A: \>FND BANK

A: \>FIND "BANK" PHONE.NUM
---------- PHONE.NUM
1ST WORLD       984-3949        BANK
3RD WORLD       394-3948        BANK

A: \>_
```

The replaceable parameter %1 has been replaced with the string BANK and lines containing this string are displayed.

In this chapter you have worked with the advanced features of DOS that have been borrowed from the UNIX operating system, an operating system that runs on large mainframe computers. The advanced features of I/O redirection, piping, and filters will be used extensively throughout the rest of this book and will give you the means to create the sophisticated utilities described in later chapters.

13

More Work with Files

To make your work with DOS easier you can create "menus" or "help" screens that can be displayed on the screen at any time. Before proceeding to the end of the tutorial in the next chapter, we'll take a look at this process and, at the same time, give you more experience with file creation and editing. The files you'll create are a DOS command menu and a batch file used to display the menu. A combination of COPY CON and EDLIN will be used to create these files.

Creating a Help Screen

Boot your system with the TUTORIAL II disk. The computer will execute the AUTOEXEC.BAT file and display the message that tells you about the DIRALL.BAT command. This single-line message is useful, but what if you wanted to have more information displayed on the screen? One way of doing this is to use TYPE to display a text file on the screen, which is how we will display the menu in this chapter. The first step is to begin creating the menu which is shown below. In the next section of this chapter, the AUTOEXEC.BAT file will be altered so that it displays the menu whenever you boot the system. You'll also create a batch file called HELP.BAT that will display the menu at any time.

The help menu below lists various DOS commands that are used often when working with DOS. The menu has a total of 24 lines, so it will display on one screen without scrolling out of view.

```
DOS COMMAND SUMMARY ---------------------------------------------
CD <directory>                    Change directories
CD \                             Go directly to ROOT directory
CHKDSK                           Check disk. Disk and memory
                                   report
DIR/P                            Paged directory listing
DIR/W                            Wide directory listing
DIR !SORT !MORE                  Sorted and paged directory
                                   listing
DISKCOPY A: B:                   Back up a diskette
FIND "string" <file name>        Find a string in a file
FORMAT B:/S/V                    Create bootable disk with DOS
                                   files
FORMAT B:/V                      Create nonbootable data disk
MORE <   <file name>             Page a file
SORT <   <file name>             Sort a file
```

Creating the Help Menu File

To create the menu, you can use a combination of COPY CON and EDLIN, first entering a rough draft of the menu with COPY CON and then using EDLIN to make corrections or alterations. COPY CON allows you to work with a full screen of text on an uncluttered display. Title centering and text alignment with screen boundaries are more easily achieved with COPY CON. Once the rough draft is entered, you can correct typing mistakes and insert or delete text with EDLIN.

Enter the File with COPY CON

Before entering the COPY CON command, clear the screen with the CLS command so that you have an uncluttered work area.

```
A: \>CLS

A: \>COPY CON:HELP.TXT
```

After you enter the COPY CON command, the cursor will blink at the beginning of the first line in the text file. Insert two blank lines by pressing

the Return key twice and then type in the title DOS COMMAND SUM-
MARY (for appearance you can also type in the dashes that were shown
in the example).

```
A:\>COPY CON:HELP.TXT

DOS COMMAND SUMMARY --------------------------------
```

Skip one space and begin entering the help menu shown above or your
own menu. Don't worry if you made a mistake in a previous line—you can
fix it later with EDLIN. After entering the last line, press F6 (or ^Z) and
Return to write the file to disk.

```
A:\>COPY CON:HELP.TXT

DOS COMMAND SUMMARY ---------------------------------------

CD <directory>            Change directories
CD \                      Go directly to ROOT directory
.
.
.

<F6> <Return>
```

Displaying the New File on the Screen

If everything went smoothly, you can use TYPE to display the help file
on the screen to see how it looks. If you need to make corrections to the
file, you can use EDLIN; we'll cover this next.

```
A:\>TYPE HELP.TXT
```

Editing the File

All the commands in the menu so far are standard DOS commands, but
in a previous chapter you created your own command called DIR-

ALL.BAT. Add this new command to the menu, using EDLIN. To begin, enter the following command:

```
A:\>EDLIN HELP.TXT
End of input file
*_
```

Remember that the asterisk is the EDLIN command prompt. Type L (LIST) at this prompt to list the file. Your screen should look like the one below if you entered the two blank lines and the menu we suggested.

```
*L

  1:
  2: *
  3: DOS COMMAND SUMMARY -------------------------------------
  4:
  5: CD  <directory>            Change directories
  6: CD  \                      Go directly to ROOT
                                directory
  7:
  8: CHKDSK                     Check disk. Disk and
                                memory report
  9:
 10: DIR/P                      Paged directory listing
 11: DIR/W                      Wide directory listing
 12: DIR !SORT !MORE            Sorted and paged directory
                                listing
 13:
 14: DISKCOPY A: B:             Back up a diskette
 15:
 16: FIND "string" <file name>  Find a string in a file
 17:
 18: FORMAT B:/S/V              Create bootable disk with
                                DOS files
 19: FORMAT B:/V                Create nonbootable data
                                disk
 20:
 21: MORE <file name>           Page a file
 22:
 23: SORT <   <file name>       Sort a file
*_
```

Your screen may look different if you entered a menu other than the one we show. If so, substitute the numbers shown on your screen for the ones we use as you work through the exercises below. To insert a line between 11 and 12, type 12I (INSERT):

```
*12I
      12:*_
```

Add the DIRALL.BAT command to line 12 and use the Tab key to move to the next column to add the description. After you press Return, EDLIN will allow you to continue inserting new lines. You can break out of the insert mode by pressing Ctrl-Break.

```
12:*DIRALL            Display all disk directories
12:*_  <Ctrl-BREAK>
```

Correcting Mistakes

EDLIN can be used to insert and delete text or to correct a typing error. As an example, change the description of the FIND command to "Find text string in a file," from "Find a string in a file." You'll first have to delete the a and insert text, so to make the alteration, type 17. Notice that FIND is on line 17 because you inserted a line at position 12. It's a good idea to relist the file after adding or deleting lines so you can see changes in line numbers.

```
*17
      17:*FIND "string" <file name>      Find a string in a file
      17:*_
```

Take the following steps to alter the line. Press the **F2** key, and then press **d.** This will copy the template out to the d in Find:

```
*17
      17:*FIND  "string " <file name>    Find a string in a file
      17:*FIND  "string " <file name>    Fin_
```

Now press the **F1** key twice, until the cursor is directly under the a after
Find:

```
*17
    17:*FIND "string" <file name>    Find a string in a file
    17:*FIND "string" <file name>    Find _
```

Press the **Del** key once to delete the a from the template and then press
the **Ins** key so that text may be inserted in the template. Next, type **text:**

```
*17
    17:*FIND "string" <file name>    Find a string in a file
    17:*FIND "string" <file name>    Find text_
```

Press the **F3** key to copy the rest of the template to the line:

```
*17
    17:*FIND "string" <file name>    Find a string in a file
    17:*FIND "string" <file name>    Find text string in a file
```

If you've made a mistake, press **Esc** to start over. Otherwise press **Return**
to confirm the changes.

List the file to make sure all the corrections are right by typing **L**. When
you're done editing, you can press E (END EDIT), and the altered file
will be saved to disk:

```
*E

A:\>_
```

Fixing the AUTOEXEC.BAT File

Now, you need to add a command to the AUTOEXEC.BAT file so that it
will display the command menu. If you insert the command TYPE

HELP.TXT in the batch file, the menu will be displayed whenever you boot the system. To edit the batch file, type:

```
A:\>EDLIN AUTOEXEC.BAT
End of input file
*
```

Type **L** (LIST) to list the file on the screen.

```
A:\>EDLIN AUTOEXEC.BAT
End of input file
*L
      1:*PROMPT $p$g
      2: PATH \
      3: DATE
      4: TIME
      5: CHKDSK
      6: .TYPE DIRALL TO SEE THE CONTENTS OF THE ENTIRE DISK
*_
```

First, you can erase lines 5 and 6. You don't really need to run CHKDSK every time you boot—this can be done manually every now and then—therefore, delete the two lines by typing:

```
*5,6D        (DELETE)
*_
```

Then list the file:

```
*L
      1:*PROMPT $p$g
      2: PATH
      3: DATE
      4: TIME
*_
```

To insert the new command in line 5, type:

```
*5I                  (INSERT)
      5 : *_
```

Enter the new command and press **Ctrl-Break** on the next line to break
out of the insert mode.

```
*5I
      5 : *TYPE HELP.TXT
      6 : _  <Ctrl-Break>
*_
```

Type **E** (END EDIT) to quit and write the file to disk. Then, press
Ctrl-Alt-Del to reboot the system and watch the AUTOEXEC file go
through its steps.

Calling for Help

There will be many times when you want to see the help menu. You could
enter TYPE HELP.TXT every time, but an easier way of doing this
would be to place the command in a batch file. The following batch file
will display the help file whenever you type HELP. To create it, type:

```
A : \>COPY CON:HELP.BAT
TYPE HELP.TXT <F6Z> <Return>
          1 File(s) copied

A : \>_
```

The help menu created in this chapter will be invaluable to you when
you need to know about a DOS command. You can also refer to App. E
for another example of a help screen that will help you with the syntax of
DOS commands.

14

Tutorial Wrap-Up

Now that you have explored the basic ideas, concepts, and tools available in DOS, the rest of this book will be easy going. Everything else you will learn is based on these concepts. In the tutorial we showed you the DOS commands and tools and what you can use them for. This chapter is a review of those lessons.

Starting the System

You should always start your system with a bootable DOS disk in the default disk drive unless you own a fixed-disk system, in which case you can start DOS from the fixed disk. If you use the disk created in the tutorial, the AUTOEXEC.BAT file will go through its paces and set up the system. If you create a new boot disk, it's a good idea to create an AUTO-EXEC.BAT file that contains the start-up instructions that set the prompt and the path and ask for the date. Remember that the prompt can be set to display the current working directory by using the command PROMPT pg. The path can be set so that DOS will look in the ROOT directory for commands and batch files by using the command PATH \.

The Boot Files

There are two DOS boot files that your system searches for when it starts. We have already discussed the AUTOEXEC.BAT file, which can be used to set the prompt, the path, and other parameters or can be used to start an application. CONFIG.SYS is another boot file that you can use for configuring and altering the functions and features of DOS. Both CON-FIG.SYS and AUTOEXEC.BAT must be in the ROOT directory to be properly loaded by DOS. CONFIG.SYS is an ASCII file that contains command lines used by DOS to tailor the system. For example, you can tell DOS to create a special device, such as a "phantom" disk drive (RAM drive), by including the RAM drive file name as a line in the CONFIG.SYS file. See Chap. 25 for a complete description of RAM drives.

The Start-Up Chain of Events

Let's go over the boot-up steps that your computer goes through when you turn it on. This will help you understand the role that the various boot files play in the start-up scheme.

1. Turn the computer on by flicking the power switch.

2. The CPU (8088, 8086, or 80286 microprocessor) kicks into action and looks to the ROM (read only memory) for its first instructions.

3. The ROM instructions for diagnosing the system are passed to the CPU. The memory is checked and the amount available is noted.

4. Next, the ROM instructions tell the CPU to check the disk drive.

5. *a.* If a DOS disk is in the drive, the CPU reads the "bootstrap" information from it. This information starts a chain of events that loads the DOS system files.

   b. If a non-DOS disk is in the drive, the system asks you to place a system disk in the drive.

   c. If there is no disk in the drive or the door is open, IBM PCs load Cassette BASIC; XTs boot the hard disk.

6. The DOS system files are loaded into memory.

7. The disk is then searched for the CONFIG.SYS files. If one exists, the instructions in it are executed. If a RAM drive is specified, for example, it is set up in memory.

8. COMMAND.COM, containing the DOS internal commands, is loaded.

9. DOS is now in control and executes the AUTOEXEC.BAT file if it is found.

You can see that the instructions in ROM "kick start" the system, much like the starter motor on a car puts the much larger engine into motion. The ROM instructions tell DOS to get the rest of its instructions from the system files on the boot disk. This is why a disk not containing the proper system files will not boot.

Internal and External Commands

The DOS file COMMAND.COM contains a set of commands called internal commands. Commands in this file are usually the most common com-

TABLE 14-1 Internal DOS Commands

Command	Description
BREAK	Checks for control break
CHDIR	Changes directories
CLS	Clears the screen
COPY	Copies files
DATE	Enters or changes date
DIR	Lists file names
ERASE	Deletes files
MKDIR	Creates subdirectories
PATH	Sets the search path
RENAME	Renames files
RMDIR	Removes subdirectories
TIME	Sets or changes the time
TYPE	Displays file contents
VER	Displays version number
VERIFY	Sets verify mode on or off
VOL	Displays disk volume

mands used while working with DOS and are kept resident in memory so that DOS does not have to read their instructions from the disk every time they are executed. At boot time the COMMAND.COM file is loaded into memory and stays there. Table 14-1 describes each of the internal commands.

Table 14-2 describes the external commands; they are not stored in memory. Since DOS called these commands from disk, you must have a copy of the files on the disk in the default drive or in a drive that you specify before executing them.

You may copy any of the command files to a disk that you will be using regularly. For instance, you can copy the CHKDSK.COM file from the DOS disk to a disk used to store utility and maintenance programs.

As you create disks to be used on your system, you will want to have some of the DOS external files on the disk so you can use them during your computing sessions. If you formatted the disk with the /S option, the DOS system files will be on the disk, including the internal command file COMMAND.COM. Not all the external commands need be on your diskettes since they take up valuable disk space. Here, we make a few recommendations of files you may want to keep on your diskettes and those you may want to discard.

FDISK, BACKUP, AND RESTORE   These files are used by owners of fixed disks. You will not need them if you have a floppy system.

TREE   If you are not using tree-structured directories you will not need this command file.

TABLE 14-2 External DOS Commands

Command	Description
ASSIGN	Routes disk request to a different drive
ATTRIB[1]	Changes read/write status of a file
BACKUP	Backs up files on a fixed disk
CHKDSK	Checks a disk and gives status report
COMP	Compares files
DISKCOMP	Compares diskettes
DISKCOPY	Copies diskettes
FDISK	Prepares a fixed disk
FORMAT	Formats diskettes
GRAFTABL[1]	Loads graphics character table
GRAPHICS	Prints graphics screen
KEYBxx[1]	Loads support program for language keyboards
LABEL[1]	Allows you to create or alter volume labels
MODE	Sets various system modes
PRINT	Queues and prints files
RECOVER	Fixes erased or damaged files
RESTORE	Restores files to a fixed disk
SELECT[1]	Specifies keyboard and country format
SHARE[1]	Loads file-sharing support
SYS	Transfers DOS
TREE	Displays the directory structure

[1]DOS-3 only

ASSIGN, COMP, DISKCOMP, DISKCOPY, MODE, SYS   You should refer to Chap. 18 to determine your need for these command files.

GRAPHICS   This file sets graphics mode on for an IBM graphics printer; otherwise it is not important.

PRINT   This file is required if you want to do print spooling; refer to Chap. 18 for a description.

CHKDSK   Always useful on any diskette.

FORMAT   Another useful file.

The DOS Editing Keys

Take the time to learn the DOS editing keys. They will save you an incredible amount of typing. As you increase in proficiency with DOS, you will occasionally find yourself "speeding." That is, you will issue commands without the cautious attitude you had as a beginner. In the process you will probably make a few mistakes such as forgetting to insert a drive specifier or leaving out a command entirely. The DOS editing keys can help you salvage incorrectly typed commands. You can refer to App. C for some examples of how the DOS editing keys are used.

Controlling the Display

As we mentioned in the tutorial, there are several ways to control the display of files and directory listing. You can press Ctrl-S to temporarily stop a scrolling display and can resume the scroll by pressing any key. On some systems, Ctrl-Num Lock may be used in the same way. Ctrl-Break can be used to stop a scrolling display completely, but scrolling may not be resumed when it is stopped this way.

Ctrl-P or Ctrol-PrtSc will cause all screen displays to be listed to the printer. This is called "printer echo." To turn the echo off, press Ctrl-P or Ctrl-PrtSc again.

Switches may also be used to control listings on the display. When using the DIR command, you may include the /P option to page the display and the /W option to display the listing in wide format. The two switches may also be used together. You can also control the listing of a file with the MORE command by simply directing the file into MORE as in: MORE < FILE NAME. This will cause the file to be paged to the screen 24 lines at a time.

File Creation and Manipulation

Any file can be created directly from the console (keyboard) using the COPY CON command, or you can use the EDLIN line editor to create or edit files. In the next few chapters, you will make extensive use of the COPY CON and EDLIN commands. Remember that whenever you create a file with COPY CON, you must place an end-of-file marker at the end of the file by pressing F6 (or Ctrl-Z). Pressing the Return key will cause the file to be written to the disk. Keep in mind that COPY CON does not back up old versions of a file but simply copies over them. EDLIN, on the other hand, will rename the old version of your file with the BAK extension. You then have a chance to retrieve the old version if necessary.

Once a file has been created, it may be moved, altered, erased, duplicated, or renamed. Files tend to grow and shrink in size during their life, and DOS will allocate more or less disk space for the file as needed. As files are erased and new files are created, DOS will tend to break files up and scatter then throughout the disk surface, filling the available space opened by erased files. Eventually this will reduce the disk read/write performance of DOS. To correct this problem, you should occasionally back up a disk by copying it, using the COPY command, not the DISKCOPY command.

You should occasionally check your diskettes with the CHKDSK command to see how much room is available and to inspect the disk surface for flaws or bad sectors. CHKDSK can also be used to determine how many files are stored on the disk in a noncontiguous form, a form that slows down the performance of the system. We will discuss this in the next chapter.

There's not a whole lot more we can say about renaming and erasing files other than what was covered in the tutorials. You cannot rename a file with an existing file name. You may wish to rename some of the DOS commands to make them easier to work with. For instance, the name EDLIN.COM could be changed to ED.COM. CHKDSK.COM could be changed to CK.COM, and DISKCOPY.COM could be changed to DCOPY.COM.

Be careful when using the ERASE command because it can be indiscriminate in its destruction. If you issue the command ERASE *.* by accident, it's goodbye data. You will lose every file. To avoid accidental erasures, list files on a disk with the DIR command before erasing so you can see if there are any important files you may want to keep. For instance, DIR *.TXT will list all files that will be erased by an ERASE command using the same parameters.

I/O Redirection, Piping, and Filters

Normally, DOS sends all output to the screen and receives all input from its keyboard. These two devices are known as the "standard" input/output (I/O) devices. Table 6-1 lists the device names that DOS gives to each of the devices attached to your computer. You can tell DOS to send and receive data from other devices by using the I/O redirection features.

You can send the directory listings to the printer instead of the screen, or you can display a file by directing it into a command such as TYPE. I/O redirection provides a useful and easy way to move data through your system. Pipes and filters, including the SORT and FIND commands, are covered in more detail throughout the rest of this book. Both of these commands can be included in batch files to create useful and powerful programs.

The Hierarchical Filing System

In the tutorial, you created a subdirectory called ARCHIVE and then another called EXAMPLES. These subdirectories are part of the hierarchical filing system of DOS-2.0 and later versions. This filing system is commonly called a tree-structured filing system because it resembles the branch structure of a tree. Figure 14-1 illustrates a typical file structure

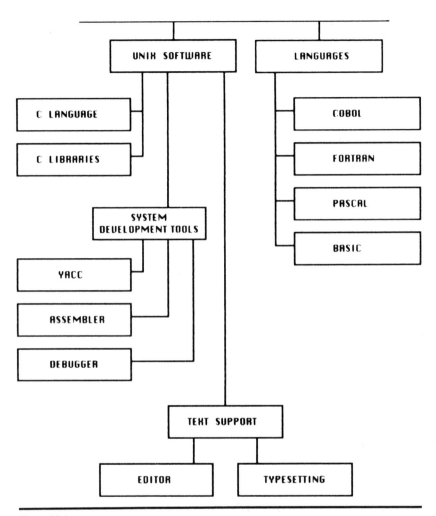

Figure 14-1

derived from the UNIX operating system, the origin of the concept of tree-structured filing. Tree structures in UNIX can get elaborate, as you can see by the illustration. You should not use complicated tree structures with DOS because they tend to slow down the performance of the system. Instead, we will concentrate on two- and three-level tree structures.

Tree-structured filing is not practical on floppy disk systems unless you have DOS-3 and high-capacity disk drives. Although you may have a need to create one or two subdirectories on a floppy disk, a complex tree structure is inefficient and degrades DOS's ability to quickly load and store files. Tree-structured filing is designed for mass storage devices such as the fixed disk. Since a single fixed disk can hold thousands of files, tree-structured filing gives you a way to keep track of those files.

Batch Files

Batch files contain a set of commands that are executed by DOS one after the other. All batch files must end in BAT or DOS will not recognize them as such. When creating batch files, be sure that you do not use the name of a DOS command as a file name. For instance, you should not create a batch file named FIND.BAT because the DOS command FIND.COM will interfere with its operation. Under DOS, files with the extension COM and EXE have precedence over files with the extension BAT.

When should you create batch files? Batch files are convenient anytime a series of commands must be repeated or if a single command is too long to be repeatedly typed over and over again on the command line. Batch files are also a convenient way to automate your system for a novice user because you can place complicated commands in batch files that have simple names like START or QUIT.

The following command is a candidate for a batch file because it requires so much typing. You could call this batch file DIRDATE.BAT because it sorts the directory listing on the date column and sends the listing to the printer.

    DIR ! SORT /+33 > PRN

Creating batch files is like creating your own special DOS commands. With the added batch file features of DOS-2 and DOS-3, you can write batch files with commands that look much like those used in programming languages. These new commands are covered in Chap. 17.

This ends the tutorial section. Our recommendation to you is that you *explore.* You have created a working copy of the DOS disk. With it, you can experiment, create files, erase them, copy them, and so forth without worrying about cluttering up the disk or destroying important data. Become familiar with the command syntax, trying different things to see what will work and what will not work. Work with the editing keys and become proficient with their use. Soon, your fingers will fly over the keyboard.

Part 2

Advanced User's Guide

Taking Care of Diskettes

Working with Diskettes

As you use your system, you will find that certain maintenance procedures must be performed as diskettes become full or old. Occasionally new diskettes must be brought into commission and will need to be formatted and labeled with an appropriate name. You should occasionally check the integrity of your diskettes with the CHKDSK command, as we will discuss in a minute. After a long period of use, the surface of a disk may begin to deteriorate and possibly produce errors; therefore you will need to be aware of the age and usage of the disk. It's a good idea to mark the date of first usage on the label of a diskette to help you keep track of its age. One way to ensure a long life for a disk is to place it back in its protective sleeve after each use, but generally, diskettes tend to have a long life.

Care should always be taken when handling diskettes, and if you have important data stored on disk, you should take extra steps to protect the diskettes. Normally, if you were to touch or damage a disk surface, you should consider decommissioning the disk after copying its files to another disk.

Checking a Disk

Diskettes become full and occasionally need to be backed up, so you should occasionally check the diskette for available space. This can be done with the DIR command, which will, at the end of its list, tell you how much space is remaining on the disk. When working with some programs, you will get disastrous results if you try to save a file on a full disk, so you should always make sure you will have enough room to work with.

If you find a disk is almost full, you can erase old files or copy them to an archive disk. Removing files from an existing disk will eventually degrade the performance of the disk because DOS will place new files in nonadjoining sectors, filling the open spaces left by erased files. DOS allocates files to available sectors whether the sectors are next to each other or fragmented throughout the disk. If you hear a lot of disk clattering when you are loading or saving files, DOS is probably working harder than it should be.

Fragmented files are not a real problem unless the fragmentation becomes excessive. You can check to see how many files are fragmented and what kind of performance you are getting from a disk by running the CHKDSK (check disk) command. "Contiguity" refers to the way files are stored on disk. If a file requires several sectors of storage and those sectors are next to each other, then the file is stored contiguously. If DOS has to store a file in nonadjoining sectors, the file is stored noncontiguously.

Using the CHKDSK Command

CHKDSK is a versatile command that reports disk status and attempts to fix errors on the disk. Here, we are interested in its ability to detect noncontiguous files. The following command will check all files in the current directory of the current drive and list those that are non-contiguous.

```
CHKDSK *.*
```

Several messages may appear. If you get the message "All specified file(s) are contiguous," then the files are stored efficiently on the disk. If there are files stored nonconcontiguously, you will see the message:

```
d:path\file name.ext
Contains nnn noncontiguous blocks
```

This message appears for each file that is broken into several nonadjoining sectors. If only three or four files are broken in this way, then the disk is still okay. If you find that many files are stored noncontiguously on the disk, you should back it up using the COPY command. The following list was produced from a disk that had been used to store WordStar documents. The disk had been in use for over six months. Many files had been created and deleted over the life of the disk.

```
      362496 bytes total disk space
       22528 bytes in 2 hidden files
      149504 bytes in 31 user files
      190464 bytes available on disk

      131072 bytes total memory
      106480 bytes free

F:\LIBRARY.DAT
      Contains 2 non-contiguous blocks.
B:\GATSBY.LET
      Contains 3 non-contiguous blocks.
B:\KANE.COL
      Contains 3 non-contiguous blocks.
B:\MONEY
      Contains 3 non-contiguous blocks.
B:\CHKDSK.COM
      Contains 3 non-contiguous blocks.
B:\XMAS
      Contains 3 non-contiguous blocks.
B:\FRENCH.TXT
      Contains 4 non-contiguous blocks.
B:\SPEECH2.TXT
      Contains 3 non-contiguous blocks.
B:\EXPOSE.TXT
      Contains 2 non-contiguous blocks.
B:\WARD.BAK
      Contains 3 non-contiguous blocks.
B:\LENNY.LET
      Contains 2 non-contiguous blocks.
B:\WARD.LET
      Contains 5 non-contiguous blocks.
B:\BYLINE
      Contains 2 non-contiguous blocks.
B:\BILINE
      Contains 2 non-contiguous blocks.
B:\JUNK.DAT
      Contains 2 non-contiguous blocks.
B:\EXAMPLE
      Contains 2 non-contiguous blocks.
```

In reading or writing a file on this disk, the drives were working much harder than they should have. Notice the CHKDSK.COM command, which we added to the disk just before running the command. It is stored in the location of a recently erased file and has been broken into three noncontiguous blocks. To correct the fragmentation problems on this disk, we copied its files to a new disk using the COPY command.

The DISKCOPY.COM command can be used to back up diskettes but you should know the difference between DISKCOPY and COPY. As covered before, DISKCOPY makes an exact duplicate of the source disk.

This means that it will copy noncontiguous files to the new disk as non-contiguous files. DISKCOPY should only be used to back up diskettes that have files stored contiguously.

Working with Applications Programs

Diskettes supplied with off-the-shelf programs such as WordStar, Lotus 1-2-3, and dBASE II do not come with the DOS system files. The DOS system files are licensed programs that must be purchased separately. Although the manuals for these software packages describe how to add DOS to the program disk, we will discuss this here to make sure that you understand the process.

There are few software packages that will run without the use of an operating system. We know of some games that boot directly without DOS, but most applications will require the DOS system files on the disk to boot properly. There are several methods you can use to do this.

1. The first method can be used with all types of software. You start DOS with your normal DOS boot disk and then insert your applications program in the disk drive. At the DOS prompt, type in the command that normally starts the application. For instance, type WS to start WordStar.

2. The second method can only be used for software that can be copied. Format a new disk with the /S option so that the DOS system files are copied to the new disk. Next, copy the files from the application to the new disk.

3. The third method is used for software that cannot be copied to other diskettes. You must copy the DOS system files to the application diskette. These packages usually have a batch file that will lead you through the install procedures.

The first method would only be used if there is not enough room on the disk for both the applications programs and DOS. Otherwise, method 1 is not practical. Method 2 is the most common. WordStar, Volkswriter, dBASE II, and other software that is not copy protected can be copied to DOS formatted, bootable diskettes. Once a software application has been installed on a disk containing the DOS system files, you can place an AUTOEXEC.BAT file on the disk that will automatically start the program when the system is turned on. You'll have to determine what the start-up command is for the application and include it as a command in the AUTOEXEC.BAT file. For instance, the start-up command for WordStar is WS. To make it self-loading you would create the following batch file:

AUTOEXEC.BAT
DATE
TIME
WS

Remember that you can put other commands in the AUTOEXEC.BAT batch file, such as DATE, TIME, PATH, and PROMPT. Some of the more common start-up commands are DBASE for dBASE II, VW for Volkswriter, Lotus for Lotus 1-2-3, MP or MP80 for Multiplan, and BASICA for the BASIC language. Owners of fixed-disk systems will usually store applications in special directories.

Occasionally, you will have to use the SYS command to copy the DOS system files to an application. The command for transferring the system files from a DOS disk in drive A to a program disk in drive B would be:

A>SYS B:

You should check the documentation for your software to see if there is a batch file that will copy the proper DOS files to the program disk and set it up for use. This batch file is often called SETUP.BAT.

Investigating a Diskette

This section will show you how to investigate an unknown or questionable diskette. For example, suppose a friend has just given you a whole box of diskettes that contains programs from various user groups, bulletin boards, and other sources. There is no documentation with the diskettes, and you are left with the task of exploring each disk. Or suppose you are taking over a computer system that was used by a former employee and find a box that holds various diskettes of unknown content.

Where do you start? The first and most obvious step is to list the files on the disk using the DIR command. Look for an AUTOEXEC.BAT file and display its contents using the TYPE command. Since AUTOEXEC is the automatic start-up command for any programs on the disk, it will probably give you a good idea of the disk contents. If the AUTOEXEC file does not exist, look for other batch files. Batch files usually contain commands or tasks that are carried out often or repetitively and may directly relate to the main use of the disk. Remember, batch files have the extension of BAT and may be read using the TYPE command.

Look for DOC (document) files and use the TYPE command to display them on the screen. Bulletin board services usually supply a document file with each program file. For example, the file SCRNSAVE.DOC will tell you all about SCRNSAVE.COM. Look for COM files. COM files are usually ready-to-run programs. If a corresponding DOC file does not exist for a particular COM file, then you could try running the program to find out what it does. This is done at your own risk. We recommend that you copy the program to a blank disk before running it. There's no telling what the program will do. The last step is to display the contents of any remaining files with the TYPE command, assuming they are standard ASCII text files.

Special Considerations for Owners of Fixed Disks

Fixed disks suffer from the same noncontiguous file problems that floppy disks do, so you should occasionally back up and then restore the files on the disk. The commands BACKUP and RESTORE are used for this purpose and will be covered in more detail in Chap. 24.

When using the FORMAT command on a fixed-disk system, you should be careful to specify that the floppy disk in drive A is the target for the formatting routine; otherwise, you could erase your entire fixed disk. This could occur if, when entering the command, you did not specify the drive to be formatted. For instance, if you were to type:

FORMAT /S

and answer Yes to the question "Insert disk to be formatted in the drive," you would completely erase the hard disk because DOS assumed the default derive was the drive to be formatted.

The following procedure will help prevent the accidental formatting of the fixed disk. Since it is unlikely that you would ever want to format anything but a floppy disk, the batch file described below will direct all formatting routines to the floppy drive instead of the hard drive. First, rename the FORMAT command to DOFORMAT and then create the batch file shown below. We assume that your hard drive is called drive C and the floppy drive is called drive A; otherwise substitute the proper drive designators for your system. Also make sure you are in the ROOT directory.

```
C:\>RENAME FORMAT.COM DOFORMAT.COM
```

Next, create the batch file:

```
c:\>COPY CON:SFORMAT.BAT
REM - PLACE A BLANK DISK IN FLOPPY DRIVE A
PAUSE
DOFORMAT.COM A:/S/V
<F6> <RETURN>
c:\>_
```

This batch file forces the formatting command, which we have renamed DOFORMAT.COM, to format the disk in drive A. We have called the batch file SFORMAT because it places the system files on the disk. To format data diskettes you can create a batch file called DFORMAT.BAT that contains the command DOFORMAT A:/V so it will format diskettes without the system files.

Making Life Easier with Batch Files

Batch files can make your day-to-day interaction with DOS and the computer much more enjoyable. In the tutorial, you created a help screen and then built a batch file that displayed the help screen. Batch files can also be used to set the system parameters when booting, as the AUTO-EXEC.BAT file does. Other batch files can find a word or combination of words in a set of files or can display a set of files on the screen, one after the other.

The following batch files will help save you time and trouble and can be entered using the COPY CON command. The first is called NOCOM.BAT; it will display a directory listing that does not include files that end in COM.

```
A:\>COPY CON:NOCOM.BAT
DIR I FIND/V "COM"

<F6> <Return>
A:\>
```

As you can see, it is much easier to type NOCOM than it is to type the command shown in the batch file. The next batch file will prevent you from erasing needed files. In the tutorial we recommended you run a DIR command before erasing files, so you can see those that might be accidentally erased. The batch file shown below displays the files that will be erased before doing so, giving you a chance to make sure they should be erased. This command is meant to be used when you are erasing with wild-card characters.

```
A: \>COPY CON:REMOVE.BAT
DIR %1/W
REM - THESE ARE THE FILES THAT WILL BE ERASED.
REM - PRESS Ctrl-Break TO STOP.
PAUSE
ERASE %1
<F6><RETURN>
A: \>_
```

To run the batch file type REMOVE followed by the names of the files to be erased. For instance, if you wanted to erase all DOC files, you would type REMOVE *.DOC. The first command in the file will place *.DOC in the position specified by %1. This will issue the command DIR *.DOC, and list all files ending in DOC. The REM (remark) and PAUSE commands will display the message and allow you to break out of the command if necessary. The PAUSE command will temporarily stop the batch processing and display the message "Press any key to continue." If you choose to continue, the ERASE command will erase all DOC files, and the batch command will end.

The next batch file performs a diskette backup. It has all the commands you would normally type when backing up a file, including the CHKDSK (check disk) command to help you determine if a backup is necessary.

```
A: \>COPY CON:NEWDISK.BAT
CHKDSK *.*
REM - IS IT TIME TO BACK UP? PRESS Ctrl-Break IF NOT.
PAUSE
REM - PLACE A BLANK DISK IN DRIVE B
PAUSE
FORMAT B:/S/V
COPY *.* B:
REM - BACKUP COMPLETE—PLACE A LABEL ON THE NEW DISK.
<F6> <Return>

A: \>
```

The first command in the batch file (CHKDSK *.*) displays the condition of the disk you want to back up. You can review the list of noncontiguous files produced by the command and determine whether the disk needs to be backed up. The REM and PAUSE statements allow you to make a decision to continue or not. The PAUSE command displays the message "Strike any key to continue." If you choose to continue, you are asked to place a disk that will be formatted in drive B. The files on the disk in drive A are then copied to it. Since you will need to check disks occasionally, this batch file will allow you to do so and to make a backup, if necessary, in one operation.

In this chapter, we have discussed how diskettes are used on a day-to-day basis and how you can use the CHKDSK (check disk) command to make sure your diskettes are in good condition. The batch files shown here are just a sample of the routines you can create to make your time with the computer easier.

16

Cut and Paste
with EDLIN

The way that text is stored within a file is not permanent. You can move whole blocks of text, insert words, correct mistakes, and delete unwanted parts. The whole process of manipulating the text within a file is known as text editing. You can think of text editing as you would the cut and paste techniques used by newspapers and advertising agencies.

There are many programs and "tools" you can use to edit documents. Word processors such as WordStar or Volkswriter can be used as can an editor such as IBM's Personal Editor. Here we will concentrate on the EDLIN line editor, which is included with DOS. In Chap. 12, you used a combination of the COPY CON command and EDLIN to work with the phone number list. In this chapter you will explore how EDLIN can be used to write short notes and memos and will also get a chance to do more work with the COPY CON-EDLIN combination by creating a screen graphics files.

What Is EDLIN?

EDLIN is called a line editor because all work on a file is done one line at a time. Each line in a file is numbered sequentially, starting with 1. To work on any line you simply type its number on the EDLIN command line. EDLIN also has various commands that can be typed on the command line with the line numbers.

EDLIN is an excellent tool for creating or editing small files such as the batch files we use throughout this book. EDLIN loads quickly compared to some word processors, providing a quick and clean way into and out of files. Once the short list of commands is learned, you may find EDLIN easier or more efficient for some tasks than full-featured word processors or editors. For example, moving a block of text within a document is accomplished much faster with EDLIN than with some word processors.

Line-Oriented Versus Screen-Oriented Editors

In a line-oriented editor you select the number of the line you wish to edit and press Return and it is displayed on the screen. You can only work on one line at a time, and cursor movement is limited to that one line. The cursor may be moved left or right but not up or down to another line.

In screen-oriented editors, a screen's-worth of the document is displayed at one time. You can move the cursor to any location on the screen by using either the up, down, left, or right Arrow keys. In this respect, screen-oriented editors are usually superior to line editors.

There are several advantages to using EDLIN, however. One is the quick loading of the program. With it you can make quick alterations to files or throw together a short batch file with a minimum of time and effort. Another advantage of EDLIN is that it creates ASCII files which, as you'll see in Chaps. 29 and 30, are an ideal format for sending to other computers over phone lines or by direct connection. The files may also be displayed on the screen with TYPE and read as normal text. Some word processors introduce special control codes and other modifications in your text files that make them unreadable or unsuitable for transporting to other computers. EDLIN does not do this.

Loading EDLIN

When you start EDLIN, a file name must be specified. If the file already exists, it will be loaded into memory for editing. If the file does not exist, EDLIN will create it. The examples below list several ways that a file called NEWFILE.TXT could be loaded. The first example assumes that EDLIN.COM is on the default drive and the file to be created or edited is on the same drive.

```
EDLIN NEWFILE.TXT
```

The next example assumes that EDLIN is on the default drive and the file, if it exists, will be read from drive B. If it doesn't exist, EDLIN will create a new file on drive B.

```
EDLIN B:NEWFILE.TXT
```

EDLIN may also be loaded from another disk by specifying the drive designator before the command. For instance, if NEWFILE.TXT was in default drive A, you could place a copy of a disk containing EDLIN in drive B and type:

B:EDLIN NEWFILE.TXT

Using EDLIN

Let's create a file called REMINDER.TXT to show some of the simple EDLIN commands. Enter the following command on the command line:

```
A:\>EDLIN REMINDER.TXT
New file
*_
```

You will see the message "New file" if the file does not exist. If the specified file does exist, EDLIN will load the file into memory. If the file will fit in available memory, EDLIN displays "End of input file." If the whole file will not fit in memory, EDLIN loads only part of the file. You may, however, load any segment of the file into memory. Also, if a file already exists, EDLIN will rename the old version of the file with the BAK extension when you save the revised version. (Files with the BAK extension cannot be edited unless you rename them before editing.)

Line numbers always start at 1 and run sequentially to the end of the file. The line numbers are dynamic, in that if you delete a line, other lines will shift up and renumber automatically. If you add a line, all remaining lines will be renumbered. If the file does not fit in memory and you want to work on a segment still on disk, you must copy the segment of the file in memory to disk before you can read the next segment. This is an inconvenient aspect of EDLIN that makes its use with large files impractical. Most of the files you will work with in this session and throughout this book are small batch files and text files—small enough to make EDLIN worthwhile.

EDLIN always keeps track of a line as the current line. The current line is marked with an asterisk in a listing of the file. If you issue a command without specifying a line number, EDLIN will assume the current line is the line you want to work with. After lines have been added or deleted, the line numbers will change, so it's important to keep track of them. Listing the file frequently will help you see changes in line numbers.

EDLIN Commands

EDLIN uses simple one-character commands. Each command is preceded by a line number that corresponds to the line you wish to edit or do an operation on. One benefit of EDLIN is that it has only a few simple-to-use and easy-to-learn commands. There are two levels of commands, the simplest of which are those used to insert, delete, and list lines. Advanced commands do the following tasks:

- Move lines
- Copy lines
- Write or read specific lines on disk
- Search for text in a file

All EDLIN commands are called by specifying the first character of the command; they are listed in Table 16-1. You don't have to type the entire command. This command character is usually preceded by a line number or range of line numbers.

Inserting Text

Now that the file is open, you can start entering text by typing I (INSERT). After typing in each line as shown in the example below, press

TABLE 16-1 EDLIN Editing Commands

Symbol	Command	Description
A	APPEND	Loads and appends lines from the file to memory for editing
C	COPY	Copies a range of lines to another line number in the file
D	DELETE	Deletes a line or range of lines
E	END EDIT	Saves file and ends editing session
I	INSERT	Inserts lines of text in front of a line number
L	LIST	Lists a range of lines on the screens
M	MOVE	Moves a range of lines to another location
P	PAGE	Scrolls through the file one page at a time
Q	QUIT	Quits EDLIN without saving changes
R	REPLACE	Replaces a string with another string
S	SEARCH	Searches for a string
T	TRANSFER	Inserts text from another file
W	WRITE	Writes lines to disk

Return. EDLIN will give you another line and will continue to give you new lines until you press Ctrl-Break. Type the following:

```
A:\>EDLIN REMINDER.TXT
New file
*I
       1: *ACTIVITIES FOR WEDNESDAY <Return>
       2:* <Return>
       3: *9:00 MEET WITH JACK
       4: *11:00 DROP OFF CAR AT GARAGE
       5: *12:00 LUNCH WITH JANE
       6: *3:00 DENTIST APPOINTMENT
       7: *7:00 CLUB MEETING
       8 *__ <Ctrl-Break>

    *__
```

After you press Ctrl-Break, the EDLIN prompt reappears and waits for another command. You can list the file as it is so far by typing L for LIST:

```
 __L
       1: ACTIVITIES FOR WEDNESDAY
       2:
       3: 9:00 MEET WITH JACK
       4: 11:00 DROP OFF CAR AT GARAGE
       5: 12:00 LUNCH WITH JANE
       6: 3:00 DENTIST APPOINTMENT
       7: 7:00 CLUB MEETING
```

Since you broke out of the INSERT mode on line eight, the file contains seven lines of text. To insert an appointment between the 9:00 and 11:00 appointment, type the following:

```
 *4I
       4: * 10:00 CALL BROKER <Return>
       5: * <Ctrl-Break>
    *__
```

The line is inserted before the line specified in the command. Press Ctrl-Break to break out of the INSERT mode and list the file again to see the new line numbers.

```
*L
        1: ACTIVITIES FOR WEDNESDAY
        2:
        3: 9:00 MEET WITH JACK
        4: 10:00 CALL BROKER
        5:*11:00 DROP OFF CAR AT GARAGE
        6: 12:00 LUNCH WITH JANE
        7: 3:00 DENTIST APPOINTMENT
        8: 7:00 CLUB MEETING

*_
```

The existing lines were shifted down and automatically renumbered when you inserted the new line. Notice that line 5 has the asterisk following the line number, indicating that this line is the current line.

The current-line marker is a convenient feature that you can use when editing. If you type L, EDLIN will list lines that surround the current line. For instance if you had a file that was 30 lines long and the current line was 15, EDLIN would display 11 lines before and after line 15. You may also list lines relative to the current line by using the plus and minus sign. Typing +10L would list the lines starting 10 lines away from the current line. Typing −10L would list 10 lines previous to the current line.

You can display a range of lines by typing the line number you want to start with, along with the L command. If you type 24L, the file will be listed starting at line 24.

Editing a Line

You can edit any line by entering its line number. Suppose the car needs to go to Stoney's Garage. To edit line 5, simply type the line number at the EDLIN prompt:

```
*5
        5:*11:00 DROP OFF CAR AT GARAGE
        5:*
```

The line is displayed with a blank line under it. This set of lines is similar to the editing template used by DOS, except that the line above is the template, which in EDLIN is visible. To copy lines from the template to the blank line press the Right arrow key (or F1), as is done in DOS. As the editing keys are pressed, the characters in the template above are copied to the new line. Press the **Right arrow key** until the cursor is under the G in GARAGE:

```
*5
    5:*11:00 DROP OFF CAR AT GARAGE
    5:*11:00 DROP OFF CAR AT _
*_
```

Now, press the Ins key to open the template so that characters can be inserted. Type in STONEY'S and press the F3 key to copy the rest of the template to the line.

```
*5
    5:*11:00 DROP OFF CAR AT GARAGE
    5:*11:00 DROP OFF CAR AT  <Ins> STONEY'S <F3> GARAGE
*_
```

Now that the changes have been made and the file is complete, you can save it on disk. To end the editing session and save the file, type E (END EDIT) and the file will be saved to disk. If you wanted to quit the editing session without saving the changes, you could type Q (QUIT). You'll want to save the file for later use, therefore type **E** and press **Return.**

Working with Advanced Commands

EDLIN advanced commands allow you to do a variety of editing tasks. Text can be moved, copied, or deleted, and you can search an entire document for a word, replacing it if necessary. Let's work with the reminder file created above to show some of these features. Open the file by typing:

```
A:\>EDLIN REMINDER.TXT
End of input file
*
```

The EDLIN prompt waits for your command. Since the file is small, the entire file is loaded into memory and the message "End of input file" is displayed. Type **L** to list the file.

Cut and Paste: EDLIN's MOVE Command

Normally, when working with text editors, you write a document and then begin altering it by moving sentences and paragraphs around. EDLIN's MOVE command will perform a cut and paste operation in your text file by letting you select either a line or group of lines and move them to another location in the text. Suppose your meeting with Jack has been moved from 9:00 to 1:00 and you want to make the change in the document. Normally, to do this, you would insert the text between lines 6 and 7 and delete line 3. An easier way to accomplish this is to use the MOVE command. To move the line enter the following command:

```
*3,3,7M <Return>
*
```

You won't see any changes as EDLIN moves the lines. Instead, you'll have to list the file to see the changes. The MOVE command takes the form:

<beginning line>,<ending line>,<destination line number>M

It allows a range of lines to be moved to a destination line number. In the example above, 3,3 represents the range of line (one line) and 7 represents the destination. All lines are renumbered after the move. To change the time from 9:00 to 1:00 in line 6, type 6 and use the DOS editing keys to alter the line.

Copying Lines

If you've ever had to retype a whole sentence or paragraph that you just typed in a previous paragraph, the COPY command is what you need. You can select a line or block of lines and duplicate them in another part of the text. EDLIN's COPY command differs from the MOVE command. COPY makes a duplicate of the line or lines at the destination location. To copy lines 1 through 5 to the end of the file and list the changes, type the following EDLIN commands:

```
*1,5,9C

*L

          1: ACTIVITIES FOR WEDNESDAY
          2:
          3: 10:00 CALL BROKER
          4: 11:00 DROP OFF CAR AT STONEY'S GARAGE
          5: 12:00 LUNCH WITH JANE
          6: 1:00 MEET WITH JACK
          7: 3:00 DENTIST APPOINTMENT
          8: 7:00 CLUB MEETING
          9: *ACTIVITIES FOR WEDNESDAY
         10:
         11: 10:00 CALL BROKER
         12: 11:00 DROP OFF CAR AT STONEY'S GARAGE
         13: 12:00 LUNCH WITH JANE
```

Deleting a Range of Lines

You'll often need to delete text in your files to clear out mistakes or unneeded text. The DELETE command allows you to delete a single line or a range of lines. To delete the lines just copied, type in the following command, which erases lines 9 through 13:

   *9,13D

Replacing Text

Occasionally, you will want to change a word throughout an entire document or replace selected words with another word. The REPLACE command allows you to replace one string of text with another. A range may be specified, and you can have EDLIN ask you for a confirmation before it replaces a string by using a question mark in the command.

The command below will replace all occurrences of :00 with GARBAGE in lines 3 through 5. We show this here for demonstration only. On the command line, the EDLIN REPLACE command follows the range of lines that EDLIN will attempt to replace text in. The string to be replaced is inserted after the REPLACE command. F6 (or Ctrl-Z) is then pressed, and the replacement string is then entered. Type the following to make the replacement:

   3,5R:00^ZGARBAGE

As the string is replaced in each line, it is displayed on the screen. Now, convert the lines back to their original contents. This time use the ?

parameter, which is placed before the REPLACE command. Type the following:

```
*3,5?RGARBAGE^Z:00
    3:  10:00 CALL BROKER
O.K.?_
```

EDLIN displays "O.K.?.," asking you if you want to replace the string in the line. You can answer Y for yes and N for no. The REPLACE command is a convenient way to change a string throughout an entire file. For instance, you can write a form letter that contains generic strings like name and date. You can then use this letter any time by replacing the dummy characters with real names and dates using the REPLACE command. If you have a long string that will be repeated several times in a file, you can place a dummy character like # in place of the string and use the REPLACE command later to replace all instances of # with the string.

As a practical example of the REPLACE command, replace Jane in line 5 with Dick and Jane.

    *5,5RJANE^ZDICK AND JANE

Searching for Text

The SEARCH command is a convenient way to find words or strings in a document. For instance, suppose you wanted to edit Table 3 within some document. You could search for the string Table 3, and EDLIN would scan the entire document and place you in the proper place within the document when the string was found. The search will end when the first occurrence of the string is found unless you use the ? parameter. If you use ?, EDLIN will display the prompt O.K.? at each occurrence of the string until you enter Y to accept the one you want. The following command will find all occurrences of :00 in the file.

    *1,8?S:00

Paging Through a Document

After editing your document, you may want to read it while still in EDLIN. The PAGE command allows you to scroll through a large document, one page at a time. You can start at line 1 by pressing 1P. To view consecutive pages after the first page, keep pressing the P key.

Transferring Lines from Another File

Occasionally, you will want to copy text from another file into the file you're working on. You could bring in a table from a spreadsheet file or some common sentences or paragraphs from boilerplate files. Boilerplate files contain blocks of text that can be used in other documents. Merging boilerplate files into the document you are working on will save you a lot of keystrokes. You can merge the contents of another file into the file you are working with by using the TRANSFER command. The contents will be inserted ahead of the line being edited. For example, to transfer a file called EXAMPLE.TXT into the current file ahead of line 5, you would type:

```
*5TEXAMPLE.TXT
```

Quitting EDLIN

When you're finished with the editing tools of EDLIN, you should exit with the E (END EDIT) command. This will save the document and any changes you made to it. The Q (QUIT) command exits EDLIN without saving the edited file. If you decide you don't want to save the file or save any changes made to an existing file, you can exit EDLIN with QUIT. Existing files will be left intact. An example of the QUIT command follows:

```
*Q
Abort Edit? Y

A:\>
```

We have only touched on the capabilities of the EDLIN commands. Since most DOS manuals have a full description of EDLIN, we will not cover it in detail here. Next, you'll see how EDLIN can be used to create screen graphics.

Being Creative with EDLIN: Screen Graphics

EDLIN is a great tool to use when creating screen graphics. In the following exercises, you will use EDLIN to create the graphics screen shown in

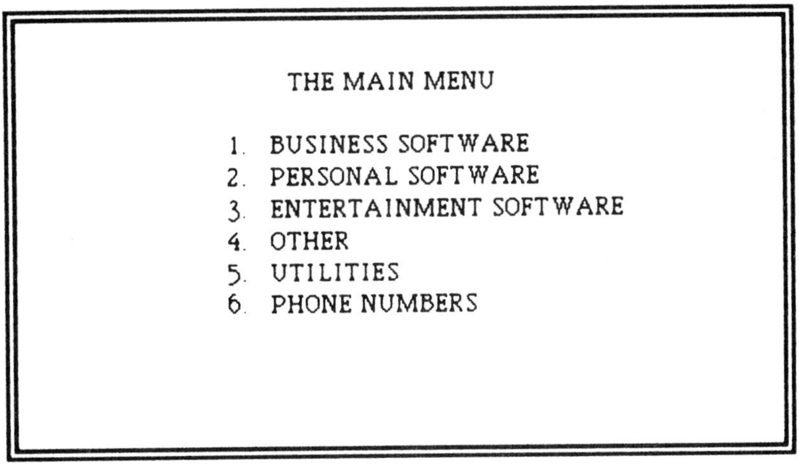

```
┌─────────────────────────────────────────────┐
│                                               │
│                 THE MAIN MENU                 │
│                                               │
│            1.  BUSINESS SOFTWARE              │
│            2.  PERSONAL SOFTWARE              │
│            3.  ENTERTAINMENT SOFTWARE         │
│            4.  OTHER                          │
│            5.  UTILITIES                      │
│            6.  PHONE NUMBERS                  │
│                                               │
│                                               │
│                                               │
└─────────────────────────────────────────────┘
```

Figure 16-1 A menu frame built with IBM's extended graphics characters.

Fig. 16-1. This screen will be used in future exercises as a border for menus and help screens. The illustration shows a menu display box that was created by using the extended ASCII set available on IBM computers (see App. A).

Combining COPY CON and EDLIN

To begin building the menu frame, use the COPY CON command to create the initial structure of the frame. We start with COPY CON because it gives you a full screen to work with when creating the initial frame, helping you center it on the screen.

The frame shown in Fig. 16-1 uses the extended ASCII graphics characters to form its border. You will not enter them at first because it is a tedious task to display them on the screen. You would have to press the Alt-ASCII code sequence a number of times to display them across the screen. Instead, you will use the asterisk character to build an image of the frame and then later replace the asterisks with the graphics characters by using EDLIN's REPLACE command.

The name of the file will be FRAME.PIC. Since the menu box can be used for many applications, you'll not add text to it yet, but instead will make copies for later use.

Start by opening the file using COPY CON:

```
A:\>COPY CON:FRAME PIC
–
```

Figure 16-2 The menu frame as it appears before editing with EDLIN.

Next, press **Return** twice to leave space at the top of the file. On the third line, press the space bar 10 times to indent the first character of the box. Enter the corner symbol (ASCII code 201) at space 11 by typing Alt-201. Next, type 58 asterisk characters; then at the end of the line, press Alt-187 to enter the upper right corner bracket:

A: \>COPY CON:FRAME.PIC

(10 spaces) (Alt-201)∗∗∗∗∗∗∗ ... (58 asterisks) ... ∗∗∗∗∗(Alt-187)

That's the top of the box. Does it look centered? You are using COPY CON for this task so that you can check centering. This is the way it will appear when displayed on the screen later as a menu. If it's not centered, you should make any needed changes now before pressing Return.

On the next line, space over 10 spaces until the cursor is directly under the left corner bracket. Press Alt-186, space over until the cursor is directly under the upper right corner bracket, and then press Alt-186 again. In the next line, make the bottom of the box by spacing over 10 and pressing Alt-200 for the bottom left corner bracket and Alt-188 for the bottom right bracket. Don't worry if the box doesn't seem to have much room. You will expand it later in EDLIN by making multiple copies of the middle line. When you are finished, press the F6 (or ^Z) key and Return. The file should look like Fig. 16-2 at this point.

Altering the Graphics Menu with EDLIN

You'll now use the editing tools of EDLIN to turn the frame into a pleasing graphics display image. Load the file into EDLIN by typing:

A: \>EDLIN FRAME.PIC
End of input file

*_

The first thing to do is replace the asterisk characters with the horizontal graphics character (ASCII code 205) using the EDLIN REPLACE command. Keep in mind that the F6 key (or Ctrl-Z) separates the search text from the replace text. Also, if you list the file first, you will notice that it is contained within five lines because you inserted two blank lines at the top. At the EDLIN prompt, type the following:

1,5R<F6><Alt-205>

EDLIN will go through an interesting display as it replaces every asterisk with the graphics character. When it is finished, you can list the file with the L command to see the changes.

Now all you have to do is expand the height of the box. This is easily done with the EDLIN COPY command. The following command will copy line 4 to lines 5 through 15. Note: A copy of line 4 is made in each new line.

*4,4,5,15C

Tyle L to list the file again. This procedure is simple compared to trying to build the box with Alt-ASCII code sequences. Type E to end edit and exit to DOS. When the DOS prompt appears, type in the following command.

A:\>TYPE FRAME.PIC

You now have a standard frame that you can use to create menus, help screens, directory titles, and so on. When you need a border for a menu or help file, make a copy of FRAME.PIC and add the menu text to the copied file. This will keep FRAME.PIC intact for other menus. Later, you will create a menu called MENU.TXT. You can copy the frame file to a file called MENU.TXT by typing:

A:\>COPY FRAME.PIC MENU.TXT

You now have a duplicate of FRAME.TXT. To keep the original file FRAME.TXT intact, you may want to file it on a disk that contains a library of screen graphics.

In this chapter we explained the EDLIN commands and how they are used to edit a simple appointment file. EDLIN is an excellent tool to use in creating or editing small files such as batch files. In the last half of the chapter, you used a combination of COPY CON and EDLIN to create a menu frame using the extended ASCII codes available on the IBM and some of the compatible computers. This file is called FRAME.TXT and will be used in later chapters.

Working with Batch Files

You have already seen how batch files can make your work on the computer much easier. In this chapter you will further explore batch files and look at some of the advanced features that have been added with DOS-2.

What Is a Batch File?

A batch file consists of a group of events that are carried out by the computer one by one until completed. Running a batch file is equivalent to putting DOS into autopilot mode. Each command in the batch file is executed, sometimes without the need for an operator to monitor the process. In this way, you can build batch files that perform tasks while you are doing something else.

Creating batch files is like creating your own DOS command. To execute the batch file, you type its name on the command line, just like you would if executing a DOS command. Batch files are like the external commands of DOS because they are stored on the disk, waiting to be used at any time. This is one of the best features of batch files; you can enter a set of DOS commands once and never have to retype the whole set again. By executing the batch file, the commands in the file are automatically placed on the command line and executed.

With DOS-2 many advanced features have been added to the DOS batch-file processor. A batch-file language now exists that contains programming features such as loops, GOTOs, and IF/THEN statements. The commands that execute these features are known as batch-file subcommands; they give you the power to write sophisticated batch files.

But what is a computer program? The best examples of programs are the DOS command files on the DOS disk. Each of these files contains a set of instructions that the computer uses to perform some task. For instance, the FORMAT command executes a set of routines that initializes a diskette. The program first asks you to place a disk in the drive and it then formats the disk. All of the instructions that tell DOS how to check the surface of a disk and then prepare it to accept files are contained in the code of the FORMAT.COM command.

When one program is finished, DOS "idles," displaying the familiar DOS prompt, until it is told to execute another program or set of instructions. As long as the instructions are usable by the computer and do not contain errors or bugs, the computer will faithfully execute the code in the program to completion. When finished, the familiar DOS prompt will reappear, waiting for a new command.

There is a difference between the way instructions appear in COM (command) programs and the way they appear in batch files. COM programs contain code that can be used immediately by the computer. The code in COM programs cannot be listed in a readable form on the screen (with the TYPE command for instance). Batch files, on the other hand, are text files that contain commands the computer must translate before executing. Batch files can be read with the TYPE command, but since they do contain text and not executable program code, they run much more slowly than COM files. Batch files, unlike COM files, are easy to write, however, because the batch file subcommands form a mini-programming language that is simple to use and easy to understand.

All programs are built from a series of commands that someone has typed using an editor or word processor, much the same as the EDLIN editor. COM programs start out this way but are eventually converted to computer code. Batch files are always stored as text files, and DOS has the job of converting these files to executable instructions every time the batch file is run.

Programming Features

Your computer can perform various tasks, depending on the instructions in the batch files. The commands available with DOS-2 can become quite elaborate. For instance, a command can pose a question to the computer such as "Is the string of text the operator just typed in equal to another string of text?" The computer can only answer this question logically— with either a Yes or No answer. If the answer is Yes, the computer can be instructed to perform one task, and if it is No, the computer can be instructed to perform another test. On a more practical level, you can write a batch file that says, "If the file name entered by the operator is

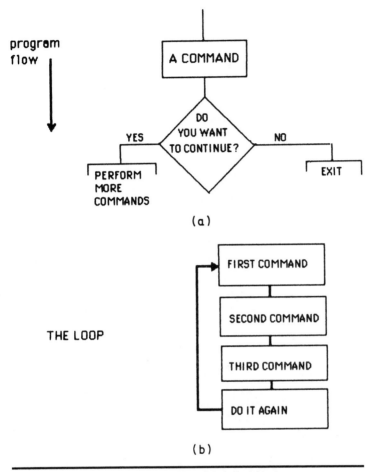

Figure 17-1 Two types of program flow. (*a*) A decision in a
program or batch file. (*b*) An endless loop.

already being used by a file on the disk, then warn the operator before
creating a new file with the same name."

Another new feature of the new DOS batch-file subcommands is the
ability to have the batch file perform a task over and over again by placing
a loop in the batch file. The loop causes the batch file to "jump" back to
a previous instruction and execute it again. You could place a loop in a
batch file that would cause a command to be executed repeatedly until
stopped by the operator (see Fig. 17-1).

In this chapter you will explore the new DOS commands and see how
batch files can be written to take advantage of these new features.

Writing Batch Files

As you may recall from the tutorial, batch files can be created in several ways. You can use a word processor, an editor like EDLIN, or you can create them with the COPY CON command. Since most batch files tend to be small, COPY CON is usually the best tool for writing the files. EDLIN can be used to write batch files or to edit existing files. When writing a batch file with COPY CON, don't forget to close the file by pressing F6 (or Ctrl-Z) and Return.

You can name a batch file with any file name as long as it abides by the file naming rules. You should not name a batch file with the names reserved by DOS for its command files and device names. A batch file name must, however, end with the BAT extension; otherwise, DOS will treat it as a regular file and will not execute it when you type its name on the command line.

Remember that the AUTOEXEC.BAT file is the only batch file that is started automatically by DOS at boot time, and it must be in the ROOT directory or DOS will not execute it. All other batch files must be called by entering their name on the command line.

Running Batch Files

To run a batch file, type its file name as a command on DOS's command line. There is no need to type in the .BAT extension. You can run a batch file from a current directory, even if the batch file is stored in another directory, as long as the search path has been set with the PATH command. Remember that PATH is used to tell DOS in which directories it should look for commands and batch files. This is a powerful feature of DOS that eliminates the need to have duplicate batch files throughout your filing system.

When you execute a batch file, DOS reads each command line one at a time and completes each command before reading another. When it gets the next batch command, it looks on the disk. A batch file is not loaded into memory when executed, therefore DOS requires that a copy of the disk containing the batch file remain in the disk drive while the batch file is executing. If you pull the disk out or forget to put it back in after DOS has executed a command on another disk, DOS will display an error message, informing you that it needs the disk that contains the batch file.

DOS does allow you to change directories as part of a batch file. You can move to a subdirectory, execute commands, and then return to the original directory. DOS will keep track of which directory holds the batch file.

Stopping a Batch File

You can stop a batch file at any time by pressing Ctrl-Break. DOS will then display the message "Terminate batch job (Y/N)?" If you answer Y for yes, the batch file will end processing and ignore the rest of the commands. If you answer N for no, the current command will be stopped, but the remaining commands will be executed.

The Batch File Subcommands

There are seven subcommands that can be used to control batch-file processing. These commands are ECHO, FOR, GOTO, IF, SHIFT, PAUSE, and REM. We will explain each in detail here, but before explaining each command, we will first discuss a feature of batch files called replaceable parameters. Remember that parameters are words, strings, or characters placed on the command that are used by a command or to control the actions of a command. A parameter following a batch-file name has special meaning, as you will see next.

Replaceable Parameters

You can include dummy parameters within your batch file which DOS will replace with values you supply on the command line when executing the file. Using replaceable parameters allows you to specify different sets of data every time you run the batch file. You can use up to 10 parameters; if more are needed, the SHIFT command can be used to extend the available set (see SHIFT). Each parameter entered on the command line is designated inside the batch file as numbers 0 through 9, preceded by the percent (%) sign. Each parameter directly relates to the position of strings on the command line. The example below will help illustrate this:

```
A:\>SEARCH B: ROUND BLUE
```

When you type in a command, the command itself (SEARCH) is parameter %0. The parameter following the command (B:) is %1, and so on. All parameters following the command take on successive parameter values.

Let's create a batch file that uses replaceable parameters. Start your computer in the normal way. If you use the disk you created in the tutorial, it will step through the AUTOEXEC.BAT file and eventually display the DOS prompt. When the DOS prompt appears, type in the following batch file.

```
A:\>COPY CON:LOOP.BAT
REM - LOOP BATCH FILE
CLS
%0
<F6> <Return>
```

Execute the command by typing **LOOP** and watch what happens. The batch file first displays the remark (REM) and then clears the screen by executing the CLS command. The last line of the batch file calls parameter %0, which is the first (and only) parameter on this command line—the LOOP command. This executes the whole sequence over again, (see Fig. 17-2). Here's what the batch file looks like when you run it:

```
A:\>LOOP

A:\>REM - LOOP BATCH FILE

A:\>CLS

A:\>LOOP

A:\>REM - LOOP BATCH FILE

    .
    .
    .
<Ctrl-Break>

A:\>_
```

The batch file will loop forever unless you stop it or the power goes off. To stop the batch file, press Ctrl-Break. This batch file is useless for normal applications, but it does show how parameters and loops can be used.

Let's add another parameter to the batch file. Using EDLIN to edit the

A:\>LOOP

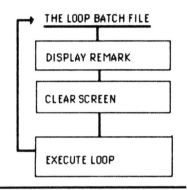

Figure 17-2   A looping batch file.

file you created above, make the changes shown in the next few paragraphs. To get into EDLIN type:

```
A:\>EDLIN LOOP.BAT
End of input file
*L                              (type L for LIST)
      1:*REM - LOOP BATCH FILE
      2: CLS
      3: %0
*_
```

Insert another parameter before the CLS command (see Fig. 17-3). Type 2I at the EDLIN prompt and enter %1. Press Return to accept the

A:\>LOOP DIR

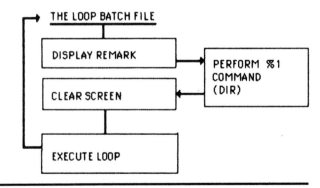

Figure 17-3   Adding a command to the batch file.

new line and press Ctrl-Break to break out of the INSERT mode. You can list the altered file to to see if the correction is okay, then press E to END EDIT, and save the changes.

```
*2I
    2: *%1
    3: * <Ctrl-Break>
*E
    1: REM - LOOP BATCH FILE
    2: *% 1
    3: CLS
    4: %0
*E

A:\>_
```

Now you can execute the new batch file, but this time you can type a string on the command line in the position of parameter %1. This string will be read into the batch file as shown below.

```
A:\>LOOP DIR

A:\>REM - LOOP BATCH FILE

A:\>DIR
    .
    .                       (the directory of drive A is listed)
    .

A:\>CLS

A:\>LOOP

A:\>REM - LOOP BATCH FILE

    .
    .
    .
<Ctrl-Break>
A:\>_
```

You can stop the command by pressing Ctrl-Break. Several interesting things have happened in this new file. When you issued the batch command, LOOP was in the position of %0 and DIR was in the position of

%1. The first time through the batch file, DIR was read into %1 and the directory was displayed. LOOP was then called again by the last line of the file, but the second time through, a parameter was not available to fill %1 and the DIR command was not executed the second time through the loop. If you want to execute DIR every time the batch file loops, the last line of the batch file would have to read %0 %1. You can try this if you like by altering the last line with EDLIN.

Once again, this batch file serves only to demonstrate the features of replaceable parameters. We can think of only a few uses for a looping batch file like the one above. For example, you could continuously run a software demonstration package or graphics animation program with a loop. You could also test the integrity of your hardware by continuously running a test program over and over again.

Let's try one more experiment with replaceable parameters. Create the following file:

```
A:\>COPY CON:SHOWFILE.BAT
TYPE %1
TYPE %2
TYPE %3
<F6>  <Return>
```

This batch file will display, using TYPE, the files that you specify as the first, second, and third parameters on the command line. Type the following at the DOS prompt to display the three files that were recently created:

```
A:\>SHOWFILE REMOVE.BAT LOOP.BAT AUTOEXEC.BAT
```

SHOWFILE will faithfully display each file on the screen, one after the other (see Fig. 17-4). Later, when we discuss batch file subcommands, you'll see how to use wild-card characters to display a whole group of files on the screen.

The REM and ECHO Subcommands

You've already seen how REM will display a message or a prompt while a batch file is executing. Remarks of the sort shown in the previous exam-

A:\>SHOWFILE REMOVE.BAT LOOP.BAT AUTOEXEC.BAT

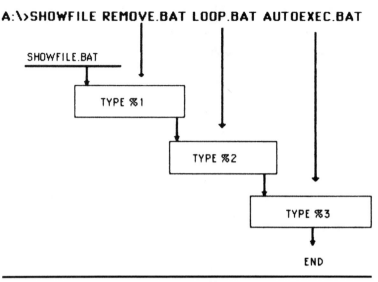

Figure 17-4   A batch file with three replaceable parameters.

ples are usually followed by the PAUSE command to temporarily suspend execution of the batch process. In the batch files that we created earlier a message such as "Do you want to continue?" is displayed, followed by the PAUSE command. This gives the operator a chance to break out of the batch file, if necessary, or to continue. You can also use the REM statement to display the title of a batch file or explain what it does. Remarks can be any string up to 123 characters long. REM must be followed by at least one space but you do not have to follow it with text. REM could be used for spacing to increase readability.

The ECHO command was also added to DOS-2. Although it is similar to REM, it is much more versatile. When you use REM in a batch file, the whole line is displayed, including the REM command itself. This tends to clutter the display and usually causes an operator to ask "what does REM mean?" ECHO allows you to inhibit the screen display of DOS commands as they execute by turning ECHO off. The first command of a batch file can contain the command ECHO OFF, which will inhibit the display of batch commands throughout the rest of the file. Messages produced by the commands themselves will not be inhibited.

If ECHO is off during execution of a batch file, you can display messages on the screen by typing ECHO <message>. In the next few sections, you will use ECHO extensively to enhance the display of batch files as they execute. You can type in the following simple batch file and run it by typing TESTECHO. TESTECHO.BAT demonstrates how the ECHO command works.

```
A:\>COPY CON:TESTECHO.BAT
ECHO OFF
ECHO
ECHO THIS IS A MESSAGE DISPLAYED WITH ECHO OFF
ECHO ON
ECHO
ECHO THIS MESSAGE IS DISPLAYED WITH ECHO ON
```

The following is displayed on the screen as the batch file executes:

```
A:\>TESTECHO

A:\>ECHO OFF
ECHO is off
THIS IS A MESSAGE DISPLAYED WITH ECHO OFF

A:\>ECHO
ECHO is on

A:\>ECHO THIS MESSAGE IS DISPLAYED WITH ECHO ON
THIS MESSAGE IS DISPLAYED WITH ECHO ON

A:\>_
```

The first line sets ECHO off so that the second line displays the off status of ECHO. The third line displays the message in the fourth line in an uncluttered way on the screen. The fifth line turns ECHO back on, but the execution of this command is not visible because ECHO was off when it was executed. The last line shows the undesirable effects of displaying messages when ECHO is on.

The FOR Subcommand

Occasionally you will want to carry out a DOS command on several files. Suppose you want to use TYPE to display the contents of three files on the screen. You could enter the TYPE command each time for each file, or you could use the DOS subcommand FOR in a batch file to perform the same task. Here's how FOR works. The command takes the form of:

FOR % %variable IN (set) DO command % %variable

This subcommand tells DOS, "FOR each member of (set), DO a command." Here's an example. If you type

FOR %%A in (MYFILE.TXT YOURFILE.TXT) DO TYPE %%A

DOS will display the two files in the parentheses. Here, two items in the set, MYFILE.TXT and YOURFILE.TXT, will each be assigned to the variable % %A and the command following the DO statement will be performed on the variable.

The first time the subcommand is executed, it uses MYFILE.TXT from the set. The subcommand would take the form:

FOR MYFILE.TXT DO TYPE MYFILE.TXT

and the file MYFILE.TXT would be displayed with the TYPE command. The second time through, the command would take the form:

FOR YOURFILE.TXT DO TYPE YOURFILE.TXT

and the file YOURFILE.TXT would be displayed with the TYPE command.

The items included in set can be specified with the wild-card characters * and ? if you want specify a whole range of files. You can also specify the items in the set with a replaceable parameter so that the items can be specified on the command line when you start the batch file. For example, the following batch file will display all files with the extension of TXT on the screen.

```
A: \>COPY CON:TYPETXT.BAT
FOR %%A IN (*.TXT) DO TYPE %%A
<F6> <Return>

A: \>_
```

The batch subcommand in the file above uses the asterisk wild-card character to specify all TXT files, and the contents of each batch file is displayed with the TYPE command. The next batch file will allow you to specify the items in set on the command line when executing the batch file:

```
A : \>COPY CON:DISPFILE.BAT
FOR %%A IN (%1) DO TYPE %%A
< ^·Z > <Return>

A : \>_
```

This file is a little more generic and can be used to display any file or group of files on the screen. Try it by typing **DISPFILE *.BAT**. Notice that it even displays its own contents. One of the most important uses of the FOR batch subcommand is to display the contents of each file on a disk or in a subdirectory. You can view the list of files and easily find files you are searching for, or you can locate files to be erased or moved to an archive disk.

The GOTO Subcommand

The GOTO subcommand causes the execution of commands in a batch file to jump to another location in the batch file. With the GOTO subcommand, a batch file no longer has to execute commands in consecutive order. When you use GOTO, control in the program jumps to the label specified in the GOTO command. The label can be placed anywhere in the batch file and must be preceded by a colon (:). GOTOs are usually used with the IF subcommand (covered next). Here's an example showing a simple application of the GOTO command you can type in and run:

```
A : \>TESTGOTO.BAT
:LABEL
ECHO HELP! I'm stuck in a loop.
GOTO LABEL
<F6> <Return>
```

Press Ctrl-Break to break out of the loop.

The IF Subcommand

The IF subcommand allows you to check for certain conditions before executing more commands. The IF subcommand contains two parts. The first part performs a test to see if a certain condition is true. If it is true, then the commands in the second part of the IF subcommand are executed. If the condition is false, the rest of the command is skipped and the next line of the batch file is executed. The IF subcommand is used frequently with the GOTO subcommand, covered previously. When a condition is met, a branch is usually made to another part of a batch file where execution continues. This branch is made with the GOTO command.

The IF command take the following form:

IF <condition> <command>

There are three conditions you can check with the IF command. The first is to check for an ERRORLEVEL code. The second is to compare two strings to see if they are equal. The third condition checks to see if a file exists on a disk.

Checking for ERRORLEVEL

ERRORLEVEL is a variable set by DOS after completion of some command. You can check the error code and perform a task depending on the type of code. When a program or DOS command successfully executes, it sets ERRORLEVEL to 0. If the program did not successfully complete, ERRORLEVEL is set to 1. Currently, only two DOS commands use this feature—BACKUP and RESTORE. You can build a batch file that executes either BACKUP or RESTORE and displays an appropriate message if the commands are completed successfully or not. Here is a sequence you could put in such a batch file that uses the IF ERRORLEVEL subcommand.

```
BACKUP C:\ A: /S
IF ERRORLEVEL 1 ECHO SORRY—THE BACKUP FAILED
```

Here, the ECHO subcommand is used to display the failure message. This message will only display if the backup did *not* work properly. Chap. 24 describes how to use ERRORLEVEL in a batch file with the BACKUP and RESTORE commands.

The Compare Condition

The next type of conditional parameter is used to compare two strings to see if they are equal or not equal. If the conditions are met, then the second component of the command, which is usually a branch to another part of the batch file, is carried out.

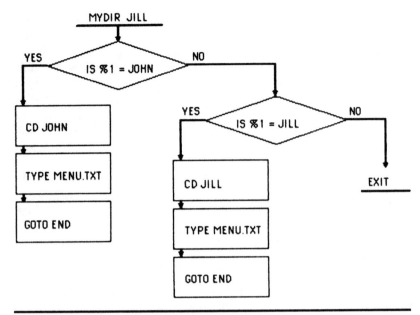

Figure 17-5   A conditionally branching batch file.

The following batch file illustrates how strings are compared. This batch file could be used on a computer that has a fixed disk and several users, each user having his or her own directory. The user enters his or her name when executing the batch file. The batch file then compares this name against others and takes appropriate action. The IF and GOTO commands are used here to transfer control to a different part of the batch file (see Fig. 17-5).

```
MYDIR.BAT
IF %1 = = JOHN GOTO JOHN
IF %1 = = JILL GOTO JILL
GOTO END
:JOHN
CD JOHN
TYPE MENU.TXT
GOTO END
:JILL
CD JILL
TYPE MENU.TXT
GOTO END
:END
```

Assume that the name of this batch file is MYDIR.BAT. When John is working on the system, he would type MYDIR JOHN. The batch file would execute and treat JOHN as %1. The first line compares %1 (JOHN) with JOHN. Since they are equal, the second part of the command, which says "go to the label JOHN," is executed. This label is the fourth line of the batch file which reads :JOHN. The batch file jumps directly to :JOHN, ignoring all the lines in between, and begins stepping through the rest of the batch file. In John's case, DOS changes directories (CD) to the subdirectory JOHN and uses TYPE to display the file MENU.TXT on the screen. The next line says GOTO END. This will cause execution to jump over the next few lines, which pertain to Jill, and go to the end of the batch file.

When Jill logs on, a different sequence occurs. She types MYDIR JILL. This time, the first IF statement fails to make a comparison because JILL does not match JOHN. The next line of the batch file is executed, which compares JILL with JILL. This time a match occurs, and the second part of the command is executed, which causes the batch file to jump to the label :JILL, skipping over all the lines in between. DOS changes directories to JILL and the file MENU.TXT is displayed on the screen. The batch file then jumps to :END, which, in this case, is the next line. We could have left this jump out but put it in for clarity.

In this example, you are on the verge of actually programming the computer. DOS batch-file processing is not really considered a programming language, so we will refrain from calling it that, but you can see the power that is available when you use batch-file subcommands to automate DOS commands.

The IF Exist Condition

There is one more IF condition that you can test. You can check to see if specific files exist on a disk. If a file exists, you can then instruct the computer to display a message or take some other action. The following batch file is an alternative to the COPY CON command. You may want to create it and use it instead of COPY CON because it will prevent you from writing over and thereby erasing existing files. As you may know, if you create a file with COPY CON you are not warned if you are about to write over an existing file. Also, COPY CON does not convert the old file to a BAK file, so you are not protected in that respect.

```
A:\>COPY CON:MKFILE.BAT
IF NOT EXIST %1 GOTO CREATE
ECHO THIS FILE ALREADY EXIST—DO YOU WANT TO WRITE OVER IT?
ECHO PRESS Ctrl Break TO STOP.
PAUSE
:CREATE
COPY CON:%1
<F6> <Return>
```

In this batch file, the NOT condition has been added to the IF statement. The first line says "If the file (%1) does *not* exist, then go to the label :CREATE." The messages following the IF statement are ignored when processing jumps to the label :CREATE. If the file specified does exist on disk, the next few lines, which display the warning messages, are executed. The batch file pauses so that you can make a decision whether to continue or not. If you press Ctrl-Break, the batch file will end and you can start over with another file name. If you press a key to continue (the PAUSE command displays the message "Strike a key when ready . . ."), the batch file executes the COPY CON command and inserts parameter %1 in the position of the file name.

Try running the batch file using a file that you know is on the disk. Then try running it with a file that is not on the disk. This batch file not only prevents you from writing over existing files, but it is much easier to type than COPY CON:<FILE NAME>.

You may have noticed that the screen was cluttered with commands as the batch file executed. You can use the ECHO command to help clean up the display. Enter the following file or use EDLIN to edit your existing file so that it looks like the one below (add ECHO OFF to the first line of the batch file and ECHO ON to the line just before the COPY CON command).

```
A:\>COPY CON:MKFILE.BAT
ECHO OFF
IF NOT EXIST %1 GOTO CREATE
ECHO THIS FILE ALREADY EXIST—DO YOU WANT TO WRITE OVER IT?
ECHO PRESS Ctrl-Break TO STOP.
PAUSE
:CREATE
ECHO ON
COPY CON:%1
<F6> <Return>
```

The first line turns off the display of all commands until the ECHO ON command is encountered. It's a good idea to turn ECHO back on just before the COPY CON command is executed so the user will know what is happening when the batch file runs. You could also place a statement here such as "You are typing characters into a file." Try running the command with a file that you know already exists to see how the batch file prevents you from writing over it.

The Pause Subcommand

The PAUSE subcommand suspends execution of the batch file temporarily and displays the message "Strike a key when ready. . . ." You can display messages in batch files with the ECHO subcommand and then pause so the reader can read the message. These messages must precede the PAUSE command.

A common method used in batch files is to display a message before a major command is executed, giving the user a chance to break out of the batch file. The following line from a batch file shows how this is done.

```
ECHO DRIVE C IS ABOUT TO BE ERASED . . .
ECHO Press Ctrl-Break to stop or
PAUSE
```

The screen display would appear as follows:

```
DRIVE C IS ABOUT TO BE ERASED . . .
Press Ctrl-Break to stop or
Strike a key when ready . . .
```

One of the most useful features of PAUSE is to allow a user to change diskettes between commands of a batch file.

The SHIFT Subcommand

The SHIFT subcommand is made to be used with replaceable parameters. Previously, when we talked about replaceable parameters, you saw how three files could be displayed with the SHOWFILE batch file. What if you wanted to display four files? You would have to rewrite the batch file to include another TYPE command, or you could use the SHIFT command for more than 10 parameters in a file. The following batch file uses the GOTO and SHIFT command to ECHO any number of parameters typed on the command line.

```
A:\>COPY CON:REPEAT.BAT
ECHO OFF
:LOOP
ECHO %1
SHIFT
GOTO LOOP
<F6> <Return>

A:\>_
```

Try running the command by typing:

```
A:\>REPEAT THIS IS JUST A TEST

A:\>ECHO OFF
THIS
IS
JUST
A
TEST
ECHO is off
ECHO is off
 .
 .
 .
```

This batch file has a bug—you'll have to press Ctrl-Break to stop it. Before looking at the bug, let's discuss how the SHIFT command works. When you called the batch file, you specified five words that occupied parameter positions 1 through 5 on the command line. In the batch file, ECHO is used to display the word at parameter position %1. How did the rest of the parameters get displayed? The SHIFT command shifted all parameters one position to the left, replacing parameter %1 with %2, and so on. After shifting the parameters, a GOTO is used to loop back to the label :LOOP and begin again.

Now let's look at the bug. After displaying the last parameter (test) on the command line, the batch file kept executing because it didn't know it was out of parameters from the command line. It will keep shifting blanks into the parameter %1 position and looping back to the :LOOP label where it attempts to echo a blank string. The ECHO command displays the status of ECHO because it doesn't have a string to display. Remember, ECHO by itself displays its current status.

To fix the batch file you must tell it that there are no more parameters on the command line. If you were to type STOP as the last parameter on the command line, you could test to see when STOP is encountered and branch to the end of the batch file when it is. Programmers refer to this as a "flag." Alter your batch file using EDLIN so that it looks like the following:

```
ECHO OFF
:LOOP
IF %1 = = STOP GOTO END      (add this line)
ECHO %1
SHIFT
GOTO :LOOP
:END                          (add this line)
```

To try the batch file again, type:

```
A: \>REPEAT this is a test STOP
```

Two lines have been added to the batch file so it will check for a flag. The first line checks to see if the parameter from the command line is STOP. If STOP is encountered, a branch is made to the label :END, and the batch file ends. If a match is not made, the batch file continues.

Notice that the IF subcommand was included within the loop. If you had placed it above the :LOOP line, the batch file would have made only one comparison the first time through the loop. Study the flow of the file. The label and location of :LOOP is noted by the batch processor. It then executes the IF statement, echoes the word, shifts the parameters, and loops back to :LOOP. Any lines that are above :LOOP are no longer considered. Only those lines contained in the loop are considered.

Another important aspect to the successful completion of this batch file is the keyword STOP. It must be specified after the last parameter. It must also be uppercase if the string you are comparing it against is uppercase. Stop is not equal to STOP. It's a good idea to get in the habit of creating and executing batch files in uppercase.

This ends our discussion of batch files. In future chapters, we will explore batch files in much more detail, using them to enhance the capabilities of such DOS commands as SORT and FIND.

Chapter 8

DOS Commands

This chapter describes most of the DOS commands and how they are used. We will elaborate on each command, showing its practical use and some tips on how to use it.

ASSIGN

ASSIGN "tricks" DOS. In the past, when PCs could only be purchased with floppy drives, many software vendors wrote applications that only recognized those drives. Later, when fixed-disks systems like the IBM XT became available, some of those programs would not work with the fixed disk because they were programmed to look for their program and data files on one of the floppy drives. The ASSIGN command fixed this problem.

ASSIGN directs all requests for one drive to another. If you own a fixed disk, you may have software that attempts to read its program and data files from either drive A or drive B, even though it is installed on drive C. ASSIGN can correct this problem by directing all requests made to the floppy drives to the hard drive instead. ASSIGN takes the form:

    ASSIGN x = y

where x is the drive that your application wants to use and y is the drive that you want the application to use. To reset drive assignments to their normal settings, type ASSIGN without specifying parameters. You can request several assignments on one line. For instance

    ASSIGN A = C B = C

specifies that all programs looking for data or program files on either drive A or B should look for data or programs on drive C instead. The command above is what you would use if you were working with a fixed disk.

ATTRIB (DOS-3 Only)

ATTRIB (attribute) allows you to set the read attribute of a file to a read-only status. This will allow you to protect the file from accidental erasure or alteration by another user. If a file's attribute has been set to read only and an attempt is made to erase the file, the message "Access denied" is displayed. If an attempt is made to alter the file with an editor such as EDLIN, the message "File is read-only" is displayed.

The format of the ATTRIB command is:

[d](path]ATTRIB [+/−R] [d:][path]file name[.ext]

where +R sets the attribute to read-only and −R resets the attribute to read/write. For example, to set the file TEST.DAT to read-only you would type:

ATTRIB +R TEST.DAT

To display the attribute of any file, type:

ATTRIB file name

CHKDSK

The CHKDSK (check disk) command displays a status report of a specified disk and also checks the diskette's directories for problems. To run the command, type CHKDSK followed by the drive designator of the disk you want to check (you don't need to specify the default drive). A display similar to the following one will appear on your screen.

```
A:\>CHKDSK

    362496 bytes total disk space
     22528 bytes in 2 hidden files
      1024 bytes in 1 directories
    143360 bytes in 32 user files
    195584 bytes available on disk

    131072 bytes total memory
    104944 bytes free

A:\>_
```

The first line indicates that the disk has about 360K of disk space. The two hidden files are the DOS system files, which are hidden to protect them from being erased. This disk has one directory containing an unknown number of files. The space used on the disk by the directory entry is 1024 bytes. There are 32 files taking up a total disk space of 143,360 bytes, leaving 195,584 bytes open for future files. The last two lines indicate the amount of total memory in the computer and the amount of system memory free for use. The CHKDSK command takes the form:

CHKDSK [d:][FILE NAME][/F][/V]

where any drive may be specified. If you specify a single file following the drive specifier, CHKDSK will display the number of noncontiguous areas (see Chap. 15) that the file occupies.

CHKDSK will automatically correct errors found in the directory table if you specify the /F parameter, and it will display a series of messages indicating its progress if you specify the /V parameter.

You can determine the extent of file fragmentation (noncontiguously stored files) by using *.* in the file name field. This is covered in Chap. 15 in more detail.

Examples of the CHKDSK Command

CHKDSK   Checks the default drive.

CHKDSK B: Checks drive B.

CHKDSK TEXTFILE.TXT   Displays the number of noncontiguous areas occupied by the file TEXTFILE.TXT.

CHKDSK B:*.*   Checks the extent of fragmentation for the entire disk in drive B. The /V parameter will display messages indicating the command's progress.

COPY

The COPY command is a *major* DOS command that is used to perform the following tasks:

- Copy files from one disk to another
- Copy files to the same disk, but with different names
- Copy input from the keyboard into a file
- Copy files to an external device such as a printer

The following examples will show you the many ways to use COPY and will help you determine which COPY command is right for your needs.

Copying Single Files

A>COPY A:MYFILE B:MYFILE   Copies the file MYFILE on drive A to drive B, giving it the same name.

A>COPY MYFILE B: Exactly the same command as above. Since A is the default drive, the source file is copied from A. The destination for the file is drive B, and the file name defaults to MYFILE.

A>COPY A:MYFILE B:OLDFILE   Copies the file on drive A to drive B, renaming it OLDFILE in the process.

B>COPY MYFILE A: B is the default drive and the file is copied to drive A.

A>COPY B:MYPROG   Copies the file MYPROG on drive B to the default drive A.

A>COPY CHAP1.TXT B:*.BAK   Copies the file CHAP1.TXT to B, renaming it CHAP1.BAK in the process.

Copying Multiple Files

A>COPY A:*.* B: Copies *all* files on A to B.

A>COPY *.* B: The same command as above.

A>COPY A:*.DAT B: Copies all files ending in DAT to B:.

A>COPY B:*.*   Copies all files on drive B to default drive A.

A>COPY B:JOE?????.*   Copies all files from drive B that have the first 3 characters JOE to the default drive A.

A>COPY *.TXT B:*.TMP   Copies all files on default drive A ending in TXT to drive B, changing the extension of each file to TMP in the process.

A>COPY *.DAT B:ARCHIVE   Combines all files on drive A ending in DAT into one file called ARCHIVE on drive B.

Concatenating Files

A>COPY   CHAP1.TXT+CHAP2.TXT+CHAP3.TXT   B:CHAPMERG.TXT   Combines the three files CHAP1, 2, and 3 into one file on drive B called CHAPMERG.TXT.

A>COPY *.TXT B:CHAPMERG.TXT   Performs the same action as the command above. This assumes that there are no other TXT files on drive A besides those we wish to concatenate. Caution: The command shown here can cause errors if a *source* file called CHAPMERG.TXT already exists.

A>COPY SECTION1.TXT+SECTION1.PIC   Here the two files are combined and given the name of the first file.

A>COPY *.DBF+*.NDX *.BAK   All files matching *.DBF are combined with those having the same file name but the extension .NDX. Each combined file is then stored with the same file name but the extension of BAK.

Copying to and from Devices

A>COPY CON: LPT1:   Typewriter mode; copies text typed at the keyboard to the printer.

A>COPY MYFILE.TXT LPT1:   Sends the file MYFILE.TXT to the printer.

A>COPY MYFILE.TXT COM1:   Sends the file MYFILE.TXT through the communications port.

A>COPY COM1: LPT1:   Copies input from the communications port directly to the printer.

A>COPY COM1: MYFILE.TXT   Copies input from the communications port into the file MYFILE.TXT.

A>COPY MYFILE.TXT CON   The same as TYPE MYFILE.TXT; displays the file on the screen.

Copying Between Directories

C>COPY C:\WORDPROC*.DOC C:\WORDPROC\ARCHIVE   Copies all .DOC files in the \WORDPROC directory to the \WORDPROC\ARCHIVE directory.

C>COPY C:\WORDPROC\ARCHIVE*.* A: Copies all files in the \WORD-PROC\ARCHIVE directory to drive A.

C>COPY A:\GAMES\ZAP1 B:\GAMES   Copies the file ZAP1 in the \GAMES directory on drive A to the \GAMES directory on drive B.

Changing the Date

Whenever a file is created, a date is tagged to it. If we wanted to change the date tagged to an existing file, we could simulate a file creation and make DOS redate the file by entering the following command:

```
A>COPY OLDFILE.TXT +,,
```

The commas trick DOS into thinking that we have specified a second source file name to be combined with OLDFILE.TXT. The file will be redated and copied to the disk with the same file name.

Verifying a Copy

You can verify that a copy of a file is exactly like the source by adding the /V switch to the end of the COPY command:

```
A>COPY MYFILE.TXT B:MYFILE.TXT /V
```

CTTY

CTTY allows you to run your computer under DOS from another computer at a remote location. When using CTTY the standard input and output of your computer are directed to the remote device. The remote device is usually connected through the COM1 or AUX port. When CTTY is executed, DOS will then look to the remote device for its input and display its output on the external device. Refer to Chap. 29 for more information on CTTY.

DATE and TIME

The DATE and TIME commands are used for entering or changing the time and date in your system's internal clock. When you type either command, you will be prompted to enter the new date or time. You can place either command in the AUTOEXEC.BAT batch file. Normally DOS will ask for the date and time when you turn the system on unless you use an AUTOEXEC.BAT file, which will bypass the normal request for date and time. To regain this feature add the commands DATE and TIME as lines in the AUTOEXEC.BAT file.

If you have added a clock/calendar board to your system, DOS will read the time and date from the board every time you boot the system, eliminating the need to enter them.

DISKCOPY

In Chap. 9 we mentioned the disadvantages of DISKCOPY and that it would create an exact duplicate of a single-sided diskette, wasting half the disk space. In this section we will talk about its advantages. When used properly, DISKCOPY is an efficient, practical utility. It can be used to make backups of disks that contain valuable data or disks that have been set up to run an application, providing these disks have been created using the FORMAT and COPY commands as described in Chap. 9 and in this chapter. A disk formatted in this way will take advantage of the full capacity of the disk.

DISKCOPY is different from COPY because it copies the whole disk at once instead of copying one file at a time. There is a considerable increase in speed when DISKCOPY is used instead of COPY because blocks of data on the disk are moved instead of single files. Owners of single-drive systems will appreciate DISKCOPY because it will make a backup of a disk with a minimum of disk swaps.

As you use your computer in day-to-day operations, you will occasionally need to back up a disk. DISKCOPY is an external program that must be loaded into memory. To run it you must place a disk that contains the DISKCOPY.COM program file in the floppy drive. You may then issue the command shown below. After the program loads, it will ask you to place a disk to be copied in the source drive. If the disk you are copying to is not formatted, DISKCOPY will format it automatically. (Owners of fixed-disk systems may use the command below to create a copy of a disk even if they only have one floppy disk drive. The command will consider physical drive A to be logical drive B and will ask that diskettes be swapped in the floppy drive as the DISKCOPY progresses.)

```
DISKCOPY A: B:

Insert source diskette in drive A:

Insert target diskette in drive B:

Strike any key when ready . . .
```

DISKCOMP and COMP

DISKCOMP compares a copy of a disk with its original. DISKCOMP is an optional routine. It is mainly used to verify that a disk made with the

DISKCOPY command was copied accurately. To compare diskettes in drive A and drive B you would type:

DISKCOMP A: B:

COMP performs a compare between two files. The format of the command is the same as DISKCOMP except that you place the file names to be compared as parameters on the command line:

COMP NEWFILE.TXT OLDFILE.TXT

FIND

We've already discussed FIND. Here we will cover it in more detail. FIND is a filter that takes data or a file from the standard input, processes it, and then outputs the altered data. For instance, FIND will read a file you specify, find all lines in that file that match a string, and then display those lines on the screen. The command takes the form:

FIND "string" file names . . .

The string should always be enclosed within quotes. File names is plural because you can specify more that one file for the search. Each file specified on the command line should be separated by a space. The capabilities of FIND are greatly increased by using it in batch files. You can place the FIND command in a batch file and use replaceable parameters as the string parameter. Wild cards may not be used for file names, although you can include the command with the FOR batch subcommand to get around this deficiency. We will discuss FIND's use in batch files later.

There are three switches you can use with the FIND command which must be placed before the string in the command:

/V   Causes all lines *not* containing the string to be displayed

/C   Causes FIND to display a count of the number of lines that have matching strings in the specified file

/N   Causes the line number of the line containing the matching string to be displayed

FIND is a useful tool to use with text documents. For instance, you can use the /C switch to display the number of lines containing a specified string. This can help you determine if a word has been used too much. The /N switch can then be used to display the numbers of the lines in which excessive words exist in the file, making the editing of the file much easier.

The following examples represent typical ways of using FIND:

FIND "CALIFORNIA" CHAP1 CHAP2 CHAP3

This example finds all the lines in the three chapters that contain the string CALIFORNIA.

FIND "BLUE" INVENTRY.DAT l FIND "ROUND" > PARTS.DAT

This is an example of combining the piping and redirection features of DOS into a FIND command. The output from the first FIND is piped into the second FIND, which sends its output to the file PARTS.DAT.

Refer to Chaps. 26 and 27 and App. E for more information on the FIND command.

FORMAT

You used FORMAT in Chaps. 2 and 9 of the tutorial to prepare a diskette. FORMAT initializes a disk in the designated drive to a recording format acceptable to DOS. It analyzes the entire disk for defective tracks and prepares the disk to accept DOS files by establishing a directory. If you specify the /S option when formatting, the DOS system files are placed on the disk, making it a bootable disk. The following switches can be used with the FORMAT command:

/S This switch copies the operating system files to the new disk, making it a bootable disk. Three files are copied; two of these files are hidden and will not appear in a directory listing. The third file, COMMAND.COM, is visible in the listing.

/B Specifying this switch will format the new disk as a single-sided disk. This switch creates diskettes that will run on IBM systems and others that have single-sided drives.

/8 The /8 switch formats a disk in the eight-sectors-per-track format. A disk formatted in this way may be read by DOS-1.1.

/V This switch allows you to place a volume label on the disk. Volume labels will help you organize your diskettes by name.

/B This switch causes FORMAT to create an eight-sector-per-track diskette with space allocated for the DOS system files. It does not place the system files on the disk. Using this feature, you can create a disk for distribution to other users without infringing on the DOS copyright. Any version of DOS may be placed on the diskette by using the DOS SYS command.

/4   Formats a double-sided diskette in a high-capacity drive. This parameter is intended to allow use of double-sided diskettes in high-capacity drives. Diskettes formatted with the /4 parameter may not be readable in non-high-capacity drives.

GRAFTABL (DOS-3 Only)

The GRAFTABL (load graphics table) command loads a table of additional character data so you can display the extended character set on the color/graphics adapter. The command allows you to display foreign language characters as well as any character that has an ASCII code of 128 through 255. To load the table, simply type GRAFTABL on the command line.

GRAPHICS

The GRAPHICS (screen print) command is only useful if you own an IBM Graphics Printer and are using a color/graphics monitor adapter. It allows you to print the contents of a graphics display screen on the printer. Because the ROMs in IBM's Graphics Printer are different from those in other printers, including the equivalent EPSON matrix printers, this command may not work on other printers.

To use GRAPHICS, type in the command on the DOS command line. The utility will be loaded in memory and remain there until you turn the system off. To print a graphics screen, press Shift-PrtSc.

KEYBxx (DOS-3 Only)

The KEYBxx command loads a foreign keyboard, replacing the standard keyboard program that resides in ROM BIOS. The xx in the command represents one of the five keyboard programs provided on the DOS disk. The xx parameter can be one of the following:

UK   United Kingdom

GR   Germany

FR   France

IT   Italy

SP   Spain

To load an alternate keyboard, type the KEYBxx command, substituting the xx with the appropriate keyboard type. For instance, to load the German keyboard, type:

KEYBGR

You can change from the alternate keyboard to the United States keyboard by pressing Ctrl-Alt-F1 and change back to the foreign keyboard by pressing Ctrl-Alt-F2. Note that you can permanently set the keyboard to an alternate keyboard on any disk by adding the KEYBxx command to an AUTOEXEC.BAT file. If you create a diskette with the SELECT command, the keyboard type can be specified.

LABEL (DOS-3 Only)

The LABEL command allows you to add a label to a disk that does not contain an existing volume label or delete an existing label. You can also alter the volume label of a disk formatted with the /V option.

Volume labels are used to identify a disk and do not serve any other purpose. The volume label given to a disk should match the volume name written on the diskette's paper label. The volume label can be up to 11 characters long.

To place a volume label on a disk, type LABEL and the new volume name. For instance, to name a disk ACCOUNTING, type:

LABEL ACCOUNTING

To change an existing volume label, type LABEL and the new volume label and press the Return key. The new label replaces the old label. To delete a volume label, do not specify a volume label; simply type LABEL and press the Return key and the old label will be deleted.

MODE

The MODE command sets the operational modes of your computer. This command operates on the hardware of your system. With it, you can set options for the display monitors, the communications ports, and the printer ports.

MODE has several options which we will not discuss in full detail here, but you should be aware of its ability to alter certain parameters on your system. MODE has four main features:

1. Alter the configuration of the line printer. (This option applies to a printer attached to the parallel port.)
   a. You can select line printers 1, 2, or 3.
   b. The characters per line can be selected as either 80 or 132 columns.
   c. The vertical line spacing can be set to either 6 or 8 lines per inch.
   d. You can continuously retry the printer if there is a time out.
2. Switch displays or change the display mode.
   a. It sets the display width for 40-column mode; used for games.

    b. It sets the display width to 80-column mode. The PC*jr* boots in 40-column mode. Use this option to change to 80-column text mode.

    c. There are various ways of switching between a monochrome monitor and a color display.

    d. It displays a test pattern used to align the display.

3. Configure the communications port.

    a. This option lets you specify the baud rate, parity, data bits, and stop bits of either the COM1 or the COM2 communications port. You may also specify whether you intend to use it as a printer port. If so, time-out errors are continuously retried on the port.

4. Redirect parallel printer output to a serial printer attached to a communications port.

    a. You may redirect the output normally directed to an LPT device to a COM port instead.

    Refer to your operator's manual for more details on how you can use the MODE command to configure your system. Note that all MS-DOS versions may not have the MODE command or may not have a full implementation of it.

PRINT

    The PRINT command will print a group of files on the printer while you are doing other tasks on the computer. Up to 10 file names can be "queued" for printing at one time. You can enter more than one file name on the command or you can specify a group of files using the global file name characters * and ?. Since PRINT operates differently depending on the version of DOS you have, you should refer to the DOS manual for more details.

    The PRINT command handles printing of files in the "background." It watches over the printing of files only when you are not executing commands at the keyboard. When the computer executes a command, the printing will slow down or stop altogether until the command is finished.

    The PRINT command is a convenient feature that lets you use the computer if you have to without interrupting the printing that is in progress.

PROMPT

    The PROMPT command is a useful and fun command that is used to change the DOS prompt. You can also use it to dazzle your friends, set screen modes, and define the keys on the keyboard.

The PROMPT command takes the form:

PROMPT string

You can enter any string as the parameter of the PROMPT command, and it will become the new DOS prompt. PROMPT has the added feature of allowing you to enter special characters called meta-strings which produce interesting and useful prompts. These meta-strings are listed in the table below for reference.

Meta-string	Prompt produced
$$	A dollar sign ($), familiar to UNIX users
$t	The time
$d	The date prompt
$p	The current directory
$v	The version number
$n	The default drive
$g	The > character
$l	The < character
$b	The : character
$q	The = character
$h	Backspaces and erases the previous character
$e	The escape character
$-	Goes to new line on screen

In the tutorial we described several ways to use prompts, one of which was the time meta-string that lets you time activities on the computer as if you had a stopwatch. For example, you can time the execution of a sort, and although it is not totally accurate (because the clock is ticking as you key in the command to start the sort), you may find it useful.

```
A:\>PROMPT $t

9:15:05.54_
```

Add the > symbol to the prompt for clarity by typing:

```
9:15:05.54 PROMPT $t$g

9:17:15.10 >_
```

To time an event, press the Return key to get the latest time and type the command as fast as possible. Here, we will time the DIR command. Be sure to note the time before it scrolls off the display. Maybe one of these days you'll find a use for this!

```
9:17:15.10>  <Return>
9:19:04.02>DIR  <Return>
 .
 .
 .
9:19:16.23>_
```

Any string can be entered as the prompt:

```
9:20:23.32>PROMPT SPEAK TO ME GREAT AND POWERFUL OZ$g
```

It's nice to have the computer at your command, but this string is too long. To restore the original prompt, type **PROMPT.**

You can embed meta-strings between other characters. The following prompt will display the time between square brackets.

```
A>PROMPT [$t] $g
[ 9:21:02.46 ] >_
```

The meta-string $h produces a backspace when placed in a prompt. We can issue a long prompt, and then backspace over it. Try this for kicks:

```
[ 9:21:47.28 ] >PROMPT ECHO ECHO $H$H$H$H$H

ECHO_
```

Did you see the echo? Press the Return key several times to see the effects of the backspace command.

The g, l, b, q, and $ prompts are used to insert the symbols they represent into a prompt. Normally these symbols are used by DOS for redirection and piping. If you need them in your prompt, you can use the meta-string version. For instance, you could create the following prompt:

```
ECHO PROMPT $P$G$G$G$G

A: \>>>>_
```

Here's another interesting prompt:

```
A: \>>>> PROMPT . . . . . . . . . . . . . . . . . . .$h$h$h$h$h$h$h$h$h
            $h$h$h$h$h$h$h$h$h$p$g

A: \>_
```

Press the Return key several times to see its effects. Note that the disk-drive light comes on every time you execute the command. When using the $p (current directory) option, DOS checks the disk in the drive to make sure its current list of files is correct.

If you have the patience, you can enter the following batch file to see the "pinwheel" prompt. (Note: Two spaces follow each slash; four follow each hyphen.) Enter it into a batch file called PINWHEEL.BAT and then execute the batch file. This will save the prompt for future use.

```
A: \>COPY CON:PINWHEEL.BAT
PROMPT / $H$H$H-     $H$H$H$H$H\  $H$H$H-     $H$H$H$H$H\
    $H$H$H / $H$H$H-     $H$H$H$H$H\  $H$H$H $n$g

<F6> <Return>
```

The $_ prompt (underline) issues a carriage return. Try the following prompt to see how it works:

```
A: \>PROMPT [$T]$_$D$_$P$G

[ 9:34:09.19 ]
Tue  4-14-1984
A: \>_
```

Have fun with the PROMPT command. You can't hurt anything by experimenting. A string that is too long will affect the environment string space and lock up the computer, so keep your strings to a minimum. If you want to experiment with long PROMPT strings, use EDLIN to enter them. You may have noticed that many prompts repeat a short string several times. You can type an asterisk for every time a string will repeat and then use the EDLIN REPLACE command to replace the asterisk with the string.

RECOVER

The RECOVER command retrieves files on a diskette that has bad sectors. Sectors are the divisions on a disk that are used by DOS to store files. If a disk has been damaged, it's possible that portions of files on the disk are stored in damaged parts. The RECOVER command will help you retrieve those files. The command, however, is not foolproof. If a file is stored in several sectors and one is bad, only the data in the good sector can be retrieved. The RECOVER command will save as much of the file as possible and flag the bad sectors on the disk so they won't be used again in the future. After recovering a file, you will normally have to edit it to repair the parts lost to bad sectors. Before using RECOVER, you should copy as many files as possible to a backup diskette.

RECOVER may also be used to retrieve files from a disk that has a bad directory. When running RECOVER for this purpose, each file on the disk is renamed with a sequentially numbered file name. You may then inspect the files and rename them after you have determined what they are.

Only ASCII text and data files should be recovered. A command file will not be usable if part of its contents have been altered or destroyed and is therefore not recoverable.

As mentioned, RECOVER works on a single file or on an entire disk. If you do not specify a file name, RECOVER will assume that you wish to recover the entire disk, in which case it will rebuild the diskette directory. The syntax of the RECOVER command is as follows:

RECOVER [d][path]file name[.ext]

or

RECOVER d:

When recovering a single file, the file is read sector by sector. RECOVER skips over the bad sectors but marks them so that they are not used again. Any data in bad sectors is lost. RECOVER does not change the file name of a file when using the single-file recovery option.

When recovering an entire disk, RECOVER will create a new directory. It is a good idea to make a backup copy of a disk before attempting to recover the entire disk. Each chain of sectors that DOS "sees" as a complete file will be given a new file name in the form:

FILEnnnn.REC

The nnnn represents a sequential number starting with 001. Be careful when using this form of RECOVER, and be sure to make backups before proceeding.

If you ever have to recover files on a disk, the disk is probably getting old and should be taken out of commission. If the bad sectors are on a fixed disk, you cannot retire the disk. The recover program will, however, mark each bad sector so that DOS will avoid the sectors when storing files.

SELECT (DOS-3 Only)

SELECT is a convenient DOS-3 program that creates a DOS diskette. The command allows you to specify the country code and keyboard code you prefer to use. The country code tells DOS the date and time format, the currency symbol, and decimal separator to use. The keyboard code tells DOS which keyboard layout you want to use. The keyboard and country code are listed in the following table.

Country	Country Code	Keyboard Code
United States	001	US
France	033	FR
Spain	034	SP
Italy	039	IT
United Kingdom	044	UK
Germany	049	GR

The command takes the form:

[d:][path]SELECT xxx yy

where xxx is the country code and yy is the keyboard code. The command uses the DISKCOPY command to make a copy of the DOS disk and then creates CONFIG.SYS and AUTOEXEC.BAT files that contain the country and keyboard commands.

SET

SET is a command used to set parameters to act as variables in programs or batch files. The parameter assigned by the SET command can be equal to a replaceable parameter in a batch file. SET does not affect commands in DOS other than those in batch files. The syntax for the SET command is:

SET [parameter = [replaceable parameter]]

The greatest value of SET is that it allows you to use the same replaceable parameter in several files without having to specify it every time you use the batch file. The parameter is set once, say at the beginning of a computing session, and stays the same during the session. For example, suppose that a user (Jane in this case) logs on to a fixed-disk system that is normally used by several different users. She sets the parameter USER to JANE by typing:

SET USER = JANE

If the following batch files are on the system, Jane can now use them without having to specify her name. The parameter % USER % is replaced in all files with the parameter set by the SET command.

MYDIR.BAT	DIRLIST.BAT	READAPPT.BAT
CD % USER %	DIR \% USER % /P	TYPE % USER %.APT
TYPE MENU.TXT		

When Jane logs on, she sets USER to JANE. The first batch file assumes that there is a subdirectory called JANE. In this batch file, % USER % is replaced with JANE in the CD command, transferring Jane to her subdirectory. The second batch file, DIRLIST.BAT, uses the replaceable parameter to specify which directory should be listed. The third batch file will display the file having the file name specified by % USER %, in this case the command in the READAPPT.BAT file becomes TYPE JOE.APT, which will list Jane's appointments. Consider what will happen when Joe logs onto the system and sets USER to JOE. Now each batch file will work for Joe as if they were designed for his use.

When using SET, the parameter may be any character string that does not include the numbers 0 through 9. You may use general names for the parameter such as USER, FILENAME, DRIVE, PATH, and TEXT. These simple names will help you remember the parameters. The replaceable parameters can also be any character string that does not include the numbers 1 through 9. Use specific parameters such as \MYDIR and JOE, as described above.

You should note the difference between the replaceable parameters used with a single batch file (%1, %2, etc.) and the replaceable parameter assigned by SET. The replaceable parameters %x used in batch files only work in the batch file that has been called whereas the parameters assigned by SET may be used by any batch file that has the corresponding parameter.

SHELL

The SHELL command is interesting in two ways. First, it calls a secondary command processor instead of the one normally used by DOS. When SHELL is used in this way, you may specify a path in front of the file name for the new command processor. This feature will be of use to system programmers who develop their own command processors.

The second use for the SHELL is to call DOS commands from a BASIC (or other) program. By placing SHELL and a DOS command as a statement in your program, a temporary exit to DOS will be invoked. This is useful for programs that must pause so diskettes can be formatted, copied, or checked. You can even use the SORT command to sort a file.

SHELL, in DOS-3, is well-documented, however, there is a problem with the command in DOS-2. When you try to get back into your program from DOS, BASIC may not remember where your program is in memory, causing the program to bomb. To get around this problem, you will need to place several statements around the SHELL command. These statements save and restore the location of your BASIC program so BASIC knows where to resume after running SHELL. This information is stored in two bytes at &H30 and &H31 (DEF SEG = 0). Before using SHELL, you must PEEK at the values in these two locations and save them as variables. Upon returning to BASIC, you must POKE these values into their original locations to make the program continue normal execution.

The listing below demonstrates how to properly code the SHELL command so that it can be executed without error. The group of lines can be used as a subroutine that might be called from a menu for example.

```
100 PRINT
110 PRINT "DOS COMMAND PROCESSOR"
120 INPUT "ENTER A DOS COMMAND OR X TO EXIT ',CMD$
130 IF (CMD$ = "X") OR (CMD$ = "x") THEN 180 'check for exit
140 DEF SEG: A = PEEK(&H30): B = PEEK(&H31) 'save the
    location at start of program
150 SHELL CMD$ 'execute the DOS command
160 DEF SEG: POKE &H30,A: POKE &H31,B 'restore program
    location
170 GOTO 100 'get more commands
180 RETURN
```

If a DOS command uses much memory, it is possible that it will not return properly to BASIC. Experiment with the DOS commands you will be using in your program.

SORT

SORT will sort any ASCII file in alphabetical or reverse alphabetical order. You can also specify the column you wish to sort on. Since SORT reads a file using the I/O redirection scheme, you must point the file to be sorted into the SORT routine. The sorted output will be displayed on the screen (the standard output device) or can be directed into another file.

SORT in DOS-2 uses the standard ASCII codes as its sort criterion. If you refer to the ASCII table in App. A, you will notice that A has a lower ASCII value than a. This means that A will come before a in a sort unless you reverse the order of the sort. Numbers come before alpha characters and many of the symbols, such as the dollar sign and the percent sign, come before numbers. SORT in DOS-3 equates lowercase a through z to uppercase A through Z and collates some extended ASCII characters, such as European characters, with the ASCII characters A through Z.

The format of the SORT command is as follows:

SORT [/R][/+n]

If you specify /R in the sort, the file is sorted in reverse order. In other words, Z would come before A. SORT normally uses the first column in any file as its sort parameter. The /+n parameter lets you specify another column for the sort.

The following example illustrates how SORT receives its input from the file UNSORTED.TXT and places the sorted output in a new file called SORTED.TXT which it creates if one does not already exist. If one already exists, SORT will copy over it unless you append the new data to it using the >> option. (Note that the append symbols >> may not work in DOS-2.1.)

Here are a few example of how SORT can by used.

SORT < UNSORTED.TXT   The file is sorted and displayed on the screen.

SORT < UNSORTED.TXT > SORTED.TXT   Creates or copies over SORTED.TXT.

SORT < UNSORTED.TXT >> SORTED.TXT   Appends the sorted text to the file SORTED.TXT.

SORT < CON > NEWFILE.TXT   Sorts data keyed in at the keyboard and places it in a file called NEWFILE.TXT.

DIR ▌ SORT /+14   The directory listing is piped into the SORT command. The listing is sorted by the fourteenth column.

FIND "GUITARS" INVENTRY.DAT ▌ SORT > GUITARS.INV
Finds the string GUITARS in the inventory file and pipes the output to the SORT command, which sends the sorted output to the file GUITARS.INV.

VERIFY

VERIFY checks to see whether data recorded to a disk has been written correctly. DOS performs a verify operation after each disk write to see if the data just written can be read without error. You can set VERIFY either on or off, but if you set VERIFY on, it will cause the system to run more slowly because of the time it takes to check the data as it is written. You can turn VERIFY on before copying a set of files and turn it off after the copies have been made. You may also want to turn VERIFY on before backing up a fixed disk, although this will significantly increase the time it takes to do the backup.

The syntax of the VERIFY command is:

VERIFY [on off]

where VERIFY is set to either on or off. You can check the current status of VERIFY by typing the command without parameters:

VERIFY

Chapter

19

Configuring Your System

Every time you start DOS it searches for the system configuration file CONFIG.SYS in the ROOT directory. Each line in the file is an ASCII text string command that tells DOS how to configure the system. The commands used in the CONFIG.SYS file are BREAK, BUFFERS, COUNTRY, DEVICE, FILES, LASTDRIVE, and SHELL.

CONFIG.SYS is like AUTOEXEC.BAT in that the commands in the file are executed when the system starts. You will not see anything on the screen, however, as the commands execute—the process is invisible to the user. The CONFIG.SYS file is optional; it is not essential to the start-up process or the operation of your computer. There are, however, several good reasons to use CONFIG.SYS, which is the subject of this chapter. If you are using a RAM drive, a mouse, or other special devices, you will need to use CONFIG.SYS to tell DOS about them.

The CONFIG.SYS file is a standard ASCII file which can be created or edited with EDLIN or any other text editor. Since the file is only read at boot time, any changes made to the file will not take effect until you reboot the system. The following commands may be included in the CONFIG.SYS file. They will be discussed in detail later.

BREAK   Specifies when DOS should check for the Ctrl-Break key sequence.

BUFFERS   Specifies how many disk buffers should be set up by DOS. Buffers hold temporary blocks of data from the disk drives and may increase the speed of access to data on a disk.

COUNTRY	Specifies the country whose date and time format you want to use (DOS-3 only).
DEVICE	Specifies other devices besides the standard keyboard, screen, and printer.
FCBS	Specifies the number of file control blocks that can be concurrently open (DOS-3 only).
FILES	Specifies how many files can be open at any given time.
LASTDRIVE	Specifies the maximum number of drives that you can access (DOS-3 only).
SHELL	Specifies the name and location of another command processor besides COMMAND.COM,

BREAK

You have already learned to use the Ctrl-Break or Ctrl-C keys to stop an executing program or batch file. Ctrl-Break can also be used to break out of various DOS commands such as COPY and COPY CON. It is a convenient way to stop a program that may be having problems or to simply interrupt a running program. You may have noticed that Ctrl-Break does not always work or that you have to press the sequence several times before the computer will respond. This will occur if BREAK is off.

Normally, DOS will only look for the Ctrl-Break key sequence when it is performing screen writes, keyboard inputs, printer outputs, or communications through a COM port. In other words, DOS will only recognize Ctrl-Break if it makes a call to one of the above devices during the execution of a program. While it is out handling the device call, it also checks for a Ctrl-Break. If Ctrl-Break has been pressed, the program will stop. This is the default configuration of the BREAK command. Setting BREAK ON will cause the system to check for the Ctrl-Break sequence more often.

The BREAK command takes the form:

    BREAK on/off

If you want to set BREAK to the on position, include the command BREAK ON in the configuration file CONFIG.SYS. This will allow you to break out of any program whenever a DOS function has been called by the program. Note that BREAK may be set at any time during a session on the computer by entering the command from the keyboard.

In the normal off position it may be hard to break out of programs that do not access the normal DOS devices often enough. Some applications, such as language compilers, do few or no operations to the standard devices until they are done with their task. You should set BREAK to on when using these applications.

BUFFERS

The BUFFERS command is an interesting feature of DOS that you can put to use, especially if you are performing many disk accesses, which may be the case when working with database applications such as dBASE II. If your program asks for data on the disk, DOS will put this data in a temporary hold area called a buffer. It will then remember what data is in the buffer so the next time you make a request for data, DOS will look in the buffer first and not on the disk. This can save a considerable amount of time if you are performing many disk accesses.

The BUFFER command takes the form:

    BUFFER = n

where n is the number of buffers you want to use. The command should be included as a line in the CONFIG.SYS file. You may specify from 1 to 99 buffers, but the default is 2. If you do not specify BUFFERS, the default will remain in effect until the system is restarted with a different value in the CONFIG.SYS file.

A buffer is an area of memory set up by DOS at boot time. It is reserved and cannot be written over by other programs. These buffers are usually 512 bytes in size. Since buffers take up room in RAM memory, the number of buffers that you specify will depend on the amount of RAM you have available. If you are working with 64K, we recommend that you stay with the two-buffer default. If you have 128K RAM, you can probably get by with two to four buffers. If you have more than 128K RAM, you can specify as many buffers as you want, although it is usually not practical to exceed 20 buffers.

You will want to specify additional buffers if you are working with applications such as databases or accounting programs in which many random accesses are made to the disk. Some applications will slow down with an increase in the number of buffers. This can occur in systems with little memory, say 64K or 128K RAM when a large number of buffers has been specified. The application will have plenty of buffers available for its data but may not have enough room left over for itself.

COUNTRY (DOS-3 Only)

The COUNTRY command is used to specify the date and time format you want to use. Information specific to the country you choose is also set, such as the currency symbol and the decimal separtator. The default value of COUNTRY is United States (001). The format of the command is:

    COUNTRY = xxx

where xxx is one of the following country codes:

Country	Code
United States	001
Netherlands	031
Belgium	032
France	033
Spain	034
Italy	039
Switzerland	041
United Kingdom	044
Denmark	045
Sweden	046
Norway	047
Germany	049
Australia	061
Finland	358
Israel	972

Note that the country code is added to the CONFIG.SYS file if you use the SELECT command.

DEVICE

The DEVICE command loads a device driver. A device driver is a program written in assembly language that tells DOS how to use a particular device. DOS already knows about the standard devices like the keyboard, screen, floppy drives, and hard disk. Special device drivers can be built to tell DOS how to handle other devices, such as RAM drives, mice, printers, and plotters.

The DEVICE command takes the form:

    DEVICE = device driver name

or:

    DEVICE = [d:][path] device driver name

When DOS is first loaded, it will load its own standard drivers used for handling the keyboard, screen, and other standard I/O devices. It will then load the drivers for the device or devices that you specified in the CONFIG.SYS file. As an example, a device called ANSI.SYS is included on many version of DOS and can be used to replace the standard keyboard and screen drivers. Using this driver will allow you to make keyboard assignments, control the screen as if it were a standard terminal, and set the screen foreground and background colors. This ANSI.SYS driver is covered in more detail in Chap. 21. To include the ANSI.SYS driver in your CONFIG.SYS file, you would add the following line:

```
DEVICE = ANSI.SYS
```

An advantage of installing devices using the DEVICE command is that it makes it easier for hardware manufacturers to interface their own devices to DOS. DOS must know how to "talk" with all devices attached to the system, and device drivers provide this link. They also provide an easy way for hardware manufacturers to attach their equipment to a computer by means of a standard interface to DOS. Previously, alterations had to be made to DOS itself.

Adding a new device to your system is as easy as specifying its device-driver file name in the CONFIG.SYS file. With the added feature of device drivers, a proliferation of external hardware devices compatible with DOS is inevitable. In the past, it was the responsibility of the manufacturers to provide the DOS alterations that made their equipment compatible. Now that device drivers are available, complicated alterations to DOS are no longer necessary.

Installing device drivers through the CONFIG.SYS file allows you to attach several different "foreign" devices to DOS at one time. Each of the drivers access DOS through a standard interface. This interface is controlled by the operating system and keeps the devices from interfering with each other. When you consider the number of devices that might be attached to a system at one time, you can see why this is important. For instance, typical devices that may be added to a system include a hard disk, mice, networks, and tape backup systems. There are also devices that alter the system such as the ANSI.SYS driver, RAM drives, and foreign language keyboard drivers.

DOS-3 VDISK Device

DOS-3 contains a device-driver file that creates a simulated disk drive by using a portion of your computer's memory as the storage medium. The simulated disk is known as a virtual disk and is sometimes referred to as a RAM drive or "phantom disk." The following characteristics apply to RAM drives:

- RAM drives are fast since they operate at the speed of your computer's memory.

- You can install more than one RAM drive because each RAM drive installed will take on a successive drive specifier. For instance, if you have two physical floppy drives known as drive A and drive B, two RAM drives would take on the drive names of C and D.

- You can specify the amount of memory to be used by each RAM drive.

- The contents of a RAM drive are lost when you turn the system off.

To install a RAM drive, enter the VDISK command in your CONFIG.SYS file in the following format:

    DEVICE = [d:][path]VDISK.SYS [bbb][sss][ddd][/E]

where d and path are the drive and path to the VDISK.SYS file. The bbb parameter is used to specify the size of the RAM drive in K bytes (the default value is 64K). The sss parameter is used to adjust the sector size in bytes. Allowable sizes are 128, 256, or 512 (the default value is 128K). If you are storing small files, such as batch files, you may want to specify a small sector size to save space. The ddd value is the number of directory entries (number of files) that the virtual disk can contain (64 is the default value). The /E parameter tells DOS to use the extended memory that is available on the IBM PC/AT computer above 1 megabyte.

The following example installs a 256K RAM drive with 512-byte sectors and 64 directory entries:

    DEVICE = VDISK.SYS 256 512 64

The next time the system is booted, the new CONFIG.SYS file is read and VDISK displays the drive designator given to the RAM drive along with the buffer size, sector size, and number of directory entries.

FILES

The FILES command allows you to specify how many files an application can open. The command provides DOS with a "handle" for each file. The command takes the form:

    FILES = nn

where nn is the number of files from 5 to 99 that are opened. Increasing the number of files has little effect on the amount of memory used since each file handle only requires an additional 39 bytes. Normally, you will not need to specify FILES unless you run into an error message warning that an insufficient number of handles is present. The FILES command should then be used to provide DOS with additional file handles.

LASTDRIVE (DOS-3 Only)

The LASTDRIVE command sets the maximum number of drives that you may access; the minimum number you can set LASTDRIVE to is the number of drives you have installed on your computer. The command is ignored in the CONFIG.SYS file if the number of drives specified is less than the number of physical drives on the computer.

The command takes the form:

    LASTDRIVE = x

where x is the alphabetic character A through Z of the last valid drive that DOS will recognize. The default value is E. For instance, to set the number of drives equal to 10, include the following command in the CONFIG.SYS file:

    LASTDRIVE = J

SHELL

The SHELL command allows you to specify the name of an alternate top-level command processor in place of the normal COMMAND.COM provided with DOS. The command takes the form:

    SHELL − [d:[path] command processor

Experienced programmers may wish to develop their own command processors. This command will load the new processors from the CONFIG.SYS file. (See Chap. 18 for a description of how to use SHELL to call DOS commands from a BASIC program.)

Creating a CONFIG.SYS File

CONFIG.SYS is an ASCII text file that you can create with EDLIN or COPY CON. If the file already exists on a disk, you can use EDLIN to alter the existing version. The following is a sample CONFIG.SYS file. Remember that any changes made to the file do not have an effect on the actual system until you reboot.

CONFIG.SYS

BREAK ON	(set BREAK to on)
BUFFERS = 4	(set up four buffers)
DEVICE = ANSI.SYS	(load the ANSI.SYS driver)
DEVICE = RAM180.COM	(install a 180K RAM drive)
DEVICE = MOUSE.SYS	(install a mouse driver)

In this chapter we have discussed each of the commands that can be placed in the configuration file CONFIG.SYS. You can use this file to help set up the operating environment of your computer. The section on the DEVICE command explains how to install a RAM drive or the ANSI.SYS keyboard driver. The section on BUFFERS explains how you can make your computer work more efficiently when working with data on disk.

20

Hierarchical
Filing Systems

When you format a disk with the FORMAT command, DOS creates a directory to keep track of the files that will be stored on the disk. A single-sided floppy disk has 64 available entries in the directory, a double-sided floppy disk has 112 entries, and a fixed disk has 512. This initial directory that is created by DOS is always known as the ROOT directory and is symbolized by the backslash (\) character in path names and file names.

Versions 2 and 3 of DOS allow you to create additional directories on a disk. Each directory can hold its own files and keeps track of its own file names. Files in one directory can have file names similar to those in other directories and they will never interfere with each other. The most important feature of these directories is that they branch from other directories, like limbs on a tree. When a structure contains several levels of directories and branching subdirectories, the structure is often referred to as a tree-structured directory or a hierarchical filing system. Figure 14-1 shows an elaborate tree-structured filing system derived from the UNIX operating system. With DOS, you don't really need to create structures that are this elaborate, but the example will give you an idea of what can be created.

Whether you own a floppy-disk system or a fixed-disk system, you may eventually find the need to create separate directories on a disk so that you can store common files together. Students could create a directory for each class they are attending and store files for each class in separate directories (see Fig. 20-1). Managers could create the directory structure shown in Fig. 20-2. Each subdirectory that branches from the ROOT directory contains programs or files related to the subdirectory headings.

In Chap. 7 you created a subdirectory, copied files to it, and used the CHDIR (change directory) command to travel to it. This single subdirec-

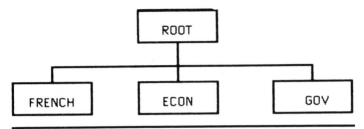

Figure 20-1 Directory structure for a student that illustrates two levels of directories.

tory was the beginning of what could be an elaborate tree-structured filing system. Why create such a structure? If you own a fixed disk, you probably know that it is capable of storing hundreds, possibly thousands of files. Tree-structured filing can help organize these files by storing them as separate groups in subdirectories. Owners of floppy-disk systems store files in a similar manner by placing common types of files on different floppy diskettes. You can think of each subdirectory as a single diskette that holds its own files.

Although the tree structure of a filing system can get elaborate, you should never create a structure more than three levels deep because a multilevel tree structure degrades DOS's ability to read and write files. We also don't recommend elaborate tree-structured filing on floppy diskettes although one or two subdirectories branching from the ROOT may be convenient and useful. One reason to create a subdirectory on a floppy disk is to create a convenient place to store files or separate them from other files. You can "hide" files away so they are not affected by global commands, for instance.

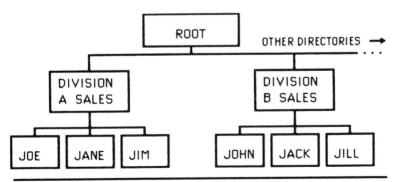

Figure 20-2 An example tree structure for a manager of a sales organization that shows three levels of directories.

Things You Should Know About
Subdirectories

- DOS will always keep track of a current directory. This directory is where DOS will default to when storing and retrieving files or looking for commands. DOS will even keep track of the current directory on another drive. The PATH command can be used to tell DOS to look for programs and batch files in other directories, but DOS will always look in the current directory first.

- We will occasionally refer to a subdirectory as a directory. Subdirectory is a term we will use when referring to a directory that branches from another directory. Subdirectories are directories in their own right. The ROOT is always a directory and never a subdirectory and all other directories can trace a path back to the ROOT, no matter how many branches they have taken.

- Directories and subdirectories are sometimes referred to as "parent" and "child" (see Fig. 20-3). The ROOT directory is the parent of all other directories. A subdirectory that branches from a directory is known as the child of that directory, although any subdirectory can also be a parent of a subdirectory.

- The path refers to the route you must take through the tree structure to reach a particular directory (see Fig. 20-4). You can execute commands on directories other than the current directory by specifying the path to that directory in the command. The last parameter in a path name may be either a directory, a file name, or a file name with wild-card characters. This means that you can refer to a whole directory, a single file in a directory, or a group of files in a directory when issuing DOS commands with paths.

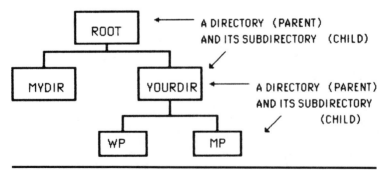

Figure 20-3   A directory structure showing the relationship between directories and subdirectories.

- You cannot erase a directory until you remove all the files within it. You also cannot rename a subdirectory. You must create a whole new directory with the name you want and then copy the files from the other directory to it.

- DOS treats subdirectories as files and even displays their names in directory listings. Each subdirectory has its own list of files. Directory names follow the same file naming rules as file names.

- The ROOT directory is created on every disk and is limited in the number of files it will hold. Subdirectories can hold any number of files and are limited only by the capacity of your fixed disk. Subdirectories grow and shrink as needed.

- Commands and batch files can be placed in a single directory such as the ROOT and can be called from any other directory. This will save space on the disk because you do not need to have several copies of the same file. The PATH command can be used to tell DOS where to look for commands and batch files.

This chapter is written primarily for owners of fixed-disk systems, but as mentioned before, owners of floppy-disk systems will benefit from this discussion as well. All examples in this chapter will illustrate a drive C prompt, which is the normal default prompt on a fixed-disk system. Owners of floppy-drive systems should substitute the designator of their default drive. This chapter is meant to be only an exercise in creating and

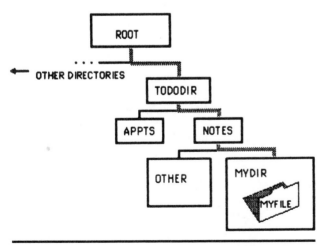

Figure 20-4 The path of \TODODIR\NOTES\ MYDIR\MYFILE.

working with subdirectories. In later chapters we will show you how to organize your system using the methods learned here.

Making a Subdirectory

Before starting the examples, make sure that the DOS prompt is set to display the current directory. This is important when you are working with subdirectories. It will help you keep track of which directory you are in by displaying the path to the directory in the prompt. Issue the following command to set PROMPT to show the current directory:

PROMPT pg

Also, make sure you are in the ROOT directory by typing the command to change directories to ROOT:

CD \

From now on we will use the abbreviated forms of the directory commands, CD for CHDIR, MD for MKDIR, and RD for RMDIR.

Once in the ROOT directory, you can create a subdirectory that branches from it using the MD (make directory) command (see Fig. 20-5). To create a directory called SAMPLES, type:

```
c:\>MD SAMPLES
c:\>_
```

Directories are always created on the default drive unless you specify another drive, and they are always created as subdirectories of the current directory unless you specify a path. The following command will create a directory called DATAEAST that branches from SAMPLES:

```
c:\>MD \SAMPLES\DATAEAST
```

Keep in mind that you were still in the ROOT directory when you created this new subdirectory. You can see this by looking at the DOS

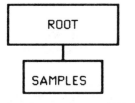

Figure 20-5 The ROOT directory showing the new SAMPLES subdirectory branching from it.

prompt, which should say C:\>. When you entered the command, the path to this new directory was specified as part of the command parameters. In the command above, \SAMPLES was included before the name of the new branching subdirectory. The backslash between SAMPLES and DATAEAST separates the two names.

In the next command, you will create a directory called DATAWEST that also branches from the SAMPLES directory, but you will use another method to create the directory. First go to the SAMPLES directory by typing:

```
C:\>CD SAMPLES

C:\SAMPLES>_
```

The prompt changes to \SAMPLES, telling you which directory you are in. Now, it will be much easier to create a branching directory because you won't have to specify a path for it. The next command creates a directory that branches from the current directory:

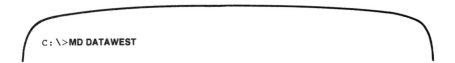

```
C:\>MD DATAWEST
```

Creating directories using this second method is the most common way to build tree-structured directories. This will help you keep better track of the structure as it is built.

Tree Structures

The new directory structure is illustrated in Fig. 20-6. This is a three-level structure, which is about the maximum number of levels you should use. If you were to add a subdirectory to either the DATAEAST or DATA-WEST directories, you would have a four-level tree structure. Tree structures larger than three levels will cause the drive to work much harder when reading and writing files, so they are not recommended.

What's in a Directory

Let's take a look at the contents of the SAMPLES directory. You should be in SAMPLES and the prompt should display C:\SAMPLES>. Type DIR on the command line:

```
C:\SAMPLES>DIR

  Volume in drive C is COMPLANDSBA
  Directory of C:\SAMPLES

  .            <DIR>
  ..           <DIR>
  DATAWEST     <DIR>
  DATAEAST     <DIR>
          4 File(s)

C:\SAMPLES>_
```

Although you have not created or copied files to this directory, a few items have been listed with the DIR command. The dot and double-dot

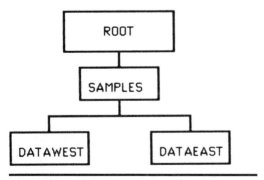

Figure 20-6 The directory structure showing the new third-level subdirectory additions.

listings are used by DOS to keep track of the current directory. Dot contains information about \SAMPLES and double-dot contains information about the parent of \SAMPLES. All directories are followed by <DIR> in the listing. The last two lines of the listing are the DATAEAST and DATAWEST subdirectories you just created. As you can see, subdirectories are listed as if they are files.

Moving Through Directories

The CHDIR, or CD, (change directories) command allows you to travel along the pathways to directories. The simplest form of the CD command is executed when you want to move to a subdirectory of the current directory. You simply enter the name of the subdirectory as a parameter of the CD command. A path is not needed since the subdirectory branches from the current directory. Since you are in the SAMPLES directory, the simple command below can be entered to move to its DATAEAST subdirectory:

```
C:\SAMPLES>CD DATAEAST

C:\SAMPLES\DATAEAST>_
```

Your current location in the tree structure is shown in Fig. 20-7. Notice that the DOS prompt has changed to show the path to our current directory. As you move through the tree structure, this prompt will keep you

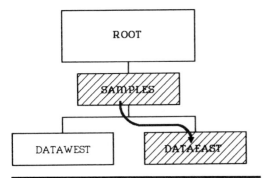

Figure 20-7 Moving from the SAMPLES directory to its DATAEAST subdirectory with command CD DATAEAST.

conveniently aware of your current location. Try typing DIR from the \SAMPLES\DATAEAST directory:

```
C:\SAMPLES\DATAEAST>DIR

  Volume in drive C is COMPLANDSBA
  Directory of C:\SAMPLES\DATAEAST

   .              <DIR>
   ..             <DIR>
         2 File(s)

C:\SAMPLES\DATAEAST>_
```

The dot and double-dot files are listed in this directory as well. We mentioned earlier that the two dots represent the parent of the current directory. The double dot can be used as a shorthand notation to refer to a parent directory in commands. Specifying the double dot as a parameter of the CD command will cause you to travel back one directory level to a parent directory:

```
C:\SAMPLES\DATAEAST>CD ..

C:\SAMPLES>_
```

Figure 20-8 illustrates how this is done.

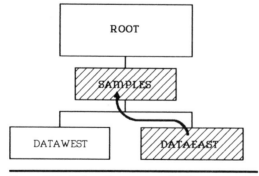

Figure 20-8 Using the command CD .. to move. back to SAMPLES.

This command essentially says "go back one directory." You can see by the DOS prompt that you are back in the SAMPLES directory. If you type the command again, you will be transferred another level back in the tree structure to the parent directory of SAMPLES, which is the ROOT directory (see Fig. 20-9).

```
C:\SAMPLES>CD ..

C:\>_
```

You do not have to step through each of the directories to get to an outer subdirectory. If you specify the full path to the target directory when typing the CD command, you will be transferred directly to it (see Fig. 20-10). For example, to get to the DATAEAST directory from the current ROOT directory in one step you can type:

```
C:\>CD \SAMPLES\DATAEAST

C:\SAMPLES\DATAEAST>_
```

Moving from the DATAEAST directory to the DATAWEST directory is an interesting exercise. There are several commands you can use to get to a directory that branches from the same path as the current directory. One method would be to drop down to SAMPLES using CD .. and then

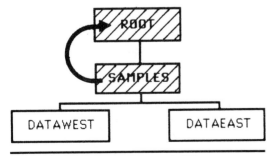

Figure 20-9 Using the command CD .. to move. to the ROOT directory.

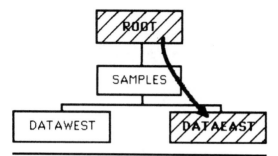

Figure 20-10 Moving through several levels of directories with one command, CD \SAM-PLES\DATAEAST.

transfer to DATAWEST from SAMPLES by typing CD DATAWEST. Another method would be to specify the full path to the directory by typing CD \SAMPLES\DATAWEST. The example below uses the first choice.

```
C:\SAMPLES\DATAEAST>CD ..\DATAWEST

C:\SAMPLES\DATAWEST>_
```

This command is the most interesting and the easiest, although it may be more confusing. The two dots indicate that you want to move *back* one directory, which places you in the SAMPLES directory. From there we travel to DATAWEST. Figure 20-11 shows this move.

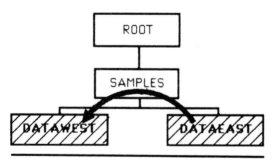

Figure 20-11 Moving to another directory on the current path with the command C ..\ DATAWEST.

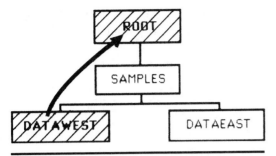

Figure 20-12 An example of moving directly to the ROOT directory with the command CD\.

You can use the double dot to travel through multiple levels by typing more than one set on a command line. For instance, you could type CD ..\.. to move back two levels. To transfer directly back to the ROOT directory from any level you can type the ROOT symbol (\) as a parameter of the CD command (see Fig. 20-12) as in the example below:

```
C: \SAMPLES \DATAWEST>CD \
C: \>_
```

Displaying Directories

If you're in a directory, you can type DIR to display its contents, but to list a directory other than that of the current directory, you must specify the path to that directory in the DIR command. For instance, to display a list of files in the SAMPLES directory you would type:

```
C: \>DIR \SAMPLES
```

To display a list of files in the \SAMPLES\DATAWEST directory, type:

```
C: \>DIR \SAMPLES\DATAWEST
```

If you were in a higher-level directory such as \SAMPLES\DATA-WEST, you could view the directory listing of its parent by typing:

```
C:\SAMPLES\DATAWEST>DIR ..
```

and to see a listing of a directory two levels down you could type:

```
C:\SAMPLES\DATAWEST>DIR ..\..
```

To list the ROOT directory from another directory you would type:

```
C:\SAMPLES\DATAWEST>DIR \
```

Copying and Displaying Files

Create the following file in the ROOT directory. You will use it in the next few exercises to see how files are copied between directories.

```
C:\>COPY CON:EXAMPLE.TXT
LINE 1
LINE 2
LINE 3
END OF FILE
<F6><Return>

C:\>_
```

To copy the file to another directory you will need to specify the path to that directory in the COPY command. To copy EXAMPLE.TXT to the \SAMPLES\DATAEAST directory, enter the following command. Figure 20-13 illustrates how it works.

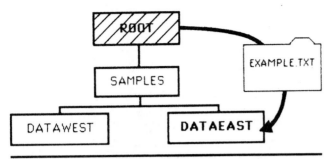

Figure 20-13 Copying the file EXAMPLE.TXT from the ROOT directory to the DATAEAST subdirectory using the command COPY EXAMPLE.TXT \SAMPLES\ DATAEAST. Note that ROOT is the current directory.

```
C:\>COPY EXAMPLE.TXT \SAMPLES\DATAEAST
          1 File(s) copied

C:\>_
```

Now, enter the DIR command to see that the file has been transferred to the DATAEAST directory. You can use the DOS editing keys to borrow characters from the previous command to build the DIR command. To do this, type in DIR and a space. Press the F4 editing key, then press the Backslash key, and then press the F3 editing key to copy the template out to the end. This trick will save you time, especially when you are working with long path names. Remember that the F4 key copies the rest of the template out past a specified character.

```
C:\>DIR \SAMPLES\DATAEAST            (type DIR <F4>\<F3>)

   Volume in drive C is COMPLANDSBA
   Directory of C:\SAMPLES\DATAEAST

   .          <DIR>
   ..         <DIR>
EXAMPLE TXT 36
          3 File(s)

C:\>_
```

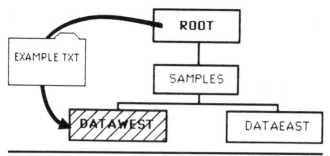

Figure 20-14 Copying the file while DATAWEST is the current directory with the command COPY \ EXAMPLE.TXT.

Sometimes it is simpler to copy a file to a directory if you are already in that directory. To try this out, go to the \SAMPLE\DATAWEST directory and type the copy command shown below (see Fig. 20-14). Compare it to the COPY command above.

```
C:\>CD \SAMPLES\DATAWEST

C:\SAMPLES\DATAWEST>COPY \EXAMPLE.TXT
       1 File(s) copied

C:\SAMPLES\DATAWEST>_
```

You still had to specify the path of the source file in the COPY command, but this time the path is much shorter (\) and easier to type. If you are copying more than one file to a directory, you can save many keystrokes when issuing COPY commands by doing so from the directory that will receive the files.

Here's an example of how to copy the EXAMPLE file from \SAMPLES\DATAWEST, our current directory, to \SAMPLES\DATAEAST. Since the file already exists in the DATAEAST directory, the command will rename it as it is copied (see Fig. 20-15).

```
C:\SAMPLES\DATAWEST>COPY EXAMPLE.TXT ..\DATAEAST\EXAMPLE2
       1 File(s) copied

C:\SAMPLES\DATAWEST>_
```

Now, list the files in the DATAEAST directory to see that the files have been copied. You will have to specify the path to the DATAEAST directory since the current directory is still DATAWEST.

```
C:\SAMPLES\DATAWEST>DIR ..\DATAEAST

   Volume in drive C is COMPLANDSBA
   Directory of C:\SAMPLES\DATAEAST

   .              <DIR>
   ..             <DIR>
EXAMPLE   TXT       36
EXAMPLE2            36
           4 File(s)

C:\SAMPLES\DATAWEST>_
```

In the COPY command above, you used the double dot (parent) to help specify the path for the copy. The path drops down one directory from \SAMPLES\DATAWEST to \SAMPLES and then points to \SAMPLES\DATAEAST. You used the same technique to get a listing of the directory. In renaming the file EXAMPLE.TXT to EXAMPLE2, you specified the new name as the last parameter in the path name of the

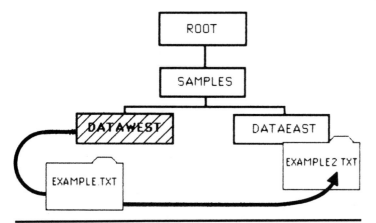

Figure 20-15 An example of copying a file from one directory to another on the same path. The copied file is renamed in the new directory. Note that DATAWEST is current directory.

directory it was to be copied to. To explain this, we must talk about path name syntax.

Path Name Syntax

Technically, the full name of the DATAWEST directory is \SAMPLES\ DATAWEST. Since the file EXAMPLE2.TXT resides in the \SAM-PLES\DATAWEST directory, its full name is \SAMPLES\DATA-WEST\EXAMPLE2.TXT. The last parameter in a path can be either a file name or a directory, but DOS will always consider it to be a directory first. Look at the COPY and RENAME command used previously to see how this works.

COPY EXAMPLE.TXT ..\DATAEAST\EXAMPLE2

COPY is the DOS command, EXAMPLE.TXT is the source file, and ..\DATAEAST\EXAMPLE2 is the destination.

When DOS executed this command, it first established the pathway to the directory that was to receive the EXAMPLE.TXT file. The COPY command was issued from the \SAMPLES\DATAWEST directory in which the file EXAMPLE.TXT resides; therefore the path was not required on this side of the command (source side). The other side of the COPY command (destination side) specifies the path to the directory to which the file will be copied. DOS's first reaction to the command above was to copy EXAMPLE.TXT to a directory called EXAMPLE2, but when it didn't find this directory branching from DATAEAST, it assumed EXAMPLE2 was the new name for the file.

Note that the first instance of the backslash in a path name refers to the ROOT directory. All other occurrences of the backslash in a path name are used to separate the directory names and file names in the path.

Displaying the Directory Structure

The DOS TREE command can be used to display the tree structure of your filing system.

```
C : \>TREE
```

To display the files in each directory add the /F parameter to the command:

```
C : \>TREE /F
```

You can pipe the screen output into the MORE command to page the listing:

```
C : \>TREE /F : MORE
```

To print the listing, enter the following command. The printout will serve as a map of your system.

```
C : \>TREE /F > PRN
```

You can also use the CHKDSK command to display the directories and their files. The following command will list each subdirectory and each file it contains:

```
C : \>CHKDSK /V
```

Setting Paths

The PATH command is important for the proper operation of DOS's hierarchical file system. With PATH you can tell DOS where to look for commands and batch files. PATH can specify more than one directory, causing DOS to search in a specified order, one directory after the other, until it finds the command.

There are two types of paths which we should clarify to avoid confusion. The first type of path is one you specify when issuing DOS commands. For example, you place a path before a file in the COPY command to tell

DOS where to copy the file. You can also place the path in a DIR command to tell DOS which directory to list.

The second type of path is the one set by the PATH command, normally as part of a AUTOEXEC.BAT file. This is the path that DOS will use when *searching* for commands and batch files. In this section, we will discuss this second type of path.

To set the search path, type PATH and the path name. The following path directs DOS to search the ROOT directory of the default drive when looking for commands.

```
C:\>PATH \
```

You can specify another drive as part of the path, but PATH will always search the current directory first before looking elsewhere for a command. This feature can be used advantageously. For instance, assume that a system contains the standard DOS files in the ROOT directory, including the DOS commands FORMAT, MODE, and TREE. You can prevent a new user who is working in a directory called \NOVICE, for example, from issuing these commands by writing batch files in the \NOVICE directory that have the same file names as the commands. These batch files would simply display a statement such as "Sorry, you can't do that from this directory" when the user in the \NOVICE directory tries to issue one of the commands. The batch file in the directory overrides the command file in the ROOT directory, displaying the message.

You can tell DOS to look in several different directories by specifying each directory in the PATH command. Each directory must be separated by a semicolon. The following PATH command would cause DOS to first look in the current directory, then in the ROOT directory, next in the TOOLS directory, and lastly in the UTILITY directory for a command or batch file.

    PATH \;\TOOLS;\UTILITY

The next PATH command will cause DOS to look first in the ROOT directory of drive C, second in the ROOT of drive A, and third in the ROOT of drive B.

    PATH \;A:\;B:\

The PATH command can be inserted into the AUTOEXEC.BAT file so that it automatically sets the path when you turn your computer on.

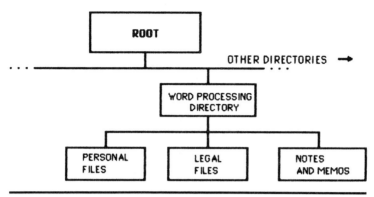

Figure 20-16   Data directories branching from an applications directory.

When using some programs, you will want to store data in subdirectories that branch from the directory holding the program files. Although not all software will allow you to do this, more is available today than when DOS-2 was first introduced. Using this feature with a word processor, for instance, you can create several directories that branch from the directory that is holding the program files. Each directory would hold different types of files, such as legal files and personal files. This saves space by allowing both subdirectories to access the same program files. Figure 20-16 illustrates a directory for a word processing program that has several subdirectories used for storing text files.

Removing Directories

We include this topic last because it is the most unglamorous feature of tree-structured filing. Eventually, you will need to remove a subdirectory because the information in it is no longer needed. If the subdirectory contains branching subdirectories, each of the subdirectories will have to be removed before you can remove the parent directory.

Let's step through the process of removing the \SAMPLES directory. First you will need to delete all the files in \SAMPLES\DATAEAST and \SAMPLES\DATAWEST. Type the following to delete the files in DATAEAST:

```
C:\>DEL \SAMPLES\DATAEAST
Are you sure (Y/N)? Y

C:\>_
```

This erases all files in the subdirectory. You cannot type RD \SAM-PLES\DATAEAST (RD stands for remove directory) until you have erased the files in the directory, otherwise DOS will display "Directory not empty." Now that the files are removed, you can remove the directory:

```
C:\>RD \SAMPLES\DATAEAST

C:\>
```

The DATAEAST subdirectory has been removed, but you still can't remove the SAMPLES directory until the DATAWEST subdirectory has been removed. The following commands will erase the required files and remove the rest of the directories.

```
C:\>DEL \SAMPLES\DATAWEST
Are you sure (Y/N)? Y

C:\>RD \SAMPLES\DATAWEST

C:\>DEL \SAMPLES
Are you sure (Y/N)? Y

C:\>RD SAMPLES
```

After removing many files and directories from a fixed disk, it's a good idea to back up and restore the disk to prevent new files from being stored noncontiguously in the sectors left by the old files. An alternative method to remove a directory is to simply back up all directories except the ones you want to remove. Refer to Chap. 24 for more details about this method.

This chapter explained the use of hierarchical filing structures and the commands used when working with them. Many examples were used to explain how files are copied to other directories and how path names are used in commands. The last section explains how to remove a directory structure. In the next few chapters we will describe various features of DOS that can be used to help enhance and automate a tree-structured filing system, and in Chaps. 23 and 24 you will see examples of ways to organize your system.

21

Keyboard and Screen Reassignments

One of the unique features of DOS is its ability to reassign the meaning of the keys on the keyboard and to alter the screen display. Using this feature, you can assign a string of characters or a DOS command to almost any key on the keyboard. After a key has been assigned, a simple press of the key will execute the DOS command or display the string.

To assign keys, the alternate keyboard and screen driver file called ANSI.SYS must be loaded into memory. This is accomplished by including its name as a device in the CONFIG.SYS file as described in Chap. 19. ANSI.SYS is a file that is supplied on the DOS disk and is loaded into the system at boot time when DOS reads the CONFIG.SYS boot file. Before proceeding with this chapter, check to make sure that your version of DOS has this driver file.

ANSI.SYS is an alternate device driver. It alters the normal portion of the operating system that controls input from the keyboard and output to the screen. Earlier, you saw that DOS has given the name CON or console to the screen and keyboard devices, the screen being the output console and the keyboard the input console. Normally, all input and output goes to the CON devices through a keyboard/screen input/output program (the console device driver) that is loaded when you turn your system on. You can replace this normal driver with the ANSI.SYS driver. When it is in use, special codes, preceded by an Escape code, can be sent to DOS where they are interpreted differently than normal keyboard input.

Any time an Escape code is sent to DOS, it will receive the next character as a special character. If the ANSI.SYS device driver is loaded, the codes following the Escape code will be translated by the driver into keyboard assignments or screen redefinitions.

There are some hitches, however. The Escape key on the keyboard cannot be used to send the Escape code. This key is used by DOS as an editing key; pressing it will cancel the command on the command line. Instead, you can send an Escape code to DOS with the DOS PROMPT command, which has an Escape meta-string, or you can build a file that contains Escape sequences and use TYPE to display the file on the screen.

Loading the ANSI.SYS Driver

The file ANSI.SYS must be loaded at boot time before any keys can be assigned. This is accomplished by placing it in the CONFIG.SYS boot file, which DOS automatically reads when it starts. The CONFIG.SYS file is a simple text file that contains the names of the device drivers to be loaded. To load ANSI.SYS, you simply add the line DEVICE = ANSI.SYS to the file.

COPY CON or EDLIN can be used to create the file. If you already have a CONFIG.SYS file, add the statement DEVICE = ANSI.SYS to it using EDLIN. If not, create the file shown below. The CONFIG.SYS file must be stored in the ROOT directory, otherwise the file will not be read when the system boots. In this respect, CONFIG.SYS is similar to the AUTOEXEC.BAT boot file. Type the following in the ROOT directory to create the file:

```
A:\>COPY CON:CONFIG.SYS
DEVICE = ANSI.SYS
<F6> <Return>
```

The driver does not take effect until you reboot your system, which you can do now by pressing **Ctrl-Alt-Del.** Once the driver is loaded, space is set aside in your computer's memory for up to 127 defined character strings.

Assigning Keys

Let's assign a key now so you can get a feel for what we are doing before going further. The simplest way to assign keys is to use the PROMPT command. If you look at the list of PROMPT meta-strings, you will notice that $e is an Escape code. By combining this Escape sequence with special codes, a key assignment can be made. Type in the following; we will explain the details in a minute.

```
A:\>PROMPT $e[0;68;"DIR"p
```

Now press the **F10** key. The DIR command appears on the command line, and you simply press **Return** to execute it. Whenever you use PROMPT to assign a key, you will lose the existing prompt. To correct this, you will need to reissue the prompt as shown below.

```
PROMPT $p$g
A:\>_
```

Let's break the PROMPT string down and look at each of its components. First, PROMPT sends the whole string to DOS for interpretation. DOS reads the meta-string $e and, upon detecting Escape, prepares to receive a set of characters it will treat differently than normal keyboard input. Because the ANSI.SYS device driver is loaded, the characters following the Escape code are used to define a key. The next character, the square bracket, tells DOS "the characters begin here."

The numbers tell DOS which key on the keyboard is to be reassigned. Each key has its own keycode. Table 21-1 shows the keycodes for the extended keys on the IBM keyboard. The string you want to assign to the key is placed in quotation marks. This is followed by the p which ends the string. When you press Return, the Escape sequence is sent to DOS and the key is assigned.

Try one more key reassignment. The following command will assign the string DIR /W to the F9 key. This time a carriage return (code 13) will be placed at the end of the string so that it will be immediately executed when you press F9.

```
A:\>PROMPT $e[0;67;"DIR /W";13p
A:\>PROMPT $p$g
A:\>_
```

TABLE 21-1 Extended Character Codes

Code	Extended key
3	Null character, NUL
15	Shift-tab
16–25	Alt- Q, W, E, R, T, Y, U, I, O, P
30–38	Alt- A, S, D, F, G, H, J, K, L
44–50	Alt- Z, X, C, V, B, N, M
59–68	F1 through F10 (F1 through F6 are normally assigned as DOS editing keys)
71	Home
72	Cursor up
73	Pg up
75	Cursor left
77	Cursor right
79	End
80	Cursor down
81	Pg dn
82	Ins
83	Del
84–93	Shift-F1 through Shift-F10 (F11 through F20)
94–103	Ctrl-F1 through Ctrl-F10 (F21 through F30)
104–113	Alt-F1 through Alt-F10 (F31 through F40)
114	Ctrl-PrtSc
115	Ctrl-Cursor left (previous word)
116	Ctrl-Cursor right (next word)
117	Ctrl-End
118	Ctrl-Pg dn
119	Ctrl-Home
120–131	Alt- 1, 2, 3, 4, 5, 6, 7, 8, 9, 0, -, =
132	Ctrl-Pg up

Compare this new string with the one shown above. We have changed the number 68 to 67, the code for the F9 key. The string in quotation marks now contains the /W parameter which lists the files in the wide format. The most important difference is the addition of the 13, which is the ASCII code for carriage return (see App. A). When you press the F9 key, DIR /W will be typed on the DOS command line and then a carriage return will be executed, which causes the command to be executed. Note in both examples that a semicolon (;) separates the components of the strings. If you forget the semicolons, the key reassignment will not work.

There are two types of key assignments: those that directly execute by issuing a carriage return and those that wait for more input. Many strings require switches or parameters; for instance, if you assign the DIR command to a string, you may want to add parameters to it such as B: or /P. Other assignments may execute immediately, such as CLS or DIR. These assignments should have the carriage return code 13 placed at the end of the string.

Finding the Keycode Numbers

To assign a string to a key, you will need to know what the keycode for the key is. This keycode tells DOS what key on the keyboard will receive the reassignment string. There are two sets of codes. The first set locates the standard ASCII keys like A and a on the keyboard. The other set of codes locates the keys that are specific to IBM-compatible computers. These keys include the F1 through F10 keys and any combination of F1 through F10 used in conjunction with either the Alt, Shift, or Ctrl key. The codes for these keys are shown in Table 21-1, "Extended Character Codes." Extended keycodes contain a zero before the keycode.

Look at the ASCII character code table shown in App. A. This table shows the ASCII codes for standard characters and numbers. For instance, the letter A has an ASCII value of 65. This is the code used to specify the A key. Note that a has an ASCII value of 97. The keycode is placed in the position following the square bracket. The following example demonstrates how you could assign % to the Equal (=) key. (Assigning % to this key will save you a lot of shifting.)

```
PROMPT $e[61;"%"p
```

In this example, the Equal key is coded 61, according to the ASCII chart. Since the Equal key is a standard key and not an extended key, the keycode is not preceded by 0.

Remember that to assign strings to any extended key, you must place a 0 before the keycode for that key. For instance, if you wanted to asssign FORMAT B:/S to the Alt-F2 key (fixed-disk users use FORMAT A:/S) you would type:

```
A:\>PROMPT $e[0;105;"FORMAT B:/S"p

PROMPT $p$g

A:\>_
```

Breaking this down you can see that:

- $e is the Escape meta-string.
- The square bracket begins the reassignment string.
- The 0 indicates an extended key.

- Keycode 105 is the Alt-F2 key.
- The string to be assigned is between the quotation marks.

Although any key on the keyboard may be reassigned, the Function keys are best used for this purpose. Do not use Function keys F1 through F6 because they are assigned as the DOS editing keys. Any combination of Alt, Ctrl, and Shift may be used with the Function keys. The total number of characters that DOS will keep track of as assignment strings is 127. If you find that this is not enough, you can create short assignment strings that call batch files.

Automatic Reassignment

The PROMPT reassignment commands can be placed in a batch file or the AUTOEXEC.BAT file. If placed in AUTOEXEC, the keys will be assigned when the system boots. As discussed above, reassigning a key will leave you with a blank prompt so the last line following the assignment strings in the batch file should set up the DOS prompt. We have included the batch file below as an example. It sets up the following key assignments:

Key	String	Explanation
Alt-F1	CD ..	Go back one directory
Alt-F2	CD \	Go to ROOT directory
Alt-F3	DIR	
Alt-F4	TYPE	
Alt-F5	A:	Use with DIR and TYPE above
Alt-F6	B:	Use with DIR and TYPE above
Alt-F7	PROMPT	Can be used for further assignments

```
A:\>COPY CON:AUTOEXEC.BAT
PATH \
PROMPT $e[0;104;"CD ..";13p
PROMPT $e[0;105;"CD \";13p
PROMPT $e[0;106;"DIR "p
PROMPT $e[0;107;"TYPE "p
PROMPT $e[0;108;"A: "p
PROMPT $e[0;109;"B: "p
PROMPT $e[0;110;"PROMPT "p
PROMPT $p$g                    (sets DOS prompt back to normal)
<F6> <Return>

A:\>_
```

The first two prompt assignments end with a carriage return because the commands are usually directly executed. The rest of the commands will accept further parameters. For instance, you can press F3 for DIR and press F6 to add B: to it. You can then add other options such as the /W or /S switches. The last prompt sets up the DOS prompt to display the current directory and default drive. To assign the keys, reboot your system or type AUTOEXEC on the command line.

Using the PROMPT command is the easiest way to assign keys. You can enter a keyboard assignment directly from the keyboard at any time. There is another way, however, to assign keys and we will cover this method in a minute.

About the ANSI.SYS Driver File

ANSI.SYS is a special driver file that controls not only key assignments, but also screen cursor positioning and colors. You can change the foreground and background colors of the screen as well as control the location of the cursor by using the ANSI.SYS driver. ANSI stands for American National Standards Institute and the ANSI driver meets the standards set by this organization. Having a standard set of sequences to control devices like the screen allows programmers to create programs that can be used on many different machines.

The full ANSI set is described in more detail in App. F. One set of codes that is of particular interest to owners of color graphics monitors is the list of Color Rendition Codes shown in Table 21-2. The following prompt will set a yellow foreground with a blue background on a color graphics monitor.

PROMPT $e[33;44m

The format for the color rendition code is as follows:

ESC[#; . . . ;#m

where # can be specified a multiple number of times in one line and takes one of the values listed in Table 21-2.

Creating Key Reassignment Files

Using PROMPT to reassign keys is not the only way to get the Escape codes to the screen. Earlier you used the PROMPT meta-string $e to produce the Escape code, adding the rest of the string to it.

TABLE 21-2 **Color Rendition Codes**

Code	Explanation
0	All attributes off
1	High intensity (boldface) on
4	Underscore (underline) on
5	Blinking on
7	Inverse video on
8	Invisible display
30	Foreground black
31	Foreground red
32	Foreground green
33	Foreground yellow
34	Foreground blue
35	Foreground magenta
37	Foreground white
40	Background black
41	Background red
42	Background green
43	Background yellow
44	Background blue
45	Background magenta
46	Background cyan
47	Background white

Another way of assigning keys is to place the Escape codes in a file and then use TYPE to display the file on the screen. ANSI.SYS must be loaded first, of course. Placing an Escape code in a file is easy with EDLIN; you can place any Control code directly in a file by pressing Ctrl-V, followed by the symbol normally used for the code. The symbol for Escape is the left square bracket ([).

The table below shows the key assignments that will be made by a file called ASSIGN.CDS. (Note: From here on we refer to the normal Function keys as F1 through F10, the Ctrl-Function keys as C1 through C10, the Alt-Function keys as A1 through A10, and the Shift-Function keys as S1 through S10.) F1 through F6 are not assigned because they are already used as the DOS editing keys.

Key	Assignment	Key	Assignment
F7	DIR	F8	TYPE
F9	A:/P	F10	B:/P
A1	CHKDSK	A2	FORMAT B:
A3	CLS	A4	COPY
A5	PROMPT	A6	*.*
A7	HELP	A8	MENU
A9	MM	A10	PM

We recommend the above assignments, but you can use any of your own by making alteration in the file we show below. Owners of fixed-disk systems will want to substitute the designator for their floppy drive for the B on key A2. The strings assigned to A7 through A10 will be used in the next two chapters to execute batch files, so keep them as we show here.

To start creating the file, get into EDLIN by typing the following command:

```
A:\>EDLIN ASSIGN.CDS
New file
*_
```

Press I for INSERT and on the first line, press Ctrl-V; ^V will appear on the line. Enter the left square bracket immediately after it.

```
*I
    1:* ^V[
```

Now, enter the rest of the string for the first key assignments. The example below shows the proper keycodes.

```
1:*    ^ V [[0;65;"DIR"p <Return>
2:*_
```

That's all there is to it. To assign the rest of the keys illustrated above, enter the following codes while in INSERT mode. The ^V character in the first part of each string is entered by pressing Ctrl-V.

```
^V[[0;66;"TYPE "p
^V[[0;67;"A:/P"p
^V[[0;68;"B:/P"p
^V[[0;31;"CHKDSK "p
```

```
^V[[0;32;"FORMAT B:"p
^V[[0;33;"CLS";13p
^V[[0;34;"COPY "p
^V[[0;35;"PROMPT "p
^V[[0;36;"*.*"p
^V[[0;37;"HELP";13p
^V[[0;38;"MENU";13p
^V[[0;39;"MM";13p
^V[[0;40;"PM";13p
```

You can add more strings to this file now or later. Remember that the assignments don't take effect until you reboot the system and use TYPE to display the file on the screen. You can place the command TYPE ASSIGN.CDS in your AUTOEXEC.BAT file. Also, don't forget to load the ANSI.SYS driver by placing it in the CONFIG.SYS file. Keep in mind that there is a limit to the number of characters you can assign. If you start running out of characters (the maximum is 127), create short assignment strings that call batch files. For instance, the last four lines shown above will call batch files called HELP.BAT, MENU.BAT, MM.BAT, and PM.BAT. We will cover this in the next chapter.

Removing Key Assignments

To remove assignments from a key, simply send the key's original code back to it. For instance, to clear a string from the F10 key (key 0;68), using the prompt command, you would type:

```
A:\>PROMPT $e[0;68;0;68p

A:\>PROMPT $p$g

A:\>_
```

To clear a whole set of assignments, like those made by the ASSIGN.CDS file, make a copy of ASSIGN.CDS, calling it RESET.CDS:

```
A:\>COPY ASSIGN.CDS RESET.CDS
```

Next, use EDLIN to alter each line in the file by replacing the string assignment with the key code for that key. The following is an example of how you would alter the first line:

Change: ˆ[0;65;"DIR"p
To: ˆ[0;65;**0;65p**

Change each line in the file. To cancel all key assignments created by ASSIGN.CDS, simply use TYPE to send RESET.CDS to the screen.

In this chapter we discussed the ANSI.SYS keyboard driver and how it is loaded into the system. We then covered key reassignment using PROMPT. Another method of assigning keys was covered in the last part of the chapter, whereby a file is built with EDLIN and then TYPE is used to display it on the screen. Removing key assignments was also covered.

22

Organizing and Automating Your System

This chapter will aid you in organizing your system, whether you are using floppy diskettes or have a fixed disk. By creating a series of menus, help screens, and Function key assignments, you can automate your computer, making it easier for you and others to use. The menu shown in Fig. 22-1 is an example of a main menu that can be displayed when the system is first turned on. It can also be displayed at any other time by pressing Alt-F9, the Function key you assigned in the last chapter as the main menu (MM) key.

Remember the file FRAME.PIC you created in Chap. 16? Now you can use it as the frame for the main menu. The Function key assignments created in the last chapter will be used to automate the computer, and many of the batch files created previously will become part of this new system.

This chapter has many functions. One is to give you more experience with editors, batch files, and DOS commands. We will also bring together many of the concepts you have learned in previous chapters and use them as tools to help create an organized system. You may not need a menu system such as the one we describe here, but the lessons learned in this chapter will help you understand some of the advanced features of DOS.

If you own a floppy-disk system, this chapter will help you create a disk that can be used as a master boot disk. The disk will contain the menus and utilities we talked about earlier. If you own a fixed disk, this chapter is the groundwork for the next chapter in which a tree-structured filing system for your fixed disk will be developed.

```
                    THE MAIN MENU

                1  DISPLAY UTILITIES MENU
                2  LIST KEY ASSIGNMENTS
                3  DISPLAY PHONE MENU
                4  DOS COMMAND HELP
                5  DOS SYNTAX HELP
                6  (FUTURE USE)
                7  (FUTURE USE)
                8  (FUTURE USE)
```

Figure 22-1

Before You Start

If you own a floppy system, refer to "Floppy-Disk Systems," below. If you own a fixed-disk system, refer to "Fixed-Disk Systems."

Floppy-Disk Systems

In the tutorial, you created a working disk that now contains text files and batch files that were created throughout the previous chapters. In this chapter, you will create a new disk and copy some of the previous files to it.

To start, pull out a new blank floppy disk, place it in drive B, and place the original DOS disk in drive A (assuming that the default drive is A). If you have a single-drive system, place the DOS disk in the drive and follow the prompts displayed on the screen. Enter the format command as shown below:

```
A:\>FORMAT B:/S/V
```

When formatting is done, DOS will ask you for a volume name. Call this disk MENUDOS. Now copy the following files from the DOS disk to the MENUDOS diskette. Use the COPY command in the form: **COPY file name B:**

ANSI.SYS	FORMAT.COM
CHKDSK.COM	SYS.COM
DISKCOPY.COM	DISKCOMP.COM (optional)
COMP.COM (optional)	EDLIN.COM
MODE.COM (optional)	PRINT.COM (optional)
ASSIGN.COM	TREE.COM (optional)
GRAPHICS.COM (optional)	SORT.EXE
FIND.EXE	MORE.COM
BASICA.COM	

We have marked some files optional. Since files take up room on a disk, you should determine if you will be using a command file enough to justify its existence on the disk. For example, DISKCOMP and COMP are used to verify copies. You may never use these (depending on how much you trust the COPY commands). The command file GRAPHICS.COM is useful only if you have an IBM Graphics Printer, so you may not need it.

Once you have copied the DOS command files, replace the DOS disk in drive A with TUTORIAL II—the disk created in Chap. 9 that you worked with in the remainder of the lessons. This disk contains several batch files that you created in previous chapters. If you don't have these files, you can go back and create them later. To copy the files to the new disk in drive B, issue the following commands (the contents of these files are listed at the end of this chapter).

A:\>COPY PRNT132.BAT B:	(prints a file in compressed print; Chap. 8)
A:\>COPY FND.BAT B:	(finds numbers in your phone number list; Chap. 12)
A:\>COPY HELP.TXT	(help menu; Chap. 13)
A:\>COPY REMOVE.BAT B:	(displays a list of files before they are erased; Chap. 15)
A:\>COPY NEWDISK.BAT B:	(disk backup batch file; Chap. 15)
A:\>COPY FRAME.PIC B:	(menu frame; Chap. 16)
A:\>COPY DISPFILE.BAT B:	(displays a group of files on the screen; Chap. 17)
A:\>COPY MKFILE.BAT B:	(checks to see if a file exist before executing COPY CON; Chap. 17)
A:\>COPY SYNTAX.MNU B:	(help screen to display DOS command syntax; App. E)

A: \>**COPY ASSIGN.CDS B:**   (keyboard assignment file; Chap. 21)

A: \>**COPY CONFIG.SYS B:**   (system configuration file containing
ANSI.SYS driver; Chap. 21)

You can create a text file called UTILITY.MNU that displays the name
and description of each of the batch and text files shown above and use it
to help you remember the names and functions of the batch files on the
disk.

Fixed-Disk Systems

If you own a fixed disk, this chapter and the next chapter will help you
set up a tree-structured filing system on the disk that centers around a
series of menus. Figure 22-1 shows the main menu which will reside in the
ROOT directory. In the system we describe in the next chapter, your fixed
disk will be organized into several different directories that are set aside
for special applications such as the storage of business software, personal
software, entertainment software, and more. The special directories can
be called BUSINESS, PERSONAL, and ENTERTAINMENT for
instance. Each of these directories will have its own menu, and you will
be able to move through the directories by using the Function keys you
assigned in Chap. 21. Since this structure will be a permanent addition to
the fixed disk, the disk should be "optimized" before you begin work.

Optimizing the fixed disk involves removing old unwanted files, backing
up the entire disk, reformatting or erasing the disk, and then restoring the
files. The BACKUP and RESTORE commands are described in Chap. 18.
When the files are restored on the disk, they will be stored contiguously,
thus more efficiently. The file structure you install will then operate at
maximum performance.

If you started with a new fixed disk when you began this book and the
only files on the disk are those you created with it, there is no need to
back up the disk. Instead, you can save the few important files that are
listed below on a floppy disk and copy them back later after formatting
the fixed disk. If you have placed other valuable files or programs on the
disk, be sure you save them to disk or use BACKUP and RESTORE
before erasing your disk as described. An explanation of these files may
be found under "Floppy-Disk Systems," above. A full description follows
at the end of this chapter.

```
PRNT132.BAT
FND.BAT
HELP.TXT
REMOVE.BAT
NEWDISK.BAT
FRAME.PIC
DISPFILE.BAT
MKFILE.BAT
SYNTAX.MNU
ASSIGN.CDS
CONFIG.SYS
SFORMAT.BAT
```

Before copying the above files back to the reformatted disk, copy the DOS files from the original DOS disk. They should be placed on the drive first so they can be quickly accessed by DOS. Don't forget the batch file SFORMAT.BAT which prevents accidental erasure of the fixed disk. You'll have to rename FORMAT.COM to DOFORMAT.COM as outlined in Chap. 15.

The Start-Up Menu

The rest of this chapter is applicable to either floppy-disk or hard-disk systems. If you are working with floppy disks, place the disk just created in the default drive. All work will be done on this disk from now on. Be sure to label it.

To begin, make a copy of the file FRAME.TXT, calling it MENU.TXT. This will leave the original file FRAME.TXT intact so that you can use it again in the future.

```
A:\>COPY FRAME.TXT MENU.TXT

A:\>_
```

You can use EDLIN to add text to this file, creating the menu shown in Fig. 22-1. If you have an editor or word processor that displays extended graphics characters, you may prefer to edit the file with that instead of EDLIN. Because EDLIN is a line editor, you may find it hard to work with and prefer to switch. Note that the menu is one of our own design; you can add any text you prefer, or you can design your own menu that is based on how you want to organize your system. You can also add your name or company name to the top of the menu for a professional look.

To start, get into EDLIN so you can edit the main menu:

```
A : \>EDLIN MENU.TXT
*
```

List the file using the **L** command. If you created a frame file using the description in Chap. 16, the ideal place for the title is in line 5. Press **5** and **Return,** and the line will appear for editing. Notice that the side walls of the frame appear on the line. You can insert text between the walls by using the **F1** editing key (or right arrow) to copy from the template. Enter the title of your choice or the one shown in Fig. 22-1 in the center of the line. Press the **F3** key to finish the line out to the right graphics character. If the title doesn't appear centered, backspace over the title and try again. If you run into problems that are beyond normal correction, exit EDLIN and start over.

Automating the Menu

The menu has selection numbers like 1 and 2, so you can automate it by creating batch files called 1.BAT and 2.BAT. The file below will create a batch file for the first menu selection. In it, the screen is cleared and a utility menu is displayed with the TYPE command. The utility menu can display the names and functions of the batch files shown at the end of this chapter.

```
A : \>COPY CON:1.BAT
ECHO OFF
CLS
TYPE UTILITY.MNU
<F6> <Return>

A : \>_
```

Each successive selection on the menu will have a similar batch file with a name that corresponds to its menu selection number. The second selec-

```
              FUNCTION KEY ASSIGNMENTS MENU

        F7   DIR              F8   TYPE
        F9   A:/P             F10  B:/P

        A1   CHKDSK           A2   FORMAT
        A3   CLS              A4   COPY
        A5   PROMPT           A5   *.*
        A7   HELP             A8   CURRENT MENU
        A9   MAIN MENU        A10  PREVIOUS MENU
```

Figure 22-2

tion, LIST KEY ASSIGNMENTS, has a corresponding batch file called 2.BAT that displays a list of key assignments. Figure 22-2 is a sample of a menu displayed when you press 2. This menu lists the assignments made by the file ASSIGN.CDS, created in Chap. 21. You can create this menu using the same process described above for creating MENU.TXT. Simply make another copy of the file FRAME.PIC, call it ASSIGN.MNU, and then add the text shown in Fig. 22-2.

The following batch files will automate the rest of the menu:

2.BAT	4.BAT
ECHO OFF	ECHO OFF
CLS	CLS
TYPE ASSIGN.MNU	TYPE HELP.TXT

3.BAT	5.BAT
ECHO OFF	ECHO OFF
CLS	CLS
TYPE PHONE.MNU	TYPE SYNTAX.MNU

Note that the menu file PHONE.MNU shown in batch file 3 will be created in Chap. 26.

The four Function keys Alt-F7 through Alt-F10 that we assigned in the last chapter will now need to be automated. These keys are an important feature of the menu system because they can be pressed by an operator to display a menu for the current directory, a previous menu, or the menu in the ROOT directory. To automate the keys, create the following batch files in the ROOT directory:

HELP.BAT   (displays the help menu in the current directory)
ECHO OFF
CLS
TYPE HELP.TXT

MENU.BAT   (displays the menu of the current directory)
ECHO OFF
CLS
TYPE MENU.TXT

MM.BAT   (goes to the ROOT directory and displays the main
ECHO OFF   menu)
CLS
CD \
TYPE MENU.TXT

PM.BAT   (goes back one directory and displays the menu)
ECHO OFF
CLS
CD ..
TYPE MENU.TXT

Activating the New System

Once all of the menu screens and batch files have been created, you can reboot the system to activate it. Before doing so, you must create one more batch file. A new AUTOEXEC.BAT file is needed that will initialize the keys and display the new menu when you turn the system on. Create the following AUTOEXEC.BAT file in the ROOT directory of the disk you are working with:

```
A:\>COPY CON:AUTOEXEC.BAT
ECHO OFF
PATH \
PROMPT $p$g
TYPE ASSIGN.CDS
TYPE MAINMENU.TXT
<F6> <Return>

A:\>_
```

The first line of the file turns the display of commands off. The second line sets the DOS search path. The third line sets the prompt to display the current directory and default drive. (PATH and PROMPT are especially important to owners of fixed-disk systems.) The next line assigns the keys by sending the assignment codes file to the console with the TYPE command, and the last line displays the opening menu.

Once you have created MENU.TXT and the AUTOEXEC.BAT file, you can reboot your system. The keys will be reassigned, and you will be able to use them to display menus, issue commands, and move through the system. If you ever want to see the menu, press Alt-FB. If the keys don't work, several things could be wrong: The CONFIG.SYS and ANSI.SYS files are not on the disk and therefore were not loaded, or the ASSIGN.CDS file is not on the disk.

Some Handy Utilities

Many of the batch files you created in previous chapters are appropriate for this disk. The batch files we asked you to copy over are listed below for reference, along with a short description.

PRNT132.BAT
MODE LPT1:132
COPY % 1 LPT1
MODE LPT1:80

(prints a file in compressed mode)

FND.BAT
FIND "% 1" PHONE.NUM

(finds a phone number in the file PHONE.NUM)

REMOVE.BAT
DIR % 1/W
REM - THESE ARE THE FILES
    THAT WILL BE ERASED.
REM - PRESS CTRL - BREAK TO
    STOP
PAUSE
ERASE % 1

(displays the files that are about to be erased so you can stop if necessary)

NEWDISK.BAT
CHKDSK *.*
REM - IS IT TIME TO BACK UP?
    PRESS CTRL - BREAK IF NOT.
PAUSE
REM - PLACE A BLANK DISK IN
    DRIVE B.
FORMAT B:/S/W
COPY *.* B:
REM - BACKUP COMPLETE—
    PLACE A LABEL ON THE NEW
    DISK.

(checks the disk for noncontiguous files; you may choose to back up if necessary)

DISPFILE.BAT
FOR % % A IN (% 1) DO TYPE % % A

(displays all files matching parameter % 1 on the screen. Wild-cards may be specified

```
MKFILE.BAT
ECHO OFF
IF NOT EXIST %1 GOTO CREATE
ECHO THIS FILE ALREADY EXISTS.
ECHO DO YOU WANT TO
ECHO WRITE OVER IT?
ECHO PRESS CTRL - BREAK TO STOP.
PAUSE
:CREATE
ECHO ON
COPY CON:%1
```

(a substitute for COPY CON. Checks for the existence of a file before creating a new one)

If you're working with a floppy-disk system, you now have a new working disk that you can use every time you boot. In Chap. 33 you will see how the features of this disk can be combined with others to create a desktop workstation. If you own a fixed-disk system, this chapter served as the groundwork for the next, so you should proceed on to Chap. 23.

Chapter

23

Organizing a Hard Disk

You are reading this chapter because you have a fixed-disk system and need some way to organize the many files you anticipate storing on the disk. In the last chapter, we established the groundwork for this chapter by creating the opening menu, assigning the Function keys, and adding a few useful batch files to the disk. In this chapter we will discuss a complete system of file organization for a hard disk.

Hard-disk systems are capable of holding thousands of files. To organize these files, you can break them up into groups and store the groups in separate subdirectories. Locating files or applications on a fixed disk that has multiple directories, however, can be inconvenient, especially if someone else has set the system up. A planned directory structure can help you become organized and stay organized. In this chapter we will create a series of directories, each with its own menu. Each directory is designed for a particular type of application or file, and each will be listed as a selection on the main menu. You can make a selection from the menu or press a Function key to get to any directory.

An Organized Directory Structure

Figure 23-1 shows the structure you can create on the hard disk. This structure will provide you with future growth by initially dividing the hard disk into several broad categories. As your needs grow, the system will grow with you. Four broad groups have been chosen. They are business applications, personal software, entertainment software, and "other", which is used for miscellaneous applications.

The DOS files and most batch files will reside in the ROOT directory level. All other programs and files will reside in subdirectories that branch from the ROOT.

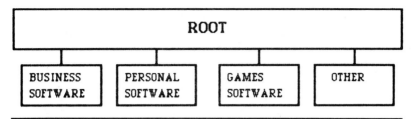

Figure 23-1 A fixed-disk directory structure that is broken into four broad categories.

Keep in mind that the menus and directories we show here are only suggestions. You can create your own structure by using the techniques shown here. In the last part of the chapter we make a few suggestions about other ways to organize a system.

Special Function Key Assignments

The Function key assignment file ASSIGN.CDS that was created in Chap. 21 and used in Chap. 22 has four assignments that are important to this chapter. These keys are listed below.

Alt-F7   The Help key. Pressing this key will issue the HELP command, which causes a batch file with the same name to be executed. This batch file will display the file HELP.MNU on the screen, providing help messages applicable to the current directory.

Alt-F8   The Menu key. Pressing this key will issue the MENU command, which causes a batch file with the same name to be executed. The file MENU.TXT in the current directory will be displayed.

Alt-F9   The Main Menu key. Pressing this key causes the current directory to be changed to the ROOT directory and causes the main menu in that level to be displayed.

Alt-F10   The Previous Menu key. This key will drop the user down to the parent of the current directory and display its menu file. It is used for moving back one directory at a time.

These keys and the menu selection batch files work like elevators, moving you through the system and saving you keystrokes. The menus will help you keep track of where you are in the system, especially after you exit from an applications program. By pressing either Alt-F8 or Alt-F9, you can display the current menu or the main menu.

The Function keys have an interesting feature in that the batch files for each reside in the ROOT directory. These files are HELP.BAT,

MENU.BAT, MM.BAT, and PM.BAT. Since the path set in the AUTO-EXEC.BAT file directs DOS to look for commands and batch files in the ROOT, only one set of these files is needed because they can be executed from any subdirectories.

The Help Menus

The contents of the help menus depend on the applications and files stored in the directory in which they reside. Their contents also depend on your needs or the needs of those using the system. If you or other users are at the novice level, help menus are appropriate, but if an experienced user is using the system, help menus only take up room on the disk.

Help menus can be used to explain procedures used in applications programs. For instance, a word processing directory could have a help menu that describes the files and routines used to produce a merged mail list. A help menu in a spreadsheet directory could list the files used to produce a quarterly budget. Note that each directory level can have its own help menu. This means that the messages in the help menus can be directly related to the task that the operator does in that directory level.

If you don't need a help menu, you can still use the Help key. Since it displays a file called HELP.MNU, you can create a file with this name that contains a list of things to do or a schedule that you are trying to maintain but need to view occasionally. For instance, the help file in a spreadsheet directory could contain a list of the sheets you need to work on before a certain date. The Help key provides a quick way to display this file on the screen whenever you need to review the schedule.

The Main Menu

The main menu we use here was created in the last chapter and is shown in Fig. 22-1. Here, we will add more selections to it so it looks like the menu shown in Fig. 23-2. This menu contains a selection number to transfer the user to each of the subdirectories.

Each of the batch files listed below will automate the menu selections we show in the illustration. Enter each batch file using the COPY CON command while in the ROOT directory.

```
6.BAT                  (business applications)
ECHO OFF
CLS
CD BUSINESS
TYPE MENU.TXT

7.BAT                  (personal applications)
ECHO OFF
CLS
```

```
CD PERSNL
TYPE MENU.TXT
```

8.BAT   (entertainment software)

```
ECHO OFF
CLS
CD GAMES
TYPE MENU.TXT
```

9.BAT   (other software)

```
ECHO OFF
CLS
CD OTHER
TYPE MENU.TXT
```

Creating the Subdirectories and Their Menus

The next step is to create the subdirectories for each of the selections. Make sure you are in the ROOT directory when you issue the following commands:

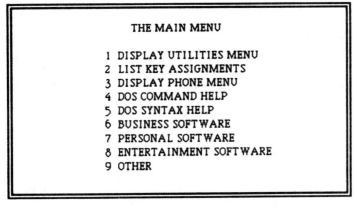

```
C : \>MD BUSINESS
C : \>MD PERSNL
C : \>MD GAMES
C : \>MD OTHER
```

Each of the subdirectory levels will need a menu of its own to display a list of the applications that reside in it. This menu will be called

```
              THE MAIN MENU

          1 DISPLAY UTILITIES MENU
          2 LIST KEY ASSIGNMENTS
          3 DISPLAY PHONE MENU
          4 DOS COMMAND HELP
          5 DOS SYNTAX HELP
          6 BUSINESS SOFTWARE
          7 PERSONAL SOFTWARE
          8 ENTERTAINMENT SOFTWARE
          9 OTHER
```

Figure 23-2

MENU.TXT in each of the subdirectories. The batch files created above transport the user to the subdirectory and then display the menu file in that subdirectory. To make the menus, copy the file FRAME.PIC from the ROOT directory, renaming it MENU.TXT in the process. The example below shows how to copy FRAME.PIC from the ROOT directory to the BUSINESS directory.

```
C:\>COPY FRAME.PIC  \BUSINESS\MENU.TXT
```

It's a good idea to copy the file to the rest of the subdirectories now while the command is still in the editing template. Perform the following steps to change the template so that it copies FRAME.PIC to the PERSNL subdirectory instead of the BUSINESS subdirectory.

1. Press **F2** and **B** to copy the template out to the B in BUSINESS.
2. Type in **PERSNL.**
3. Press the **Del** Key twice to remove the two S's left from the word BUSINESS.
4. Press the **F3** key to copy the rest of the template out.

Repeat a similar process for each of the other directories, changing the directory name in the command as needed. Here are the commands you will need to type to copy FRAME.PIC to each of the subdirectories.

```
C:\>COPY FRAME.PIC  \BUSINESS\MENU.TXT

C:\>COPY FRAME.PIC  \PERSNL\MENU.TXT

C:\>COPY FRAME.PIC  \GAMES\MENU.TXT

C:\>COPY FRAME.PIC  \OTHER\MENU.TXT

C:\>
```

Editing the Subdirectory Menus

Once the files are copied to the subdirectories, you will need to add the names of the applications you have in the directory to the menu. We recommend a title for each of the menus in addition to the normal selections.

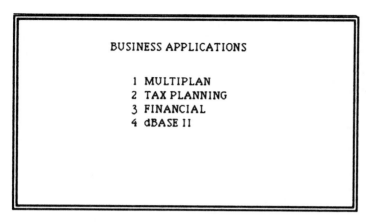

BUSINESS APPLICATIONS

1 MULTIPLAN
2 TAX PLANNING
3 FINANCIAL
4 dBASE II

Figure 23-3

To edit the menu in the BUSINESS directory, travel to the BUSINESS directory and use EDLIN to add the title. Figure 23-3 shows a sample BUSINESS directory menu with a title and selections.

Final Tasks

The last thing you have to do is create batch files for the menu selections in each subdirectory. Some of these batch files will simply start an applications program. Others will transfer to another subdirectory before starting the application. It all depends on how many applications you will have in each of the major subdirectories.

For example, assume that the BUSINESS menu has selections for Multiplan, a tax package, a financial analysis package, and a database. Figure 23-4 represents the tree structure of these directories branching from

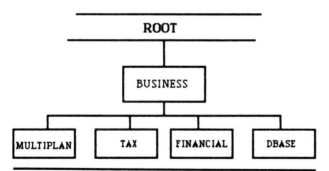

Figure 23-4 The BUSINESS directory showing several branching applications subdirectories.

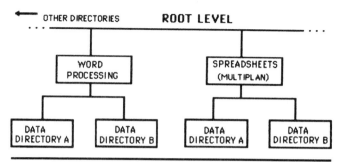

Figure 23-5 A typical tree structure showing the APPLI-
CATIONS directory in which the program files are stored
and the branching subdirectories for data files.

BUSINESS. Here, the directory BUSINESS is analogous to a lobby that
leads into the subdirectories. The PERSNL directory contains the program files for a word processor. Several subdirectories branch from this
directory, each holding similar data files created by the word processor.
Some branching subdirectories hold data and others hold program and
applications files.

The design is completely open for expansion. You can add more directories to the ROOT level or continue to add branching subdirectories to
any of the other directories.

Other Ways to Organize Your System

In this section, we offer several suggestions about other ways you can organize your system. You have already seen how to organize by dividing the
directories into a broad range of applications such as business software
and personal software. You, no doubt have some idea about what your
own needs are by now and will have to tailor your system to fit those
needs. The remaining portion of this chapter suggests several other types
of directory structures you might want to consider.

First look at Fig. 23-5 to see a possible directory structure that allows
files created by an applications program to be stored in several separate
subdirectories. This figure illustrates two subdirectories branching from
the ROOT directory. The SPREADSHEETS subdirectory has its own
branching subdirectories that are used to store data files. The WORD
PROCESSING subdirectory has a similar structure. When using either
the spreadsheet program or the word processing program, you can make
your current directory one of the branching data subdirectories and then
set the path so that program files are read from the parent directory. Note
that this structure maintains the preferred three-level limit of
subdirectories.

Figure 23-6 illustrates a variation of the previous structure. Here, the

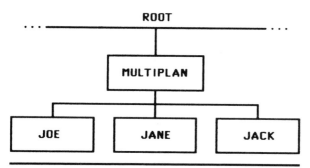

Figure 23-6 In this directory structure, users access the program files in Multiplan from their own sub-directory levels.

MULTIPLAN subdirectory has branching user directories. A user working with the system makes his or her current directory the branching subdirectory that bears the user's name. This directory holds the data files that were created with the Multiplan program that resides in the parent directory. Each of the branching subdirectories can access Multiplan in the parent directory and share its program files. This method is the most space efficient because the program files are shared.

The last example illustrates a system that has several users. This structure gives each user his or her own branching directory. Each directory has branching subdirectories for data or applications programs. This type of structure can be inefficient if program files are duplicated in other directories. It assumes that each user's software is different from software used by the others (see Fig. 23-7).

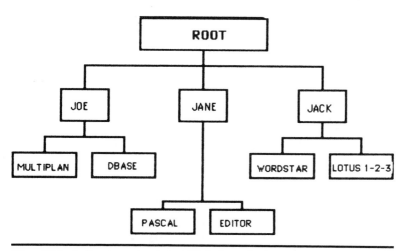

Figure 23-7 A directory structure with independent user directories and applications directories.

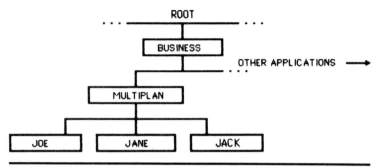

Figure 23-8

Handling Several Users on a Menu-Driven Filing System

Suppose that a fixed-disk system is organized with the menu filing system described in the first part of this chapter and with the filing structure shown in Fig. 23-8. The BUSINESS directory contains a menu similar to the one in Fig. 23-3. Several people use this system, as can be seen by the branching user data directories in Fig. 23-8. As users boot on the system, the main menu appears and directs them to the application they wish to work with. A way is needed to direct users to their own data directories when they select an application from one of the menus, the BUSINESS menu in this case.

The SET command, described in Chap. 18, can be used to make each of the menu batch files work independently for each authorized user logging on the system. Assume that Jane logs on and wants to use Multiplan. If she types SET USER = JANE, the following batch file will transfer her to the subdirectory JANE that branches from the Multiplan directory when she makes selection 1 from the business applications menu.

```
1.BAT
ECHO OFF
CLS
CD MP\%USER%
PATH ..
MP80
PATH \
CD \
TYPE MENU.TXT
```

This menu selection batch file is much more complicated than the others, so we'll study it. The third line is the important command that transfers JANE to her Multiplan data directory. It uses the replaceable parameter

USER that was set to JANE when Jane logged on. In this case, the third command in the batch file becomes CD MP\JANE and Jane is transferred to her data directory.

The path is then set so that DOS searches for the Multiplan program files in the parent directory. The command MP80 executes Multiplan. As Jane works with Multiplan, files are read and stored in her data directory. When Jane exits Multiplan, the batch file resumes, resets the path, makes the current directory the ROOT, and displays the main menu in the ROOT directory.

When Joe logs on, he sets USER to JOE, so the menu selection batch file will now transfer him to the JOE data subdirectory. Other menu selection batch files that change directories can also use the replaceable parameter %USER% to switch users to their appropriate data directories.

If you followed the examples in this chapter, your fixed disk now contains a directory structure that will help you stay organized and will also grow with you as your needs grow. You can expand the system at any time by adding new applications directories to the ROOT or by expanding on one of the main subdirectories. The menus can be updated at any time with EDLIN or other editors as software is added to the system.

24

Fixed Disk Backup
and Restore

There are several reasons to back up a fixed disk. The first is to protect valuable data. The second is to change noncontiguous (fragmented) files to a contiguous state as described in Chap. 15. The third is to simply rearrange the directory structure of your fixed disk when you feel you need a change. Backing up to protect data should be done as often as you feel it is necessary. Backing up for the second reason should be performed every several months or after many files have been altered, expanded, or deleted. The third reason for backing up is unique. You can eliminate entire directories of data by not including them in the backup.

Fixed disks tend to be very reliable, but when they fail, you will be glad that you have a backup set of data. If the drive goes down and has to go in for repair, your data is protected. The shop may even loan you a machine to use until the defective drive is repaired. In this case, you will have the data on diskettes for use on the borrowed machine.

Since the backup procedure will allow you to select specific directories for backup, you can choose which directories you want to save and discard those that are no longer needed. After backing up the directories you want to save, you can reformat the fixed disk and restore the saved directories to the disk.

Backing up a fixed disk is a tedious task, but it is the price paid for the convenience and speed that a fixed disk offers. The standard procedure to back up a fixed disk with DOS is to copy the data files from the fixed disk to a set of floppy diskettes. A 10-megabyte disk will require up to 30 diskettes for storage. Fortunately, the procedure is semiautomatic. It will copy all specified files and directories and prompt the operator for new diskettes. An operator should stand by to monitor the process and insert new diskettes when needed.

The backup will not always require 30 diskettes. If the fixed disk is only half full, then approximately 15 diskettes will be needed. If you find that the backup procedure is inconvenient, you may want to look into a tape backup system. These systems will back up an entire fixed disk to magnetic tape in a small amount of time compared to disk back up and will usually do so unattended.

Backing up the Fixed Disk

The DOS BACKUP command is used to back up the fixed disk. Before you start the backup process, you must first format the number of diskettes you will need to store the contents of the fixed disk. Since BACKUP is a procedure that runs continuously from start to finish, you cannot interrupt it. If you do not have enough diskettes on hand, you cannot stop to format another and may have to perform the backup all over again. You can determine the number of diskettes you will need by running the CHKDSK command. CHKDSK shows the number of files and the amount of space in use on the fixed disk. You should subtract the bytes available on disk from bytes total disk space to determine the total amount of room required for the files. Divide this number by the amount of space on a floppy disk, which is approximately 360,000 bytes. For example, assume a 10-megabyte fixed disk is half full. The computations below show the procedure for determining how many diskettes to format before the actual backup. All figures are rounded.

First, run CHKDSK:

```
c:\>CHKDSK

        10600000 bytes total disk space
          22000 bytes in 3 hidden files
          52000 bytes in 8 directories
        4600000 bytes in 363 files
        5926000 bytes available on disk
```

Subtracting 5,926,000 from 10,600,000 gives a total in-use disk space of 4,674,000 bytes. Dividing this by 360,000 (approximate space on a diskette) you get roughly 13, the number of diskettes you will need to do the backup. To be on the safe side, format an extra diskette. Label each diskette with a number starting with 1.

How to Enter the BACKUP Command

The format of the BACKUP command is shown below. A path name may be specified so that you can back up specific directories. Wild-card characters may also be specified so that you can back up a range of files.

BACKUP [d:][path][file name][.ext] [d:][/S][/M][/A][/D:mm-dd-yy]

The four switches are used to control which files and directories are copied. These switches are covered below. BACKUP does not actually copy subdirectories to the floppy diskettes. It names each file with the full path name to that file. For instance, if you have a file called SAM-PLE.DAT in a directory called \TESTS\GROUP1, the file will be stored on disk with the name \TEST\GROUP\SAMPLE.DAT. The following parameter may be specified with the command:

/A   Adds the backup files to a currently existing backup diskette instead of erasing the files on the backup

/S   Backs up all branching subdirectories

/M   Backs up only files modified since the last backup

/D   Backs up files that have changed since specified date

Backup Procedures

Before starting, be sure you have a set of formatted diskettes ready. Once the procedure starts you cannot stop unless you start from the beginning again. To back up the entire fixed disk, type:

```
C : \ >BACKUP C:\ A:/S
```

This command will copy all files in all directories to the floppy diskettes. The backslash following C: indicates that the ROOT directory is the starting point for the backup. All files will be copied to the diskettes in drive A. The /S switch indicates that all files in all subdirectories are to be copied.

To obtain a printout of the files, type:

```
C : / >BACKUP C:\ A:/S > PRN
```

This command prints a listing of all the files that are being backed up to the floppy diskettes.

To back up only files that have been modified, type:

```
C:\>BACKUP C:\ A:/S/M
```

This command is identical to the one above except that the /M switch has been added. This switch causes only files that have been modified since the last backup to be copied. This is a powerful feature that will save you a lot of time. Every time a file is created or modified, DOS sets a switch in the file name location so that it knows the backup status of the file.

To back up files after a specified date, type:

```
C:\>BACKUP C:\ A:/D:04-14-84
```

This command allows you to specify the date of the files to be copied. If you enter the date every time you boot the system, all files will contain a date stamp of the day they were created. Otherwise, DOS places an obscure date such as 01-01-80 on each file.

To back up specific directories, type:

```
C:\>BACKUP C:\TESTS A:/S
```

This command backs up all the files in the TESTS directory and all the files in all the directories that branch from the TESTS directory (see Fig. 24-1).

To back up specific files, type:

```
C:\>BACKUP C:\TESTS\*.DAT A:/S
```

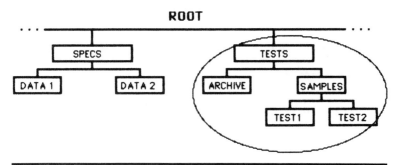

Figure 24-1 The TEST directories and subdirectories are backed up by the command BACKUP C:\TEST A:/S. None of the other directories that branch from ROOT are backed up.

Backs up all the files that have the extension of DAT that are in the TESTS directory.

Backup Strategies

How often you back up the fixed disk depends on how important and timely the data on it is. You may need to back up daily, in which case you can use the /M parameter. In other cases, you may feel comfortable backing up about once a month. There are several strategies you can use when backing up a fixed disk.

One of these is to keep two complete sets of backup diskettes. Using this strategy, you back up the entire hard disk on a regular interval, say once every two weeks. The first two weeks, you use the first set; the second two weeks you use the second set. You then repeat this process every month, switching sets as needed. This procedure ensures that you always have a complete set of backup diskettes safely stored away, even while you are backing up to the other set. There is a chance that something could happen to the fixed disk during backup or that one set of backup diskettes could be damaged. Also, if you have two sets of backup diskettes, you can store one set in a separate location.

Another method, which will help make the actual backup easier, is to back up often, say every other day, using the date parameter (/S) to back up only those files created since the last backup. This makes the backup an ongoing process and is superior in some aspects to backing up with the /M parameter. You must be sure to enter the date every time you boot the system so that all new files are tagged with the current date.

You can extend the interval between backups by manually backing up files as they are created or altered. Suppose that you have a backup set of

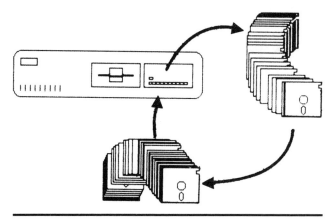

Figure 24-2 The rotation method used to back up a fixed disk. One set always holds the most current data.

diskettes created with the BACKUP command and that you are backing up every two weeks. In between backups you can copy all newly created or altered files to floppy diskettes so that you have a secure copy of them until they can be added to the backup set during the next BACKUP session. Once BACKUP has been performed, you can erase the temporary-hold diskettes and begin collecting new files on them until the next backup (see Fig. 24-2).

A Backup Batch File

Since the BACKUP procedure is so tedious and time consuming, many people, especially professionals, prefer to have someone else handle the backup procedure. The following batch file will perform the backup and monitor the process, looking for errors or problems. When a problem occurs, a message is displayed that directs the operator to take appropriate action. If you created the menu system described in Chap. 23, you may want to include this batch file as a selection on the menu called BACKUP.

```
BACKITUP.BAT
ECHO OFF
CLS
ECHO DISK BACKUP PROCEDURE
ECHO ARE THE FLOPPY DISKETTES FORMATTED AND READY?
ECHO PRESS CTRL-BREAK IF NOT
PAUSE
CLS
ECHO BACKUP IN PROGRESS—DO NOT DISTURB
```

```
BACKUP C:\ A:/S
IF ERRORLEVEL 0 ECHO BACKUP COMPLETED SUCCESSFULLY
IF ERRORLEVEL 1 ECHO SOMETHING IS REALLY WRONG!
IF ERRORLEVEL 3 ECHO WHY DID YOU STOP THE BACKUP?
IF ERRORLEVEL 4 THERE HAS BEEN AN ERROR—SEE THE BOSS!
```

This batch files uses the **IF ERRORLEVEL** batch file subcommand to display messages on the screen depending on the exit code from the BACKUP procedure. These codes are as follows:

0   Normal completion

1   No files were found to back up

3   Terminated by user (Ctrl-Break)

4   Terminated due to error

Restoring Files to the Fixed Disk

The RESTORE command is used to place files back on the hard disk that have been backed up with the BACKUP command. Files that are backed up to diskettes using the BACKUP command are unusable unless they are restored to the fixed disk using the RESTORE command. RESTORE will place all files specified on the backup diskettes back on the fixed disk. The format for RESTORE is:

```
RESTORE d: [d:][path][FILE NAME][.ext][/S][/P]
```

With RESTORE, you can specify any directory and any file to be restored to the fixed disk. The /S parameter works as it does with the BACKUP command in that it will restore all subdirectories branching from a specified directory. The /P option is very important. It checks to see if a file on the hard disk has been altered since the last backup by checking the date of the file on the backup diskette. This would indicate that the file on the backup is no longer the most recent copy. The operator is prompted before the RESTORE procedure actually writes over any files that have been changed. You can then choose to restore a file or not.

You can create a batch file to make the RESTORE procedure easy for untrained operators just as BACKITUP.BAT was created for the backup procedure. The following batch file restores files and can be included as a menu option in the menus created in Chap. 23. The error codes in RESTORE are the same as those in BACKUP.

```
RESTORIT.BAT
ECHO OFF
```

```
CLS
ECHO DISK RESTORE PROCEDURE
ECHO DO YOU HAVE THE BACKUP DISKETTES?
ECHO PRESS CTRL-BREAK IF NOT
PAUSE
CLS
ECHO FILES BEING RESTORED—DO NOT DISTURB.
RESTORE A: C:\/S/P
IF ERRORLEVEL 0 ECHO RESTORE COMPLETED SUCCESSFULLY
IF ERRORLEVEL 1 ECHO SOMETHING IS REALLY WRONG!
IF ERRORLEVEL 3 ECHO WHY DID YOU STOP THE RESTORE?
IF ERRORLEVEL 4 THERE HAS BEEN AN ERROR—SEE THE BOSS!
```

This chapter explains how to protect the files on your fixed disk. The BACKUP command attempts to make the job of backing up the fixed disk as easy as possible. Although an entire fixed disk requires 30 or more diskettes for a complete backup, you can simplify backing up your files by backing up only changed files or files that have been created since a particular date.

Tips, Tricks, and Techniques

Now that you've covered the features and commands of DOS, you can start looking at special techniques that will enhance their use. This chapter discusses various tips, tricks, and techniques that you will find useful when you are working with batch files, pipes, and filters. The first part of this chapter describes various batch file techniques, and the last part lists an assortment of tips and tricks.

Enhancing a Batch File's Appearance

By now you've seen how batch files appear on the display screen as they execute. In this section we'll cover how you can improve the visual appearance of batch files as they run. One way is to turn the ECHO command off so that as the batch file executes, the screen display appears less confusing to an untrained operator. Once ECHO is off, messages can be displayed on the screen from the batch file without the normal screen clutter.

The batch file below demonstrates one way to use ECHO to produce blank spaces on the screen and enhance the visual appearance of a running batch file. The lines shown below could be included in any batch file.

```
ENHANCED.BAT
ECHO OFF
CLS
ECHO .
ECHO .
ECHO .
ECHO A MESSAGE GOES HERE
ECHO .
ECHO BATCH FILE COMMANDS GO HERE
```

In this batch file ECHO is turned off initially and the screen is then cleared with the CLS command in preparation for the first message. The periods are used to insert spaces on the screen as the batch file executes. You can use any character you want for this spacing, but you must use a character; otherwise, DOS will interpret the ECHO command as a request to display the on/off status of echo.

You may notice that the batch file takes a while to run. This is because DOS reads commands from the disk one by one. To increase the speed of batch files that display messages you can place the messages in another file and display the file as part of the batch file routine. The TYPE command can be used to display the file. Let's simulate the batch file created above but use this new technique. Create the message file shown below and then create the batch file following it.

```
A:\>COPY CON:MESSAGE.TXT
    .
    .
    .
THIS IS A MESSAGE
    .
LAST LINE
<F6>  <Return>

A:\>COPY CON:MESSAGE2.BAT
ECHO OFF
CLS
TYPE MESSAGE.TXT
<F6>  <Return>

A:\>_
```

Now, run the batch file. The execution time for the new file is much faster because it does not have to execute one line at a time. Instead, the whole message is displayed at once when the file is typed to the screen. This technique will be used from now on in all batch files that display long messages.

Here's an example of a message that could be used with the BACK ITUP.BAT file that was created in Chap. 24. The message is a text file that is displayed on the screen by the command TYPE BACKITUP.MSG in the BACKITUP batch file.

BACKITUP.MSG

HOW TO USE THE BACKITUP BATCH FILE:

Make sure that you have formatted the proper number of diskettes before starting this batch file. If you haven't done this yet, press Ctrl-Break to stop this routine. Refer to my notes on how to calculate the number of diskettes required. When you're done with the back up, place the diskettes in the safe.

Thanks.

Checking for Parameters on the Command Line

If your batch file uses replaceable parameters to collect variables from the command line, it should check to make sure that parameters have been placed on the line before proceeding. If the parameter is not present and the batch file continues to execute, it will eventually "crash" when it gets to the command that needs the parameter. Checking for parameters is important to batch files because many times you or an operator will forget to enter the parameters when executing the batch routine.

The following batch file checks to see if a parameter has been entered. The third line checks for the existence of a parameter; it is a standard routine that you can include as part of any batch file that uses replaceable parameters.

```
CHECK.BAT
ECHO OFF
CLS
IF "%1" = = "" GOTO HELP
IF %1 = = JOHN GOTO LABEL1
IF %1 = = JILL GOTO LABEL2
:HELP
- routines to help operator -
GOTO END
- the rest of the batch file -
```

The third line checks for parameters by comparing parameter %1 against a blank string inside the quotation marks. If a parameter is not entered on the command line (e.g., the operator entered CHECK and nothing else), parameter %1 is blank. Therefore the IF statement in line 1 becomes: IF " = = " GOTO HELP, and since the variables on both sides of the equal signs match, the batch file branches to the label HELP.

If the operator enters CHECK JOHN for instance, the IF statement on line 3 becomes: IF "JOHN" = = "" GOTO HELP. This statement is not true, so the next line of the batch file is executed. In this line the IF statement becomes IF JOHN = = JOHN GOTO LABEL1, which is true, so the batch file branches to LABEL1.

The CHECK.BAT file below is a modification of the previous batch file and will display a help message if a branch is made to HELP. If the operator forgets to enter a parameter on the command line, the file MES-SAGE.TXT is displayed on the screen. Remember, this is the message display technique described in the first part of this chapter. MESSAGE.TXT can contain instructions for using the batch file or a list of possible parameters that can be placed on the command line.

```
CHECK.BAT
ECHO OFF
CLS
IF "%1" = = "" GOTO HELP
IF %1 = = JOHN GOTO LABEL1
IF %1 = = JILL GOTO LABEL2
:HELP
TYPE MESSAGE.TXT
GOTO END
  .
  .
  .              (the rest of the batch file)
:END
```

You can also display a message that informs the operator about the syntax required to use the batch file. For instance, in the batch file above, the message following :HELP could be:

```
ECHO To use this command type: CHECK (your name)
```

In the batch files above, selections were made depending on the parameters from the command line. For instance, if the parameter was JOHN, then a branch was made to LABEL1. If you changed LABEL1 to JOHN, then you could replace the command IF %1 = = JOHN GOTO LABEL1 with GOTO %1. When the operator types CHECK JOHN, parameter %1 becomes JOHN and the GOTO command becomes GOTO JOHN, causing the batch file to jump to the label JOHN. This technique is covered below under "Simplifying the Sort Command" and is a more efficient way of branching in a batch file.

Batch Files that Automatically Stop

In Chap. 17 you created a batch file that used the SHIFT batch file subcommand to continuously read parameters from the command line until the keyword STOP was encountered. The file is shown below as it appeared in Chap. 17.

```
REPEAT.BAT
ECHO OFF
```

```
:LOOP
IF %1 = = STOP GOTO END
ECHO %1
SHIFT
GOTO LOOP
:END
```

This batch file goes through a loop, echoing each parameter until it encounters the word STOP, in which case it branches to :END and stops execution. To use the routine, the operator must remember to enter the keyword STOP as the last parameter on the command line. You can use the parameter checking routine described above to detect the absence of parameters on the command line instead of using this keyword technique. Here's how it's done.

```
REPEAT.BAT
ECHO OFF
:LOOP
IF "%1" = = "" GOTO END
ECHO %1
SHIFT
GOTO LOOP
:END
```

This batch file will exit when the command line has no more parameters. It uses a loop and the SHIFT command to continue reading parameters from the command line until there are none left. SHIFT moves each parameter on the command line over, successively making each parameter %1. The GOTO command causes the batch file to loop back to the label :LOOP where the next parameter is read. The third line checks to see if the parameter just read is "empty," and if so, a branch is made to :END. This batch file can be used in a variety of situations. You can insert your own command in place of the fourth line.

From now on, routines similar to the one described above will be used to check for errors and parameters when a batch file is running.

Making Selections on a Menu

If you read Chaps. 22 and 23, you are familiar with the process of automating menus with batch files. It is described again here for reference. If a menu has selections preceded by numbers such as 1, 2, and 3, you can automate the selection numbers by creating batch files with similar file names. Suppose you have a selection on a menu that reads "3 - SYSTEM SHUTDOWN." The following batch file will automate this menu selection.

```
3.BAT
ECHO OFF
CLS
ECHO RETURN THE DISKETTES TO THEIR SLEEVES.
ECHO TURN THE COMPUTER AND THE PRINTER OFF.
ECHO GOOD NIGHT!
```

This shutdown routine is helpful to beginning and inexperienced users who are not sure what to do when they are finished with the computer.

Using Files to Answer Questions

Many DOS commands such as DISKCOPY and FORMAT will ask you to enter Y or N if you want to continue with a command or run it again. If you are annoyed by these questions or would like to speed up the execution of commands, you can use the I/O redirection features of DOS to direct the answers to the questions from a file into the command as it executes. To see how this works, create the following file:

```
NO.ANS
<Return>
N
<F6>  <Return>
```

The first line of the file NO.ANS contains a carriage return that will respond to the question "Strike any key when ready." The second line contains a response to the question "Copy another (Y/N)?" If you enter the command shown below, DOS will accept answers to its questions from the NO.ANS file. Place a blank disk in drive B before proceeding.

```
A:\>DISKCOPY A: B: < NO

Insert source diskette in drive A:

Insert target diskette in drive B:

Strike any key when ready          (first line of NO.ANS used here)

Copying 9 sectors per track, 2 side(s)

Copy complete

Copy another (Y/N)? N               (second line of NO.ANS used here)

A:\>_
```

Logging Time on the System

You can keep track of the time and dates you use your computer with the following routines. The routines copy the starting time and current date into a file called TIME.DAT when you first start the system. When you are ready to quit, you can execute the QUIT batch file shown below to record your log-off time in the file. You can then use TYPE to display TIME.DAT and see your elapsed time on the system. This routine also demonstrates an interesting use of the I/O redirection facilities.

```
LOGON.BAT
DATE
TIME
DATE> TIME.DAT
ECHO LOG-ON TIME: >> TIME.DAT
TIME >> TIME.DAT
```

The first two lines request the current date and time and update the system clock. The last three lines are written to the TIME.DAT file. When the third and fifth lines are executed, you will be asked for the date and time again. These requests come from DOS and cannot be suppressed, so ignore them and press Return. (The time and date entered by the first two commands of the batch file are used.) The fourth line places the message "LOG-ON TIME:" into the file.

The next batch file places the log-off time into the file TIME.DAT. You would execute this file just before turning your system off.

```
QUIT.BAT
ECHO LOG-OFF TIME: >> TIME.DAT
TIME >> TIME.DAT
```

When you run this batch file, the message and time are appended to the file TIME.DAT. You can then display the file TIME.DAT on the screen to see your elapsed time on the system. If you add the following lines to the end of QUIT.BAT, you can keep a permanent log of your time on the system in a file called TIMELOG.DAT.

```
TYPE TIME.DAT >> TIMELOG.DAT
ECHO -------------------------- >> TIMELOG.DAT
```

The temporary time file is now appended to the permanent log file called TIMELOG.DAT. Here's what the contents of TIMELOG.DAT might look like after several days.

```
A: \ >TYPE TIMELOG.DAT
Current date is Wed 4-04-1984
LOG-ON TIME:
Current time is 1:29:05.73
LOG-OFF TIME:
Current time is 3:15:13.79
_____
Current date is Thu 4-05-1984
LOG-ON TIME:
Current time is 10:12:05.87
LOG-OFF TIME:
Current time is 10:43:06.31
_____
Current date is Fri 4-06-1984
LOG-ON TIME:
Current time is 1:02:31.30
LOG-OFF TIME:
Current time is 3:23:18.73
_____

A: \>_
```

Moving Through Directories

If you have a multidirectory tree structure, you may have noticed that the commands for moving through these directories can become long. The menu system we described in Chap. 24 can help you move through the system by automating the CHDIR (change directory) commands, but there may be times when you want to move directly to a subdirectory without going through the menus. You can place the CD commands in a batch file to make them more convenient to use. For instance, if you wanted to move to the \SAMPLES\DATAEAST\ARCHIVE directory, you would have to type the following:

CD \SAMPLES\DATAEAST\ARCHIVE

You can instead place the command in a batch file called GOARCHV:

GOARCHV.BAT
CD \SAMPLES\DATAEAST\ARCHIVE

Suppose that \SAMPLES\DATAEAST has several subdirectories and you would like to use a batch file to transfer to one of the subdirectories. You can use replaceable parameters in a batch file so that you can specify which branching subdirectory you want to be placed in. The following batch file will cause the destination directory name specified on the command line to become %1 in the CHDIR command.

GOTODIR.BAT
CHDIR \SAMPLES\DATAEAST\%1

Another way of using replaceable parameters in this type of batch file is to use the SET command. If there are several users on a system who have their own special directories, a batch file similar to the one below could be used to transfer users to their directories. The parameter %USER% is set by users to their user passwords or log-on names when they log onto the system at start-up time.

CDMYDIR
CD \USERAREA\WPFILES\%USER%

When Jane logs onto the system, she types SET USER = JANE so that the variable %USER% in any batch file becomes JANE. The CDMYDIR batch file above would execute the command \USERAREA\WPFILES\ JANE when Jane is on the system. Note that the SET command can be included in a log-on batch file which we will describe in the next chapter.

Listing Directories

You have seen several ways of listing directories in this book that use everything from wild-card characters to the FIND command. Here is another directory listing routine that will demonstrate replaceable parameters in batch files.

The following batch file will sort the directory listing by the parameters you specify on the command line. You can specify the drive to list, the column to sort on, and a keyword to search for.

DLIST.BAT
ECHO OFF
CLS
DIR %1: ¦ FIND "%2" ¦ SORT /+%3

If you type DLIST B COM 17, the third line in the file would become: DIR B: ¦ FIND "COM" ¦ SORT /+17. The COM files on drive B would be listed by file size (column 17). You can improve the batch file by adding the instructions shown below.

DLIST.BAT
ECHO OFF
CLS

```
IF "%1" = = GOTO HELP
DIR %1: | FIND "%2" | SORT /%3
GOTO END
:HELP
ECHO DLIST format: DLIST (drive) (keyword) (sort column)
:END
```

The new instructions include the standard routine used to check for parameters on the command line. If parameters have not been entered, a branch is made to :HELP and the message describing how to use the batch file is displayed.

A Simple Way to Sort Directory Listings

Here's another way to sort the directory listing which we show to demonstrate how selections can be made with batch files. This batch file does not require the operator to know the column number of the category to be sorted. Instead, the operator enters the name of the column to be sorted. For instance, to sort the directory listing by file size, you specify SIZE on the command line instead of 17. This batch file uses the GOTO selection routine described earlier.

```
SORTBY.BAT
ECHO OFF
CLS
IF "%2" = = "" GOTO HELP
GOTO %2
:HELP
ECHO SORTBY.BAT Syntax: SORTBY drive parameter
ECHO parameter can be either NAME, EXT, SIZE, or DATE
GOTO END
:NAME
DIR %1: | SORT
GOTO END
:EXT
DIR %1: | SORT /+10
GOTO END
:SIZE
DIR %1: | SORT /+17
GOTO END
:DATE
DIR %1: | SORT /+24
GOTO END
:END
```

Typing SORTBY A: DATE would cause the batch file to jump to the label :DATE and execute the command following it, which sorts the directory listing by date. Note: Set caps lock on when working with this batch file.

Changing the Color of Your Screen

Using a batch file similar to the previous one, you can select foreground and background colors on a color graphics monitor. Refer to Chap. 21 for a description of using the ANSI.SYS screen driver. A description of the ANSI.SYS driver options are listed in App. F.

The batch file shown below sets the foreground colors for red, green, and blue. You can add the full selection shown in App. F to this file if you want. The second to the last line in the batch file resets the prompt to normal.

```
COLOR.BAT
CLS
IF "%1" = = "" GOTO HELP
GOTO %1
:HELP
ECHO COLOR.BAT Syntax: COLOR color
ECHO color can be either RED, GREEN, BLUE, or RESET
GOTO END
:RED
PROMPT $e[31m
GOTO END
:GREEN
PROMPT $e[32m
GOTO END
:BLUE
PROMPT $e[34m
GOTO END
:RESET
PROMPT $e[0m
:END
PROMPT $p$g
```

This batch file has the standard header that checks for parameters. If the user enters a command such as COLOR RED, the batch file jumps to the label :RED and executes the PROMPT command to assign a red foreground.

Working with RAM Drives

If you have enough memory in your system, you can turn part of that memory into an area that DOS treats as a disk drive. The advantage of creating an emulated disk, sometimes called a RAM drive or E-disk, is speed. Files are read and written to a RAM drive up to 10 times faster than they are on a regular floppy drive. This speed can significantly improve the performance of your database programs, word processor, and other applications. The disadvantage of RAM drives is that you can lose the data stored in them in a flash if the power goes out.

RAM drives are available commercially, but owners of IBM PC-DOS can create a RAM drive from a listing supplied with the DOS manual, although you will need an assembler to create the drive. An alternative is to obtain the assembled program from your computer store or a users' club or request a copy from us (see Appen. H). To install the RAM drive, place the command DEVICE = RAMDRIVE in a CONFIG.SYS file. The name RAMDRIVE refers to any of the names given to the many versions now available ranging in size from 64K to 360K. The IBM RAM drive will take the drive designator of the next available drive. If you have two floppy drives called A and B, the RAM drive will take the designator of C.

Once you have the RAM drive installed, you will need to copy files to it. This is where batch files come into action, The following batch file will copy all files from a boot disk to RAM drive C. After the files have been transferred, the batch file changes the default drive to C and starts an application.

```
AUTOEXEC.BAT
DATE
TIME
COPY *.* C:
C:
(command to start application)
```

The next batch file runs WordStar from a RAM drive. In this batch file, the Prokey keyboard enhancement program is executed and the special key instructions used with WordStar are loaded. Next, the files needed to run WordStar are copied to the RAM drive by the command COPY WS*.* C:. The command B: changes the default drive to drive B so that it becomes the default drive (data files will be read from this drive). WordStar is then executed from the RAM drive in the last command.

```
AUTOEXEC.BAT
DATE
TIME
PKLOAD
PROKEY WS.PRO/R/K-
COPY WS*.* C:
B:
C:WS
```

Using WordStar with a RAM drive increases the performance of the program. WordStar, however, must be installed so it looks for its program and overlay files on drive C. You can set this feature with the Winstall installation program that is supplied with WordStar.

Batch Files on RAM Drives

RAM drives open new possibilities for batch files. As you may know, batch files run slowly because each command in the batch file is read from disk. Many of the batch file routines described in this book will run faster if you copy them to a RAM drive before use. You should also copy the command files that your batch files use to the RAM drive. In most cases these files will be FIND.EXE, SORT.EXE, and MORE.COM.

The following batch file will show the difference in speed between a batch file executed from a floppy drive and one executed from a RAM drive. To see the difference in speed, create the batch file and address file shown below on a floppy disk.

```
LABELS.BAT
ECHO OFF
:LOOP
COPY ADDRESS.TXT LPT1
GOTO LOOP
```

```
ADDRESS.TXT
(blank line)
MY RETURN ADDRESS LABEL
20 N. BATCH STREET
SANTA BARBARA, CA 93105
(blank line)
(blank line)
```

If you run the batch file from the floppy disk, you'll have time to read a few chapters from *War and Peace* as it executes. Press Ctrl-Break to stop the routine and then copy the batch file and address file to your RAM drive and run it from there. The difference in speed should convince you of the advantage to using a RAM drive.

Be careful when using RAM drives. There is always the possibility that you could lose your data, so the best course of action is to keep your data files on a normal drive and run the programs from the RAM drive. The SORT command is an excellent example of a command that operates much faster from a RAM drive.

We have covered various techniques and tips to help you create batch files that look better and run better. Many of the tips used here, such as the parameter checking routines, should be used in all of your batch files, when appropriate.

26

Batch File Routines

Password Systems

If you have a fixed-disk system that several people are using or if the system is located in an area in which access must be controlled, you can create a password program with batch files to prevent access to the system or to simply route individual users to their own directories. The example batch files below serve to route individual users to their directories and can be used to prevent access to the system to some degree.

The AUTOEXEC.BAT file shown below executes normally, setting the system date, prompt, and path. It then asks the user to enter a password. When the user executes the LOGON batch file, also shown below, the password is checked and if it is legal, the user is transferred to his or her directory. If the password does not match a legal password, the user is asked to reenter a correct password.

```
AUTOEXEC.BAT
ECHO OFF
PATH \
PROMPT $p$g
DATE
TYPE ASSIGN.CDS
ECHO PASSWORD REQUIRED. TYPE: LOGON [password]
```

The last line of this file asks the user to enter a password. By entering LOGON and the password, the LOGON batch file (see below) is executed.

```
LOGON.BAT
ECHO OFF
CLS
```

```
IF "%1" = = "" GOTO TRYAGAIN        (check for a blank)
IF %1 = = JOHN GOTO JOHN
IF %1 = = JILL GOTO JILL
ECHO ACCESS DENIED—SORRY            (no match)
GOTO END
:TRYAGAIN
ECHO PASSWORD NOT ENTERED
GOTO END
:JOHN
CD JOHN                             (go to John's directory)
TYPE MENU.TXT                       (display the menu)
GOTO END
CD JILL                            (go to Jill's directory)
TYPE MENU.TXT                       (display the menu)
:END
SET USER = %1
```

In the LOGON batch file above, line 3 checks to see if a password has been entered. If one has not been entered, a branch is made to :TRY-AGAIN, the message PASSWORD NOT ENTERED is displayed, and a branch is made to the end of the file. If JOHN is entered as the password, a match is made in the fourth line, and a branch is made to the label :JOHN. The same process occurs if Jill enters her password. If a wrong password is entered, no matches are made, and the sixth line of the file executes, displaying the access denied message.

This batch file is not meant to be completely foolproof. An experienced user who really wanted to get into the system could do so by simply bypassing the menu. The batch file does serve to ensure that users are in their own directories.

To put this batch file to work on your system, determine the log-on codes for each user and substitute them in the batch file for JOHN and JILL. You can add more password names if you wish by adding more IF statements like those in lines 3 and 4. If you add more names, you will also need a label for the GOTO portion of the IF statement. For example, when Jill logs on the system, the GOTO branches to the label :JILL and the CD command is executed to transfer Jill to her directory. You will need a similar label for each name you add, followed by a command. In our LOGON batch file, the current directory is changed to the owner's directory. You can place your own commands or even messages in this position.

The last line of the LOGON batch file assigns the user's password to the environment string USER (for information on SET, see Chap. 18). In this way, the current user's log-on code can be used as a variable in other batch files throughout the system. See "Sending and Receiving Mail" below for an example.

SET can also be used in the menu selection batch files that were covered in Chaps. 22 and 23. The following example demonstrates how a batch file can use a variable string assigned with the SET command. In it, %USER% can be set equal to the password or code of each user who logs on the system. The batch file then operates as if it were designed specifically for that user. If Jill logs on through the LOGON.BAT file above, %USER% would be Jill and the TYPE command would display the message file in Jill's subdirectory by issuing the command TYPE\ JILL\MESSAGES.TXT.

5.BAT (from a menu selection that displays
ECHO OFF messages)
CLS
TYPE \%USER%\MESSAGES.TXT

Log-on Messages

A log-on message is a text file displayed on the screen at boot time. This can be a simple one line message like "Welcome to the system" or a complete menu, as seen in Chaps. 22 and 23. You can also have messages that are displayed only under certain conditions. For instance, you can create files that contain appointments and activities for a particular date that display on the screen when the date arrives. Consider the following file names:

04-23-84.TXT
12-25-83.TXT

The file name contains 8 legal and acceptable characters. The contents of these files might contain appointments, activities, or other information pertaining to the date specified by the file name.

The IF EXIST batch subcommand can be used in a batch file to search for a file that matches the date entered by the operator at boot time. The format for the date is mm-dd-yy, the same format used in the file names.

The following batch file will search for a file that has a file name that matches the date entered by the operator.

DT.BAT
ECHO OFF
IF "%1" = = "" GOTO NODATE
DATE %1
IF EXIST %1.TXT MORE < %1.TXT
GOTO END
:NODATE

```
ECHO DATE NEEDED—TRY AGAIN
:END
```

Here's how the batch file works. You execute it by entering DT and the date in the form mm-dd-yy. For example DT 4-14-84 would execute the batch file, assigning 4-14-84 to %1. The third line sets the systems date to 4-14-84. The fourth line then searches the disk for the file 4-4-84.TXT, using the batch subcommand IF EXIST, and executes MORE < 4-4-84.TXT if the file is found. MORE filters the file to the screen one page at a time so the operator can read it.

For this batch file to work properly, the operator must enter the date as a parameter on the command line and in the correct format. You can place a message in the AUTOEXEC.BAT file that will tell the operator how to use the DT batch file and how to enter the date in the correct format. To make the changes you can use EDLIN as described here to alter AUTOEXEC.BAT. First, remove the DATE command from the file and change the last line so that it contains the message shown below.

```
AUTOEXEC.BAT
ECHO OFF
PATH \
PROMPT $p$g
DATE
TYPE ASSIGN.CDS
ECHO ENTER DATE IN THE FORM: DT mm-dd-yy
```

If you are using the LOGON.BAT file described earlier, the message should be added to the end of the LOGON.BAT file instead of the AUTO-EXEC.BAT file. Normally, you would want to log onto the system before reading the date files. Here's what the log-on chain of events looks like if you are using the LOGON batch file:

1. Boot the system

2. AUTOEXEC.BAT

3. LOGON.BAT

4. DT.BAT

Creating the Dated Messages

You can create a message with COPY CON or EDLIN; however, EDLIN should be used to add messages to an existing file because it keeps the file intact. COPY CON cannot be used for adding to a message because it copies over an existing file, erasing its contents.

Deleting Outdated Messages

The ERASE command can be used with wild-card characters to remove old messages. Since the first two characters of the file name are numbers that represent the month, you can delete a whole month's worth of message files at one time by using wild-card characters. To delete all message files for the month of February you would type ERASE 2-*.*. Note the dash after the 2. This helps differentiate between other files that may contain the number 2 in the first position of the file name such as a menu batch file like 2.BAT.

Sending and Receiving Mail

This section is once again directed toward systems that are being used by more than one user. The objective is to create a mailbox for each user so mail can be sent among the users. If you are a single user, you may be interested in this routine so that you can send reminders to yourself. We will create two batch files for use in this mail routine. The first file is called READMAIL.BAT and the second file is called SENDMAIL.BAT.

The routines rely on the environment string %USER% which must be set at boot time by a batch file similar to the LOGON batch file discussed previously. The READMAIL batch file uses the environment string %USER% to determine which file to read. When you want to read your mail, you simply type READMAIL and the batch file displays the file that matches the name in the variable %USER%. Users may write mail to each other by using the SENDMAIL routine below, specifying the recipient's USER name as a parameter on the command line. Here is the READMAIL.BAT file:

```
READMAIL.BAT
ECHO OFF
CLS
MORE < %USER%.MAL
```

Suppose John logs onto the system through the LOGON batch file or a similar file that sets the environment string %USER% to JOHN. If John types READMAIL, the batch file will display the file JOHN.MAL (MAL is an abbreviation for MAIL) one page at a time. To write mail, the batch file SENDMAIL.BAT is used.

```
SENDMAIL.BAT
ECHO OFF
CLS
IF "%1" = = "" GOTO NONAME
```

```
ECHO YOU ARE IN EDLIN WRITING MAIL TO %1
ECHO BE SURE TO TYPE YOUR NAME AND DATE.
EDLIN TEMP.MAL
COPY %1.MAL+TEMP.MAL %1.MAL
ERASE TEMP.MAL
ECHO %1'S MAIL FILE APPENDED
GOTO END
:NONAME
ECHO YOU DIDN'T ENTER A NAME AND WILL HAVE TO START OVER.
:END
```

Let's study this batch file. The first two lines are the standard batch file set-up commands. The third line checks to see if a parameter has been entered. If not, the batch file branches to :NONAME and displays the message following the label. Assume that John has logged onto the system and he enters SENDMAIL JANE. JANE becomes parameter %1. The sixth line executes EDLIN with the file name TEMP.MAL. John types in the messages he wants to send to Jane using EDLIN in the normal way. After exiting EDLIN, the batch file takes control again, appending TEMP.MAL to JANE.MAL. By appending files in this way, new messages can be added to existing message files. After the files have been appended, TEMP.MAL is erased.

Later, when Jane logs onto the system, she sets %USER% to JANE and types READMAIL. The READMAIL batch file executes the command MORE < JANE.MAL, displaying the message file that John just appended.

Phone List Management

In this section, we will present a phone number management system that uses batch files to sort, search, and list a phone number list. The menu shown below automates the system by displaying selection numbers for the various batch files. You can create this menu by using EDLIN and call it PHONE.MNU.

```
-----------------------------------------------------------
       T E L E P H O N E   D I R E C T O R Y
          1)    FIND NAME  <1 name>
          2)    LIST ALL
          3)    ADD NAME
          4)    PRINT DIRECTORY
          5)    RETURN TO MAIN MENU
-----------------------------------------------------------
```

First, determine if the phone routines should be placed in a subdirectory. If you already have menu selection batch files such as 1.BAT and 2.BAT in your current directory for another application (such as the menu created in Chaps. 22 and 23), you should create a new directory for the phone routines. You can call this new directory PHONE.

Creating the Phone List

You can use COPY CON to create your phone list and EDLIN to make corrections to it. We show the fictitious list created in Chap. 12 as an example, but you can substitute your own list. Be sure to type everything in capital letters so the search routines will have a better chance of finding a match. You should also use the Space Bar instead of the Tab key to space between columns since a tab is seen as one character by some DOS commands such as SORT. Tabbing could cause problems later when you wish to sort the phone list by a particular column.

PHONE.NUM

JOE	837-3848	FRIEND
BOB	205/456-8734	BROTHER
SALLY	562-2346	AGENT 47
MR. ROOTER	769-3847	PLUMBER
1ST WORLD	983-3583	BANK
3RD WORLD	934-3857	BANK
DR. FEELGOOD	987-2039	FAMILY DOCTOR
DR. EYEBALL	485-3859	EYE DOCTOR
DR. STANDRITE	485-3434	CHIROPRACTOR

Each of the batch files below contain the same starting and ending commands: ECHO is turned off in each file and the screen is cleared. After each file performs its task, the phone menu is displayed again, except in the last file, which will display a main menu in the ROOT directory if one exists.

```
1.BAT                              (searches for a name in the phone list)
ECHO OFF
CLS
IF "%1" = = "" GOTO HELP           (check for parameter)
FIND "%1" PHONE.NUM                (search for string)
ECHO .
PAUSE
GOTO END
:HELP                              (display error message)
ECHO Enter a string to search for
```

```
:END
CLS
TYPE PHONE.MNU                                    (display menu)
```

2.BAT   (list the phone list one page at a time)
```
ECHO OFF
CLS
ECHO PHONE LIST:
MORE < PHONE.NUM                (direct the file into the MORE command)
ECHO .
PAUSE
CLS
TYPE PHONE.MNU
```

3.BAT   (add names or alter the list)
```
ECHO OFF
CLS
ECHO You are in EDLIN editing the file PHONE.NUM
EDLIN PHONE.NUM
SORT < PHONE.NUM > PHONE.NUM                      (resort the list)
CLS
TYPE PHONE.MNU
```

4.BAT   (print the list)
```
ECHO OFF
CLS
ECHO Is the printer on and the paper aligned?
ECHO .
PAUSE
ECHO PHONE LIST > LPT1                            (print title)
ECHO ————— > LPT1                                 (more titles)
COPY PHONE.NUM LPT1                               (print the file)
CLS
TYPE PHONE.MNU
```

5.BAT   (return to the ROOT and displays MAIN.MNU)
```
ECHO OFF
CLS
CD \
TYPE MAIN.MNU
```

Once each of the batch files is created and the menu is created, all you
have to do is enter TYPE PHONE.MNU to display the phone menu. You
can create a batch file that will do this. If you placed the phone routine
in a separate directory, you can create the following batch file in the
ROOT directory to call the routines:

PHONE.BAT
```
ECHO OFF
CLS
CD PHONE
TYPE PHONE.MNU
```

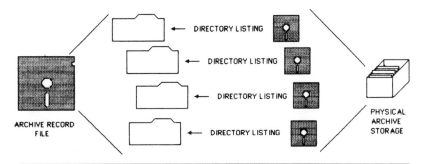

Figure 26-1 The directory listing from each diskette that is going to storage is copied to a file on the archive record diskette.

Once this batch file is created, all you have to do from the main ROOT directory is type PHONE to use your new phone management system.

The Disk Archivist

The batch file routines discussed in this section will keep a log of the files you have stored on floppy diskettes. Each disk is considered a volume and has a volume name which you will want to label on the outside of the diskette. A volume file will be created for each of the diskettes and this volume file will hold a list of the files on that diskette. Each of these volume files will be kept on a special archives diskette (or subdirectory if you own a fixed disk). We will then be able to search through this list of files to find a volume that holds a particular file. The illustration in Figure 26-1 may help clarify this process. The menu below is used for the archive routines.

```
          D I S K    A R C H I V E    M E N U
   1) ARCHIVE A DISK. Enter 1 and an 8-character volume name.
                 Example: 1 VISIDATA

   2) DISPLAY A LIST OF VOLUMES.
   3) DISPLAY A LIST OF FILES IN A VOLUME.
           Example: 3 VISIDATA

   4) SEARCH ALL VOLUMES FOR A FILE.
           Example: 4 MYPROGRAM

   5) RETURN TO MAIN MENU.
```

Selection 1 is a batch file that asks you to place the disk to be logged in drive B. The routine will then read the list of file names on the disk and store them in a file on the ARCHIVE disk. The name of the file in which the file names are stored is the parameter you specify on the command line and should be the volume name of the disk being logged.

The second batch file displays all volume names on the archives diskette, and the third batch file displays a list of file names in any volume. The fourth batch file searches all volume files on the archives diskette for a keyword you specify. It produces a display that lists each volume name and any matching strings within that volume. When you find the file you are looking for, you can then refer to the actual diskette that holds that file. The fifth batch file returns the user to a main menu in the ROOT directory if one exists.

```
1.BAT                                          (archive a diskette)
ECHO OFF
CLS
IF "%1" = = "" GOTO HELP                        (check for parameters)
IF EXIST %1.ARC GOTO NOWAY                      (file is already on disk)
PAUSE PLACE THE DISK TO BE LOGGED IN DRIVE B
CLS
ECHO FILE BEING LOGGED
DIR B: | SORT > %1.ARC              (copy the directory to the volume)
ECHO LOG COMPLETE
GOTO END
:HELP
ECHO ENTER A VOLUME NAME
GOTO END
:NOWAY
ECHO FILE ALREADY EXIST—TRY ANOTHER VOLUME NAME
:END
PAUSE
CLS
TYPE ARCHIVE.MNU
```

```
2.BAT                              (display current volume names)
ECHO OFF
CLS
DIR *.ARC /P                       (list all files ending in .ARC)
PAUSE
CLS
TYPE ARCHIVE.MNU
```

```
3.BAT                              (display file name list in a volume)
ECHO OFF
CLS
IF "%1" = = "" GOTO HELP                       (check for parameter)
MORE < %1.ARC                          (filter the file to the screen)
GOTO END
```

```
:HELP
ECHO ENTER A VOLUME NAME
:END
PAUSE
CLS
TYPE ARCHIVE.MNU
```

4.BAT   (search for a keyword among all the volumes)
```
ECHO OFF
CLS
IF "%1" = = "" GOTO HELP                          (check for parameter)
FOR %%A IN (*.ARC) DO FIND "%1" %%A                    (find keyword)
GOTO END
:HELP
ECHO ENTER A SEARCH STRING
:END
PAUSE
CLS
TYPE ARCHIVE.MNU
```

5.BAT   (return to a main menu in the ROOT directory)
```
ECHO OFF
CLS
CD \
TYPE MENU.TXT
```

In this chapter, we have discussed several routines that work by themselves or can be linked together to form a start-up chain of events. This chain of events starts with the AUTOEXEC.BAT file setting the system prompt, path, and other start-up procedures. A password program then takes control, directing users to their own directories or preventing access to the system by unauthorized people. Another batch files searches for dated files and displays them when the dates match.

The last half of the chapter explains how to develop a phone number look-up routine and a disk archive routine.

Chapter

27

Data Storage and Retrieval

In this chapter we'll really put the computer to work by having it search and sort through data files for information. We'll show you various ways to handle data files and see how the FIND command can be used to search for information. We will also show two methods of using DOS as a simple database management system. The first method involves storing and searching for information in a single file. The second method involves storing and searching for data in multiple files that reside as a group in a single directory.

Data Storage and Retrieval, Method One

Data files are a convenient place to store product inventories, price lists, mailing lists, phone numbers, and other information that needs to be searched or sorted. With the DOS FIND command, we can search through these files to obtain specific items and list them on the screen or printer.

Suppose you have the following file on disk and want to find information in the file by matching several criteria. It contains data in uppercase characters to increase the chances of finding keywords. The name of this file is PARTLIST.DAT

PARTLIST.DAT:

PART #	SIZE	WEIGHT	COLOR	SHAPE
45-67	10	30	RED	ROUND
45-68	10	30	RED	SQUARE

45-69	10	25	RED	ROUND
45-70	10	25	RED	SQUARE
46-14	13	35	BLUE	ROUND
46-15	13	35	BLUE	SQUARE
46-16	13	30	BLUE	ROUND
46-17	13	30	BLUE	SQUARE
47-36	15	40	BLACK	ROUND
47-37	15	40	BLACK	SQUARE
47-38	15	35	BLACK	ROUND
47-39	15	35	BLACK	SQUARE

We can use the FIND command to locate specific items in the parts list as in the example below in which we are looking for all round items. Note that ROUND is entered in capital letters.

FIND "ROUND" PARTLIST.DAT

produces the list:

———— PARTLIST.DAT

45-67	10	30	RED	ROUND
45-69	10	25	RED	ROUND
46-14	13	35	BLUE	ROUND
46-16	13	30	BLUE	ROUND
47-36	15	40	BLACK	ROUND
47-38	15	35	BLACK	ROUND

If you want to search through the file for an item that matches several criteria, you must break the file down into smaller and smaller parts. Assume that you are looking for a round part that has a weight of 35 pounds. You could enter the following commands, which direct the output from one search into a file that can be searched again using the second keyword.

FIND "ROUND" PARTLIST.DAT > TEMP.DAT

This command directs the output of the FIND command into a temporary file called TEMP.DAT, which now contains all the lines containing the keyword ROUND. The next step is to search TEMP.DAT for our second keyword, 35, which produces the list shown below.

FIND "35" TEMP.DAT

———— TEMP.DAT

| 46-14 | 13 | 35 | BLUE | ROUND |
| 47-38 | 15 | 35 | BLACK | ROUND |

A more convenient way to do the same task is shown below. You can use DOS's piping feature to pipe the output of one search into another search by typing:

FIND "ROUND" PARTLIST ! FIND "35"

which produces the output:

46-14	13	35	BLUE	ROUND
47-38	15	35	BLACK	ROUND

Using the piping feature, you can also send the output to the SORT command. Here the keyword ROUND is located in the PARTLIST file and piped to the sort command, which sorts on the twenty-fifth column, the weight column.

FIND "ROUND" PARTLIST ! SORT /+25
—————— PARTLIST

45-69	10	25	RED	ROUND
46-16	13	30	BLUE	ROUND
45-67	10	30	RED	ROUND
47-38	15	35	BLACK	ROUND
46-14	13	35	BLUE	ROUND
47-36	15	40	BLACK	ROUND

The FIND /V switch allows you to list all lines in a file except those containing the specified keyword. You can use this feature with the PARTLIST file to list all lines that do not contain the string RED:

FIND /V "RED" PARTLIST
—————— PARTLIST

46-14	13	35	BLUE	ROUND
46-15	13	35	BLUE	SQUARE
46-16	13	30	BLUE	ROUND
46-17	13	30	BLUE	SQUARE
47-36	15	40	BLACK	ROUND
47-37	15	40	BLACK	SQUARE
47-38	15	35	BLACK	ROUND
47-39	15	35	BLACK	SQUARE

The next command uses the piping feature to further break the list down. Here, RED is eliminated and ROUND is extracted from the remaining lines.

FIND /V "RED" PARTLIST ¦ FIND "ROUND"
—————— PARTLIST

46-14	13	35	BLUE	ROUND
46-16	13	30	BLUE	ROUND
47-36	15	40	BLACK	ROUND
47-38	15	35	BLACK	ROUND

To print a list of the lines produced by any FIND or SORT command, you can use the I/O redirection features to direct it to the printer:

FIND "ROUND" PARTLIST > LPT1

A Search Batch File

In the examples above we used several FIND commands or a single command containing a group of FINDs, to locate lines in a file. The batch file below will help make the process easier by automating the FIND commands. With it you can enter as many keywords as you want, and the batch file will break the list down into smaller and smaller results.

```
        SEARCH.BAT
 1      ECHO OFF
 2      CLS
 3      IF "%1" = = "" GOTO NONAME
 4      SET FILENAME = %1
 5      SHIFT
 6      IF "%1" = = "" GOTO NOKEYS
 7      FIND "%1" %FILENAME% > TEMP.DAT
 8      SHIFT
 9      IF "%1" = = "" GOTO NODATA
10      :LOOP
11      FIND "%1" TEMP.DAT > TEMP2.DAT
12      COPY TEMP2.DAT TEMP.DAT
13      SHIFT
14      IF "%1" = = "" GOTO NODATA
15      GOTO LOOP
16      :NONAME
17      ECHO NO FILE NAME SPECIFIED. START OVER.
18      GOTO END
19      :NOKEYS
20      ECHO NO SEARCH CRITERIA SPECIFIED. START OVER.
21      GOTO END
22      :NODATA
23      ECHO SEARCH COMPLETE. TEMP.DAT NOW HOLDS SEARCH
        RESULTS.
24      ECHO PART #    SIZE    WEIGHT    COLOR    SHAPE
25      MORE < TEMP.DAT
26      :END
```

To explain how this batch file works, we will assume that an operator has entered the following command, producing the results shown.

SEARCH PARTLIST.DAT ROUND RED 25 <Return>

SEARCH COMPLETE. TEMP.DAT NOW HOLDS SEARCH RESULTS

————— TEMP.DAT

45-69   10   25   RED   ROUND

The batch file above has been numbered so that we can step through and explain each part. We will use the search command just typed in our explanation. The first two lines of the batch file are the standard batch file set-up commands. Line 3 checks to see if %1 has been entered. Initially %1 is the name of the file to search, but it will be changed by the SHIFT subcommand as the batch file progresses. If the file name has not been entered, the batch file branches to line 16, the :NONAME label and displays the message on line 17.

If a file name was entered on the command line, the SET command in line 4 sets the parameter %FILENAME% equal to parameter %1, the file being searched. Line 5 then shifts the parameter line so that, in the example above, ROUND becomes parameter %1. Line 6 is another check routine. It checks to see if a keyword has been entered on the command line. This keyword occupies the position on the command line following the name of the file to be searched. If this keyword has not been entered, the batch file branches to the label :NOKEYS and displays the message on line 20. If a keyword was entered, batch processing continues with line 7.

Line 7 is the first search command. It searches the file represented by %FILENAME% (PARTLIST.DAT in this example) for the keyword now parameter %1 (ROUND). All lines matching the keyword in the file are directed into the file TEMP.DAT.

Line 8 shifts the parameters on the command line so that RED becomes parameter %1. The IF command in line 9 checks to see if parameter %1 is empty and if so, the batch file ends. In the example above, RED occupies this position, so processing continues.

Line 10 is the start of a loop that continues to process more parameters from the command line. Line 11 searches for the keyword in the TEMP.DAT file and directs its output to the TEMP2.DAT file. TEMP2.DAT now holds the latest search results. The old search results in TEMP.DAT are no longer needed, so TEMP2.DAT is copied over the old file in line 12. This is important if we loop back through this part of the batch file again because line 11 searches TEMP.DAT, not TEMP2.DAT. Line 13 shifts the parameters on the command line again and line 14 checks to see if there are more parameters. If so, line 15 is executed; otherwise the batch file branches to the label :NODATA.

When the file has been searched for the keywords, the results are placed in the file TEMP.DAT and are listed on the screen. The ECHO command in line 24 displays the column titles on the screen and the MORE command in line 25 pages the results on the screen.

The batch process may take a while on floppy-disk systems, but it should finish in a reasonable time on fixed-disk systems. For maximum speed, you can copy SEARCH.BAT and the file to be searched to a RAM disk. The DOS commands MORE.COM and FIND.EXE must also be copied to the RAM disk.

Creating the Data Files

We will briefly describe a method used to append data to a data file such as the file PARTLIST above. This method will make it easier to place items in specific columns of a data file. In the example above, you were able to sort the file by columns because we had aligned each data type in the file with the one above it. For instance, in PARTLIST.DAT, the part numbers were in column 1, the size was in column 2, and so on. Aligning data in this way will give you much more control when you are sorting the file.

When entering data in a file, it is handy to have a ruler as a guide to show which columns are used for each data type. This is especially true if you are appending to an existing file or an inexperienced user is entering data. The ruler shown below could be used to help align data fields in PARTLIST.DAT.

```
PART #     SIZE      WEIGHT       COLOR      SHAPE
+......... +......... +............ +.......... +............
```

This ruler can then be included in a batch file that opens a temporary file for input and displays the ruler as a guide to the operator who is entering data. When the operator closes the data input file, the batch file resumes and appends the temporary file to PARTLIST.DAT. PARTLIST.DAT is then sorted by the first column. Here is the batch file that will do this:

```
ADDATA.BAT
ECHO OFF
CLS
ECHO PART #     SIZE        WEIGHT     COLOR      SHAPE
ECHO +—————+—————+—————+—————+—————
```

```
COPY CON:TEMP.DAT
COPY PARTLIST.DAT+TEMP.DAT PARTLIST.DAT
SORT < PARTLIST.DAT > PARTLIST.DAT
ECHO FILE APPENDED AND SORTED
```

There are two things that you should note when you are entering files that will be sorted with the DOS sort command. First, SORT can get confused if you use the Tab key to space to the different columns. It "sees" the tab as a single character instead of the multiple spaces you saw when writing to the file. You should use the Space Bar to create the proper spacing between fields.

Another potential problem with SORT is that it does not consider numbers to have a value other than their ASCII code. For instance, the numbers in the first column are sorted by the first character of the number, not the value of the number. Because of this, 100 would be placed before 20 in a sort. Keep this in mind when using or creating part numbers.

Other Types of Data Files

The file above is an example of an inventory data file; however, you can create other types of data files. This section will give you a few examples of line-oriented data files, giving you ideas for data files of your own. The examples below can be searched in the same way as the file shown above. The fields of each record are aligned so they can be sorted.

We've been talking about files in the context of data files stored on a diskette. Here we will refer to the paper files you store in a file cabinet. Suppose you need to keep better track of the information being stored in the files. This information might be product brochures, product announcements, technical notes, recipes, or news items. Whatever the information is, you need a better way to keep track of it. The following headers could be used to create data files to log this information:

```
                                            HANGING          FOLDER
KEYWORD        SHORT DESCRIPTION            FILE NAME         NAME
+————————+———————————————+—————————+————
HAMBURGER      MEAT LOAF RECIPE             RECIPES           H
FREEZER        FOOD FREEZING TECHNIQUES     FOOD STORAGE      FREEZER
or
```

```
KEYWORD                                                      FOLDER
HANGING        SHORT DESCRIPTION            FILE NAME         NAME
+————————+———————————————+—————————+————
PAN            PANNING TECHNIQUES           PHOTO TIPS        P
FILM           FILM TYPE ANALYSIS           BENCHMARKS        F
```

You could use a file header like the one below to keep track of important magazine articles. This file is called SCIENCE.NWS (after *Science News* magazine).

KEYWORD	DESCRIPTION	ISSUE
MAYA	MAYA TOMB DISCOVERED, GUATEMALA	V.125 #21
COMPUTERS	FIFTH GENERATION COMPUTERS & JAPAN	V.125 #22
TECTONICS	PLATE MOVEMENT AND EARTH ROTATION	V.125 #23

Special Techniques: Data Coding

In the line-oriented data files we have been using so far, you may have noticed that there may not be enough room on a single line for an adequate description. Since the FIND command displays the whole line of a keyword and nothing else, we are limited to placing descriptions in the single line length. To save space on the line, we can code keywords into one or two character codes. The example file below will show how this is done. The file we show below is designed to be used with the PRNTLIST label printing program in Chap. 32. This program separates the fields in each line of the data file and prints them on separate lines of continuous roll mailing labels.

The coding we will use in the data file is listed in the following table:

Code	Profession	Code	District
@1	Doctor	@7	Downtown area
@2	Teacher	@8	Uptown area
@3	Attorney		
@4	CPA		

You can, of course, use as many codes as you want. We only include a few here for the example. The codes will go in the first field of each line as shown below.

CODE	NAME	ADDRESS	CITY,STATE,ZIP
@1 @7	JACKSON, JANET	1324 WALNUT	CITY,CA,93105
@3 @8	SMITH, JOHN	10 E. FOURTH	CITY,CA,93001
@2 @7	LILEY, PAUL	100 W. FOURTH	CITY,CA,93003

Once the file is entered, it can be updated by using a batch file similar to ADDATA.BAT. You can also locate information by using the FIND command, or you can use SEARCH.BAT to locate multiple parameters.

The codes are a useful way to specify several search parameters. For instance, assume that the file above is called MAILLIST.DAT. The following command would find all doctors in the downtown area:

FIND "@1" MAILLIST.DAT ¦ FIND "@7"

This file can be piped into the PRNTLIST BASIC program shown in Chap. 32. The program is a filter that you can create and use with data files like the ones created here. PRNTLIST will separate the name from character positions 11 through 30, the address from positions 31 through 55, and the city, state, and zip from positions 56 through 80. These strings will then be printed on standard 1-inch by 3-inch mailing labels. The fields allow 10 character positions for the search code, 20 for the name, 25 for the address, and 25 for the remaining characters.

Data Storage and Retrieval, Method Two

The second method of data storage and retrieval involves using subdirectories to store data files. In method 1 above you searched for data on single lines within one file. In this method you will search for data in groups of files that are stored together in a subdirectory. Think of the way a 3 by 5 card filing system is used. The top of the card usually contains keywords that describe the information in the body of the card. The body of the card has text information. Compare this type of file to the line-oriented file described earlier. This is the major difference between the two methods we describe in this chapter.

Each of the cards you will use in this filing system is a file on the disk. The files will be grouped in directories with other files that contain similar information. Since the files in these directories contain similar information, you can do searches on all the files in the directory to locate the keywords that they have in common.

The following example will help explain the structure and operation of this method. The ROOT directory will hold a batch file called FINDIT.BAT. Branching from the ROOT will be several subdirectories, each holding a specific type of data or information file (see Fig. 27-1). We will call these subdirectories data storage directories, or DSD's.

In the example we show here, a DSD called MUSIC that holds files cataloging an album collection will be created. Each file will hold information about each album in the collection. The search routines will search through every file in a DSD for a keyword. For instance, to find a specific song, SEARCH.BAT would search each file in a specified DSD and list the names of those that contain the keyword you entered.

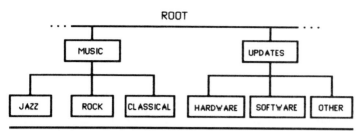

Figure 27-1 Using directories to store data files helps break the files into smaller groups.

To show how the system works, assume that a DSD called JAZZ exists on a disk. The JAZZ directory contains the following files, among others:

RAMPAL1.JZZ
SUITE FOR FLUTE AND JAZZ PIANO
JEAN-PIERRE RAMPAL, FLUTIST
CLAUDE BOLLING, PIANIST/COMPOSER

SIDE 1:
BAROQUE AND BLUE
SENTIMENTALE
JAVANAISE

SIDE 2:
FUGACE
IRLANDAISE
VERSATILE
VELOCE

JAMES1.JZZ	JAMES2.JZZ
BOB JAMES/TOUCHDOWN	BOB JAMES/"H"
SIDE 1:	SIDE 1:
ANGELA	SNOWBIRD FANTASY
TOUCHDOWN	SHEPHERD'S SONG
I WANT TO THANK YOU	BRIGHTON BY THE SEA
SIDE 2:	SIDE 2:
SUN RUNNER	THE WALKMAN
CARIBBEAN NIGHTS	THOROUGHBRED
	REUNITED

Each file could contain more information if you felt it necessary. You could place a short description of the album or the artist in the file. Now, assume that you are searching for the song "The Walkman." You know its in the JAZZ DSD, and you know it's in one of the JAMES files, but you're not sure which one. The following batch file, which resides in the ROOT directory, will search each file in the specified directory for a string:

```
SEARCH.BAT
ECHO OFF
CLS
CD %1                               (move to the appropriate directory)
FOR %%A IN (*.*) DO FIND "%2"       (search for the file)
CD ..                              (go back to original directory)
```

Running this file with the following command will produce the results shown below:

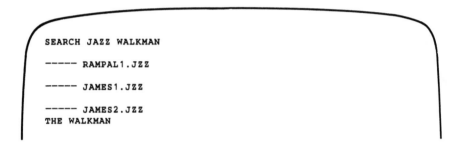

```
SEARCH JAZZ WALKMAN

----- RAMPAL1.JZZ

----- JAMES1.JZZ

----- JAMES2.JZZ
THE WALKMAN
```

You can see by the listing that the file JAMES2.JZZ contains the song. The batch file changes directories to the one specified on the command line (parameter %1). In the example above, JAZZ was specified. The FOR command then searched through all the files in the JAZZ directory for the string specified in parameter %2.

The SEARCH batch file will search every file in the specified directory for the keyword. Since searching every file takes time, you should limit the number of files in each directory. Divide your files into as many categories as possible. For instance, the broad category JAZZ could be broken down into early jazz, modern jazz, and other categories.

Using the System

The files in the subdirectories can be created with EDLIN or any word processor that produces ASCII files. This is important because some word processors convert the text in files to text that you may not be able to find with the FIND command. Generally, most files will be small and can be created with COPY CON and edited with EDLIN. As the number of DSD's grows, you may want to create a file in the ROOT directory called CONTENTS.DSD which lists the type of data stored in each DSD. You can use the SEARCH batch file above to locate information in this file and help you determine which DSD contains the data files you are searching for.

We have demonstrated two methods of using DOS as a database management system. This is a logical task for a disk operating system and one that DOS does very well. Keep in mind that the routines work best on a fixed disk, but you can get some improvement in the speed by using a RAM drive.

28

Working with a Printer

The printer is one of the biggest assets to your computer system; without it there would be no hard copy. In this chapter we will briefly discuss how a printer is connected to your system and how to control your printer, especially a dot matrix printer, from DOS.

Serial and Parallel Connections

There are two ways to connect a printer to your system—either through the serial port (COM) or the parallel port (LPT). Both of these ports provide a specific type of connection and cabling for the printer, but there is usually no reason to prefer one over the other. The serial port is usually reserved for communications, so you may want to save this port for that purpose. However, if your printer is more than 10 feet from the computer, you should use the serial port because the signal running through a serial connection will not become degraded with distance (as long as it's not excessive). Most PCs have parallel ports intended for the connection of a printer. You cannot, however, exceed 10 feet when using a parallel connection without a loss in the quality of the signal.

As we discussed previously, each port on your computer is given a specific device name by DOS. This device name is reserved and cannot be used in other file names. The parallel ports are known as LPT1 (line printer 1), LPT2, or LPT3. The communications ports are referred to as COM1 and COM2. Although DOS has reserved the names for these devices, they will not always be implemented as hardware on your system. Most PCs come with one parallel and one serial port, designated as LPT1 and COM1.

If you are connecting a serial printer to one of the COM ports, you will need to tell DOS that a printer instead of a communications device is connected to the port. The next section will discuss this.

Connecting a Serial Printer

There are two MODE commands you must use to tell your computer that a printer is attached to one of the communications ports. These commands can be added to the AUTOEXEC.BAT file so that the ports are initialized every time you boot the system. The first command sets the parameters of the communications port and the second command tells DOS that a printer, rather than a communication device like a modem, is attached to the port.

To issue the first command, you must know the baud rate of your printer, which can be found in its operator's manual. The MODE command takes the form shown below.

    MODE COMx:baud rate,parity,data bits,stop bits, P

The baud rate is the most important option of the MODE command when you are connecting a printer. If your printer operates at 1200 baud, you can type the following command, which sets all other parameters on the line to their default value.

    MODE COM1:1200

Next, you must tell DOS to send the printer output that is normally directed to the LPT port to the COM1 port instead. The following MODE command will accomplish this. In it, LPT1 is set equal to the COM1 port.

    MODE LPT1:=COM1

DOS will now direct all printer output through the communications port. You may specify any one of the LPT or COM devices as long as you have the actual hardware interfaces installed in your system.

Standard Printer Controls

There are several ways to control your printer from DOS once it has been attached and configured. If you press Control-P or Control-PrtSc, you can echo the screen output to the printer. Pressing either key again will set the printer echo off. Keep in mind that printer echo will slow the computer down because it must wait for the printer.

You can print the contents of any text screen by pressing Shift-PrtSc. This is useful for documenting a keystroke sequence or printing the screen output of a program or command. If you have an IBM Graphics Printer, you can issue the GRAPHICS command to reproduce a graphics screen on the printer.

Working with Control Codes

Most printers on the market will print enhanced characters. For instance, with the IBM Graphics Printer and the Epson series of printers, you can underline text, strike characters several times for a boldface effect, and condense or expand the type. How do you tell the printer to enhance some characters and not others? You will see how in the following discussion of printer Control codes.

A printer Control code is a sequence of characters sent to the printer to alter one of its features, such as a type style or the number of lines printed per inch. When you are sending a code to the printer, a way is needed to tell the printer that it is about to receive a special code intended as a change mode command instead of a character to be printed. This is usually accomplished by sending an Escape code to the printer before the Control code.

The printer manual will describe the Control codes used to change its modes. These codes can be sent to the printer from various sources, one of the most common being a BASIC program. Most commercially available programs have their own way of sending Control codes to a printer. In this chapter we will describe how you can send them from DOS.

In the examples that follow, we will describe the Control codes used by IBM and Epson dot matrix printers. Many of these codes will be similar to the ones used by other printers, so if you own a different type of printer, you can still follow along. If you own a letter-quality printer, you cannot set certain features such as condensed and double wide printing, but the methods we describe here can be used to set various other modes, as long as you know the Control codes.

Table 28-1 lists the most common Control codes for the IBM and Epson matrix printers. This table is not a complete list, but it does show those used to control type styles. If you refer to your printer manual you will notice other Control codes used to control such things as graphics, line spacing, and paper feed.

Figure 28-1 shows the various printer modes that are set by the codes in Table 28-1. Any of the codes may be combined for special effects. For instance, you can combine emphasized with double strike to form titles and headers.

The code ESC ! is available on the Epson FX-80 and FX-100 printers.

TABLE 28-1 Printer Control Codes

ASCII code	Control character	Description
14		Sets enlarged mode (one line only)
20		Cancels enlarged mode (set by above)
	ESC W1	Sets enlarged mode on until set off
	ESC W0	Sets above enlarged mode off
15		Sets condensed mode
18		Cancels condensed mode
	ESC 4	Sets italics (Epson only)
	ESC 5	Cancels italics (Epson only)
	ESC −1	Sets underline
	ESC −0	Cancels underline
	ESC E	Sets emphasized mode
	ESC F	Cancels emphasized mode
	ESC G	Sets double strike mode
	ESC H	Cancels double strike mode
	ESC M	Sets elite mode (Epson FX-80)
	ESC P	Sets normal pica (Epson FX-80)
	ESC S0	Sets superscript mode
	ESC S1	Sets subscript mode
	ESC T	Cancels superscript or subscript
	ESC @	Resets all codes to normal

This code allows you to select a combination of the above type styles by sending a single control sequence to the printer. This code will set the type styles on the printer as they are shown in Fig. 28-2.

Sending Codes to the Printer

Make sure your printer is connected and the power is on. Most of the codes we have listed may be sent to the printer by using the DOS COPY

ENLARGED MODE
CONDENSED MODE condensed mode
ITALICS MODE   italics mode
UNDERLINE MODE   underline mode
EMPHASIZED MODE   emphasized mode
DOUBLE STRIKE   double strike
ELITE MODE elite mode
REGULAR PICA MODE   regular pica mode
SUPERSCRIPT SUBSCRIPT

Figure 28-1

MODE #0, NORMAL TYPE
MODE #1, ELITE TYPE
MODE #4, CONDENSED MODE

MODE #8, EMPHASIZED MODE
MODE #16, DOUBLE-STRIKE MODE
MODE #17, DOUBLE-STRIKE, ELITE
MODE #20, DOUBLE-STRIKE, CONDENSED
MODE #24, DOUBLE-STRIKE, EMPHASIZED

MODE #32, ENLARGED TYPE
MODE #33, ENLARGED ELITE
MODE #36, ENLARGED CONDENSED

MODE #40, ENLARGED EMPHASIZED
MODE # 48, ENLARGED, DOUBLE-STRIKE
MODE #49, ENLARGED, DOUBLE-STRIKE, ELITE
MODE #52, ENLARGED, DOUBLE-STRIKE, CONDENSED
MODE #56, ENLRGD, DBL-STRK, EMPHASIZED

Figure 28-2

command. They are entered at the keyboard by using the Alt key in combination with the numbers on the numeric keypad. For instance, to sound the bell on your printer, enter the code shown below. Remember that you must hold the Alt key down while entering 7 on the numeric keypad. The numbers on the top row of the keyboard will not work.

```
A:\>COPY CON LPT1
  <Alt-7> <Return>
  <F6> <Return>
            1 File(s) copied
A:\>_
```

Let's discuss what has happened. First, you used the COPY command to send the code to the printer. In this case, you are sending something from the console to LPT1. If you look in the ASCII code listing in App. A you will see that the ASCII value 007 has been designated as the beep or bell. All computers and related devices such as printers that use the ASCII coding scheme recognize 007 as the bell. The Alt-numeric keypad sequence allows you to enter ASCII codes at the keyboard and have them sent to files or devices. In the example above, the bell sounded on the printer when the file was closed and sent to the printer.

Take a closer look at the ASCII codes in App. A. Notice that ASCII value 010 is a line feed, so if you wanted to produce a line feed on the screen, you could type Alt-10. If you type Alt-13, a carriage return is executed, duplicating the action performed by the Return key. To see how a sheet of paper can be form-fed on the printer, enter ASCII code 12 in a file as shown below:

```
A:\>COPY CON LPT1
  <Alt-12> <Return>
  <F6> <Return>

A:\>_
```

If you can send these simple codes to the printer, you should also be able to send the more complicated printer control codes that are listed in Table 28-1 and Fig. 28-2. Most of these codes are preceded by ESC, so you will have to perform an extra step to get the printer to recognize them.

Let's look at the easy ones first. To turn condensed on you need to send ASCII code 15 to the printer. Open a file on the keyboard using COPY CON and while the file is open, type in the text and Control code shown below. This will demonstrate how Control code sequences can be used to set type styles.

```
A: \>COPY CON LPT1
<Alt-15>
This is a sample of the condensed type style on my printer.
THIS IS AN EXAMPLE OF UPPER-CASE CONDENSED TYPE.
<F6> <Return>

A: \>
```

The two lines should have printed on your printer in condensed mode. The example above set the condensed mode on, so if you send another file to the printer, it will also be printed in condensed mode. Create the following file to be sent to the printer:

```
A: \>COPY CON:TEST.TXT
CONDENSED
CONDENSED
<F6> <Return>

A: \>_
```

Now send the file to the printer by typing:

```
A: \>COPY TEST.TXT.LPT1
```

To set another type style on the printer, enter the following, which sets the double wide mode.

```
A : \>
COPY CON LPT1
<Alt-14>THIS IS A TEST OF ENLARGED
<F6> <Return>

A : \>_
```

The string is printed on the printer, but if you look at the printout you will notice that it doesn't look enlarged compared to what is shown in Fig. 28-1. The reason for this is that you haven't turned the compressed mode off yet and the printer is printing a combination of compressed and enlarged.

Table 28-1 indicates that Alt-18 is used to turn compressed off, so you will need to send this code to the printer if you want to print in the enlarged mode. If you look at the table, you will notice that the code used to set enlarged on (code Alt-14) is the one that turns itself off after every line. If you want to set enlarged on for more than one line, you'll have to send Esc-W1 to the printer.

Let's turn compressed off. The easiest way is to simply turn the printer off and then back on, which resets the printer to its default mode. To turn condensed off from the computer, type the following:

```
A : \>COPY CON LPT1
<Alt-18>
<F6> <Return>

A : \>_
```

You can check to see that condensed has been set to off by sending the file TEST.TXT to the printer again.

```
A : \>COPY TEST.TXT LPT1
```

Control Codes Preceded by Escape

Looking at Table 28-1, you will notice that the majority of the printer Control codes are preceded by Esc. To enter an Escape code, you can type Alt-155, which displays a cent sign on the screen. You can then place the appropriate Control code next to it. For example, the following file will print several different type styles on the printer.

```
A:\>COPY CON:PARTY.TXT
<Alt-14> <Alt-155>E    COMPANY PARTY

THE ANNUAL COMPANY PARTY WILL BE HELD SEPTEMBER 25th.

<Alt-155>F
<Alt-15>SIGN BELOW IF YOU WILL BE ATTENDING<Alt-18>
<F6> <Return>

A:\>_
```

In the example above you created a file that can be edited if necessary. The file contains embedded printer Control codes that will set type styles on the printer when copied to it. In the first line, double strike is set on (one-line-only mode) by entering Alt-14. Emphasized is then turned on by entering Alt-155 and E. (Note, E must be capitalized.) The first line of text is printed as a large heading. The next line is printed in enhanced mode because the enlarged mode turns itself off after the first line. In the third line, emphasized is turned off by entering Alt-155 (Escape) and F. The last line of the file is printed in condensed mode by typing Alt-15 before the line. Alt-18 is then entered to turn condensed off.

To send the file to the printer, type:

```
A:\>COPY PARTY.TXT LPT1
```

If you have an Epson FX-series printer, you can use the mode select control code. This code is the sequence ESC ! followed by the number of the type style code shown in Fig. 28-2.

You can see how to control the printer by sending the printer Control codes to it from the keyboard or embedded within a file. Next, we will discuss a way to make the whole process even easier.

Making Control Code Files

In this section, you will build a separate file for each of the printer Control codes. Once each code is in a file, you can concatenate the Control code files with text files to produce special effects. You can store these codes in a subdirectory if you wish in order to keep them separate from other files. To create a directory called PRNCDS, you would type:

```
A:\>MD \PRNCDS

A:\>CD \PRNCDS

A:\PRNCDS>_
```

Once inside the new directory, you can start creating each of the Control code files by entering the codes shown below. Remember to press F6 (or Ctrl-Z) and Return to close each file. We do not include all of the Control Codes here, only those you will find most useful.

File Name	Control Code	Explanation
WIDE	<Alt-155>W1	Turns enlarged on; use capital W
WIDEOFF	<Alt-155>W0	Turns enlarged off; use capital W
CONDENS	<Alt-15>	Turns condensed print on
CONDOFF	<Alt-18>	Turns condensed off
ULINEON	<Alt-155>-1	Turns underline on
ULINEOFF	<Alt-155>-0	Turns underline off
EMPHON	<Alt-155>E	Turns emphasized on
EMPHOFF	<Alt-155>F	Turns emphasized off
2STRKON	<Alt-155>G	Turns double strike on
2STRKOFF	<Alt-155>H	Turns double strike off
RESET	<Alt-155>@	Clears all modes

There are several ways to use the above Control code files. You can copy them to the printer to select or cancel any printer mode, or you can concatenate them with text files as we will demonstrate here. Create the following two files for use as an example.

```
A:\PRNCDS>COPY CON:FILE1.TXT
THIS IS FILE 1
THIS IS LINE 2 OF FILE 1
<F6> <Return>

A:\PRNCDS>COPY CON:FILE2.TXT
THIS IS FILE 2
THIS IS LINE 2 OF FILE 2
<F6> <Return>

A:\PRNCDS>_
```

Now issue the command shown below to concatenate the above two files with the printer Control code files. In this example, the first file will be printed enlarged emphasized, and the second file will be condensed emphasized.

```
A:\PRNCDS>COPY WIDE+EMPHON+FILE.TXT+WIDEOFF+CONDENS+FILE2.TXT+
          RESET LPT1
```

The command combines several files to create the final printed document. First, the enlarged and emphasized printer files are concatenated to FILE1.TXT. Next, enlarged is set off and condensed is set on by concatenating the proper printer Control files. The COPY command then sends the combined files to the printer.

Think about how you could use this concatenation feature with your text files and the printer Control codes. Most electronic spreadsheet programs allow you to save spreadsheets in special print files. Since these files are normally stored as ASCII text files, they can be combined with other text files and the printer Control codes we show here, producing an attractive document with multiple type styles.

A Printer Code Batch File

The following batch file uses many of the techniques described in Chaps. 25 and 26 combined with the Control codes covered in this chapter. To run the batch file, type **SETTYPE** on the command line, along with one of the parameters listed in the file. You can specify more than one type style on the command line to get a variety of styles. We have only included a few styles here so that the batch process does not execute too slowly. You can add more codes if you wish.

```
SETTYPE.BAT
ECHO OFF
IF "%1" = = "" GOTO HELP
ECHO SETTING PRINTER TYPESTYLES
GOTO %1
:LOOP
SHIFT
IF "%1" = = "" GOTO END
GOTO %1
:HELP
ECHO USE THE CODES BELOW AS PARAMETERS FOR SETTYPE
ECHO --------------------------------------------
ECHO WIDE (sets enlarged mode on)
ECHO COND (sets condensed mode on)
ECHO ULINE (sets underline mode on)
ECHO EMPH (sets emphasized mode on)
ECHO BOLD (sets double strike on)
ECHO RESET (resets printer to normal mode)
GOTO END
:WIDE
ECHO (Alt-155) W1 > LPT1
GOTO LOOP
:COND
ECHO (Alt-15) > LPT1
GOTO LOOP
:ULINE
ECHO (Alt-155)-1 > LPT1
GOTO LOOP
:EMPH
ECHO (Alt-155)E > LPT1
GOTO LOOP
:BOLD
ECHO (Alt-155)G > LPT1
GOTO LOOP
:RESET
ECHO (Alt-155)@ > LPT1
:END
```

29

Communications

Your personal computer communicates to the outside world through its COM or communications ports. DOS allows you and your programs to talk to these devices, which are usually plugs attached to the back of your computer. Keep in mind that not all PCs are equipped with serial ports, or asynchronous communications adaptors as IBM refers to them. An asynchronous adapter is standard on the IBM PC/XT.

Through the asynchronous (COM) port you can connect directly to another computer or link with a modem, which in turn links to the telephone lines and a computer at a remote location. The remote computer may be another PC or your company's mainframe computer. You can also connect to local or national bulletin boards, banks, Western Union, and The Source.

With DOS you can have two serial ports which are assigned the device names COM1 and COM2. You can set the operational parameters of both ports by using the DOS MODE command. DOS-2 also has a command called CTTY, which allows you to run your computer from a remote location.

What Is Serial Communications

There are two ways in which your computer talks to the outside world—parallel communications and serial communications. Parallel connections are usually used to connect printers. Serial connections are usually used for communicating with other computers through modems or direct connections.

One of the main differences between the two interfaces is the way they transmit signals over their cables. Internally, your computer recognizes

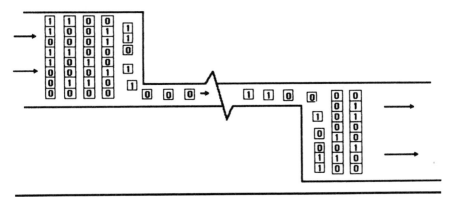

Figure 29-1 In serial communications the bits are sent across the line one at a time and reassembled on the receiving side.

each character as an 8-bit code in which each bit can be either on or off. (Note that the standard ASCII characters use only 7 bits; see App. A.) In other words, each character is a string of zeros or ones placed together to form a code the computer understands. For instance, your computer knows the letter A as 01000001 and the letter B as 01000010. To print the letter A, the computer sends the above code through the interface to the printer. To send an A to a remote computer, 01000001 is sent through the COM port. How this code is sent through the interface is one of the main differences between serial and parallel communications.

Figure 29-1 illustrates a serial connection. Here, the zeros and ones are sent serially to the printer, one at a time, over a single wire. Figure 29-2 illustrates the parallel connection. Here the signals are sent over eight wires, each signal arriving at the printer at the same time. The parallel connection may at first appear superior because each bit needed to form a character arrives at the printer at the same time. The parallel connection, however, cannot exceed 10 to 12 feet without a loss in signal quality

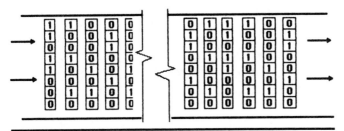

Figure 29.2 A parallel connection sends all 8 bits at once.

because the bits may become "out of sync" as they pass through the connection. Serial interfacing, then, becomes a superior interfacing method for devices that are at a distance from each other or when you need to communicate over the phone lines.

It doesn't matter which connection you use to install a printer. You might think that serial interface would be too slow for a printer, but in reality most printers are so slow that they can never keep up with the speed at which data is sent to them. Parallel connections are superior when you have two high-speed devices connected to each other. The components inside your computer are connected in parallel, transmitting data at the highest speeds possible.

When transmitting over the phone lines, you must use serial interfacing since the phone lines use only one wire for transmitting data. To connect to a phone line you will need a modem. A modem is a device that converts signals from your computer to signals that can be transferred over the phone lines. A modem is usually also required at the other end of the phone connection to convert this data back to a form that the receiving computer can understand.

Not all communications between computers require modems. If you have two computers close to each other, they can be directly connected with a serial cable. Connecting computers in this way is a common method that is used to transfer files from one type of computer to another. A modem is not required because the computers are connected directly together and understand each other's signals. A special cable is required, however, which we will discuss in a minute.

Communicating with Modems

To communicate with other computers, you will first need a serial interface card, or an asynchronous communications adapter. This is a card that fits into one of the slots on the back of your computer. The card allows you to attach a modem to your computer. Figure 29-3 shows how this installation is made.

When two computers are connected together or a computer is connected to a modem, certain standards of communications are required. Otherwise, one computer might try to send something when another is not ready to receive it. The standard used by PCs is known as RS-232-C. This standard was established by the Electronic Industries Association (EIA) in 1969. RS stands for Recommended Standard. 232 is the identification number for the standard and the C represents the latest revision. Briefly, under this standard an interface can have up to 25 wires connected between 2 devices. Each of the wires is used for a specific purpose such as

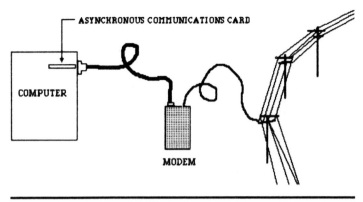

ASYNCHRONOUS COMMUNICATIONS CARD

COMPUTER

MODEM

Figure 29-3   Connecting a modem.

transmitting data or sending status codes. Most of the pins have been assigned a function by the EIA standard.

In most cases, all you will have to do to communicate with another computer through a modem is simply connect a standard RS 232-C cable between your computer and the modem. Everything else should already be set to the standards set by RS-232-C. The cable should have a DB-25 connector at each end. This connector has the 25-pin connections described above. In some cases, you may need another type of connector, such as a DB-9. You should check both connectors on your equipment before buying the cable. Connectors have gender and will be either female or male. Almost all modems have female connectors, so you will need a male connector on one side of the cable. The serial card on your system may have either a male or female connector. Once again, check your configuration before buying.

Modems come in several varieties. Most modern modems are known as direct connect modems. They use a standard phone connector to connect directly into the phone lines. Modems for microcomputers come in either 300 baud or 1200 baud. This is the speed at which your modem communicates over the phone lines. You will have to set your computer so that its "talks" at the same speed as your modem. This is usually set by a communications software program or can be set with the DOS MODE command.

Direct Connection Between Two Computers

In some cases, you will want to make a direct connection to another computer. This computer may be in the same room or close enough that a

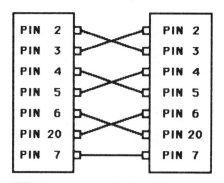

Figure 29-4 Crossover cable for connecting two IBM personal computers.

modem is not required. Many times files will need to be transferred from one computer to another. You may want to transfer files on one type of disk format, say CP/M, to your DOS formatted diskettes. The best way to do this is transfer the files directly between computers. In the next chapter we will discuss file transferring in more detail.

To connect two computers together you will need a null-modem cable, or modem eliminator as it is sometimes called. This cable makes each computer think that it is communicating with a modem. Basically, the cable reverses the connection of several wires, so that one computer's transmit data line is connected to the other computer's receive data line. Figure 29-4 illustrates the wiring of a null modem cable.

When computers are connected in this way, a much faster baud rate may be used (baud rate is a measure of the speed that data moves between devices). In some cases, a baud rate of up to 9600 baud may be used, as compared to a maximum rate of 1200 baud for most microcomputer modems.

Communications Software

In most cases, when connecting two computers together, you will need communications software to handle the "handshaking" between the two computers. Handshaking refers to the ability of the computers to signal each other when they are ready to send or receive data. Communications software should also have the capabilities of "uploading" and "download-ing" files. This refers to their ability to be able to send files stored on disk to another computer and to store files on disk that are being sent from another computer. Software that does not have this capability should not be considered.

Using the MODE Command

The DOS MODE command allows you to initialize and set the parameters of a communications port. With it, you can set the baud rate, parity, data bits, and stop bits of either COM1 or COM2. For modem communications on the PC, this will be either 300 or 1200 baud. When issuing MODE to configure a COM port, you *must* specify the baud rate.

Parity is a state set to either N (none), O (odd), or E (even) and is used to perform error detection. The default becomes E if you do not specify parity when issuing the MODE command. The number of data bits is either 7 or 8, with the default being 7. This is the number of bits used to represent an ASCII character. Stop bits represent the end of transmission of a character. The default is 2 if the baud rate is 110, otherwise the default is 1.

To issue the mode command, simply type MODE followed by the name of the COM port you want to use. The default values for all other parameters will be taken if not specified. For example, the following command will initialize COM1 to 1200 baud, with even parity, 7 data bits, and 1 stop bit:

```
MODE COM1:1200
```

CTTY: A Unique DOS Command

The CTTY command (change console) allows you to operate your computer from a remote location. CTTY changes the standard input and output console to an auxiliary console. For instance, you can access data on a PC you have at work (referred to here as the host computer) from a PC you have at home (remote terminal). CTTY allows you to operate in full DOS mode from the remote computer. The full set of DOS commands will work from the remote terminal with the exception of COPY and BASIC, which could give you some problems. For instance, when using the COPY command to create files, as in COPY CON, you must type COPY COMx:FILE NAME, instead.

Certain keyboard keys don't work at all. For instance, if you are using a PC as a remote terminal, the Function keys and the Arrow keys will not work. This could cause some problems with editors like EDLIN. Another problem occurs with some communications programs—pressing Ctrl-Break can knock you completely out of your program and destroy the connection.

If you plan to use CTTY, it's a good idea to temporarily set up both pieces of equipment next to each other and experiment with the commands before you go remote. Find out what you can and can't do and be careful not to press Ctrl-Break, a habit you may have picked up trying to stop scrolling displays. To set up your equipment for direct communications, use the modem-eliminator cable described above. We were able to operate at up to 4800 baud when directly connected in this manner. We did experience some problems at 9600 baud.

To use CTTY with a direct connection, first set up the host computer by initializing COM1 and setting CTTY. Type the following:

    MODE COM1:1200
    CTTY COM1

The cursor will sit there, doing nothing. If you have a "dumb" terminal directly connected, the DOS prompt will appear on the remote terminal. You can now operate the host computer with normal DOS commands. If you are using a PC as a remote terminal, you will first have to get it into terminal mode. Various communications programs such as PC-TALK and IBM's Asynchronous Communications Support software will allow you to do this. Once in terminal mode, you can operate the host computer.

If you are using modems, you will first have to set the modem to autoanswer (AA) mode. Once the host is set to automatically answer, you can call it from the remote terminal and operate as if in normal DOS. To do this, type the following at the host computer. The example shown below is for a Hays-Stack SmartModem. Once the connection is established, you will be able to operate from the remote site.

    MODE COM1:1200
    COPY CON COM1   (sets HAYS SMARTMODEM register 0 to the auto-
    AT S0 = 1   answer state)
    <F6> <Return>
    CTTY COM1

30

File Types and File Transferring

There are many types of files. The DOS command files are programs that only the computer can use. Text files, on the other hand, contain standard text characters that can be displayed and read on the screen. Standard ASCII text files created on one computer can even be read by other computers. We will discuss files and file types here and then discuss how you can transfer your files to other computers.

Text Files

Characters entered into text files usually follow the ASCII coding scheme shown in App. A. Under this scheme, each character is given a code that is recognized by any computer that uses the ASCII standard. If you have a file that contains standard ASCII characters, you will be able to transfer this file to another computer and use it in the normal way. Almost all major computer manufacturers today support the ASCII format, so the standard ASCII text file has become a medium for transferring information among computers. When you connect your computer to a modem and communicate with another computer over the phone lines, the computers are most likely using the ASCII standard or some derivative of it. If you've owned a computer previous to the PC you are using now, you can use the files created with this computer, as long as they are normal text files that follow the ASCII format. Some alterations may be required, but in general the files should be compatible. The topic of this chapter is how to go about transferring these files.

The files you created in previous chapters using EDLIN and COPY CON are standard ASCII text files. These files contain the characters coded 32 through 126 in the ASCII chart. Some word processors store their text in standard ASCII files but place special formatting characters in the file that are not in the range of the normal text characters. You may have trouble transferring these files from computer to computer or over the phone lines and therefore will have to remove the special codes before doing so.

WordStar, for example, stores characters in its files in an 8-bit instead of a 7-bit format. If you display a WordStar file on the screen using TYPE, you will notice that some of the text is not recognizable. WordStar files can be transferred to other computers but can only be read by another WordStar program unless you make alterations to the file.

BASIC programs can be stored as ASCII files and are transferrable to other computers in this format. Since many computers use the BASIC developed by Microsoft, your BASIC program files can be used on a variety of different computers. To store a program created with the BASIC interpreter in ASCII format, you will need to specify the A (ASCII) SAVE option (refer to the SAVE command in the BASIC manual).

Files containing ASCII characters should transfer to other computers with little trouble. Once the file has been transferred, you may need to make some alterations before it is useful. Carriage returns and formatting codes sometimes cause a problem and will need to be removed from the file before it can be used. There are programs available from user's groups and computer stores that will do this.

Recently, several file interchange formats have been developed for microcomputers. The first of these was the DIF format, which became popular with VisiCalc and is used primarily for spreadsheet files. DIF files contain the ASCII representation of the spreadsheet and contain printable data only, not the formulas and relationships of the original worksheet. Another interchange format is the Symbolic Link (SYLK) developed by Microsoft, which will store the original formulas and relationships of a spreadsheet file for use on another machine. This format is mainly used for Microsoft's Multiplan spreadsheet program.

Program Files

DOS program files have the extension COM and EXE. The difference between these two is not important here—but in a nutshell, COM programs load faster and require less space in memory than EXE files. EXE files are more flexible in their use of the facilities of the computer. Any COM or EXE file name can be executed by simply typing it on the command line. Most of the command files supplied on your DOS disk are COM files. Off-the-shelf programs are usually COM or EXE files.

COM and EXE files cannot be transferred to another computer without special handling. It is unlikely that you would want to transfer these files in the first place because the receiving computer may not run them without special modifications.

Transferring Files

If you owned another computer before buying your DOS-compatible computer, you probably have a lot of files that you would like to use on your new computer. If you used Microsoft BASIC on your previous computer, most of the BASIC program files can be used with the BASIC that comes with DOS (BASIC is supplied with most PC and MS-DOS compatible computers). You may also have a need to exchange files with other users or to retrieve files from bulletin board services and users' clubs. There are several ways to transfer these files to the PC.

One way to exchange files between computers is to connect them together through the phone lines, as described in Chap. 29, and send files between them with a communications program capable of handling files. This process, however, should not be undertaken if you have a lot of files. It is meant for people who want to download an occasional file from a friend or bulletin board. Phone communications between microcomputers usually occurs at 1200 baud, a communications speed which is too slow for transferring a large number of files in a reasonable period of time.

To transfer files between computers, you will need a communications program that is capable of sending and receiving files. PC-TALK is a program available to all PC users under a unique concept called Freeware. The Freeware concept allows you to make as many copies of the program as you like without infringing on copyrights. You can distribute these copies to anyone who needs a communications program. If you like and use the program, you are encouraged to send a $25 donation, which entitles you to updates as they become available. The program is available from most users' groups or from Freeware, The Headlands Press, P.O. Box 862, Tiburon, CA 94920. Complete documentation is on the disk as an ASCII document file. PC-TALK supports file uploading and downloading, plus the ability to transfer COM and EXE files, if necessary.

If you need to transfer a large number of files to your PC, the direct connect method discussed in Chap. 29 is best. You will need to place the two computers next to each other and connect them with the modem-eliminator cable illustrated in Fig. 29-4. Once the connections are made, you will still need a communications programs in each computer to handle the file transfers. PC-TALK is a good program to use on the IBM for transferring files; you will need another commmunications program for the other computer if it is not PC compatible.

There are several commercially available programs that handle file transferring. One program called MOVE-IT, (available from Woolf Software Systems, 23842 Archwood Street, Canoga Park, CA 91307) allows you to transfer files to and from noncompatible computers using wild-card characters. For instance, you can transfer all files on a disk by specifying the *.* option. Another program is Xeno-Copy, (available from Vertex Systems, 7950 West 4th Street, Los Angeles, CA 90048), which allows you to read or write many different disk formats on your own computer. A large number of different disk formats and operating systems are supported. The file transfer takes place in your PC without additional hardware, and the actual disk is all you need.

Collecting Free Software

If you own a modem, you can begin building a software collection by retrieving files from your community bulletin board or from other sources such as The Source. Most of the programs found on bulletin boards are in public domain and are available for noncommercial use. Since many of the programs are created by hobbyist who developed the programs for special applications, you will usually find interesting and useful software.

Most programs available on bulletin boards are either in ASCII format or in a binary format. Many of the ASCII format files are BASIC programs and many of the binary format files are COM and EXE files that will require special software for transfer. If you have a copy of PC-TALK III, you will be able to transfer files in binary format. Most COM and EXE program files have an accompanying document file that explains how they are used. These document files will usually have the same file name, but will have an extension of DOC.

Bulletin boards provide a unique way for you to build up a free library of software for the cost of a phone call. For more information, contact your local users' group. For information on utilities, refer to App. H.

31

An Introduction to BASIC

The purpose of this chapter is to get you to do something you may not have done otherwise: computer programming. This is an introduction to the BASIC programming language. We hope to persuade you that programming is easy as well as fun. Once you get started, we know you will become enthused about the capabilities of BASIC and the control you can have over your computer.

This chapter will introduce you to Microsoft BASIC. This may seem an odd subject to find in a book about computer operating systems, but almost all versions of PC and MS-DOS come with BASIC, so we must at least introduce you to it. Of course, we do not have the space to cover the language in full detail, but the topics we cover here will get you started.

There are many good tutorial BASIC books available, many of which are written specifically for the BASIC available on the PC. You should understand that the BASIC manual that comes with your computer operating system is a reference manual. It is not designed to teach you how to program; instead it will help you use the language as you become familiar with it. If you know the language, these books are invaluable. If you are new to programming and the BASIC language, then consult one of the BASIC tutorials.

What Is BASIC

BASIC stands for Beginner's All-purpose Symbolic Instruction Code. It was originally developed at Dartmouth in the 1960s, but it has grown and expanded much since then. In a nutshell, BASIC was designed as an easy-to-learn language that could be used to teach programming. It has grown in popularity among computer users who do not need a professional programming language such as Fortran, Pascal, or C. BASIC *is* easy to use and easy to learn. The best part is that it comes free with most versions of DOS.

A computer that can't be programmed is like a tape recorder that doesn't record. Programming allows you to bring out the real power of the computer. With BASIC, you can design programs to do everything from playing games to keeping track of your stock portfolio.

Computer programmers spend many hours discussing the benefits of one programming language over another. Although BASIC provides a quick and easy way to program, many programmers find it cumbersome. If you are committed to learning how to program and want a sophisticated language, then you may want to look at the structured languages like Pascal. On the other hand, if your intentions are not so sophisticated, BASIC is an excellent language. Over the years it has grown in sophistication and power. Many experienced programmers have commented on the power and features that Microsoft BASIC has attained compared to other versions of BASIC.

One of the reasons BASIC is so attractive is that it is an interpretive language. In other words, you can write a program and run it on the spot. BASIC will interpret the statements you type in and convert them to the code the computer needs. If there are problems (commonly referred to as bugs), you can stop the program, fix the bugs, and run it again. Other languages like Pascal do not have this feature. You must first write the code for the program with an editor. Then, you exit the editor and pass the text file containing the program code through a compiler. A compiler interprets the statements in the file to those the computer understands. If you run into problems along the way or when running the program, you must go back into the editor, alter the program, and then recompile it. All of this takes time. The advantage of a compiled language is that you end up with a program that executes much faster and is easier to debug or modify.

Many people feel that the advantages of compiled languages do not outweigh the advantages of interpreted languages. The convenience of being able to see small programs or segments of your program run immediately has helped keep BASIC alive and well. Many BASIC programmers are happy with the language and simply don't have the need for a professional language. Generally, if you're writing small programs or just an occasional program, BASIC is for you.

Pick up any computer magazine and you will probably find a BASIC program listing somewhere inside. Since BASIC is similar among all types of computers, it has become a sort of universal language. Owners of IBM PCs and most owners of compatible systems have the ability to use this code on their computers. In this respect, we can all share programs, either through the magazines, books, or users' clubs. BASIC programs written on other types of computers may even run on your PC with some modifications. Many experienced programmers have spent long hours developing BASIC programs that you may be able to use, and they make this code available through various sources.

Where to Start, Getting Information

There are several good books available that teach BASIC in a step-by-step manner. Courses are available on many campuses (if seats are left). Many books are available that contain prewritten program code. Not only does this provide you with a cheap source for programs, but you will learn a lot about the language by entering the code into your computer.

The best way to learn the language is to experiment with it. Start out with simple 5- to 10-line programs that don't do much of anything except help you learn. One of the nice features of BASIC is that you can easily expand a simple program by adding more lines to it.

The Steps to Writing a Program

There are several ways to write computer programs. The common method with professional languages is to write the code for the program with an editor. BASIC comes with a built-in editor, so we can simply go into BASIC and start writing programs.

To get into BASIC, insert the disk containing BASICA.COM or BASICA.EXE. (Note: Although there are two version of BASIC, we only talk about the advanced version, BASICA, here.) To start BASIC type:

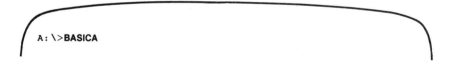

```
A:\>BASICA
```

You will see the BASIC prompt Ok and a blinking cursor. At this point, you can start entering your program. BASIC actually has two operating modes, direct mode and programming mode. In direct mode, you can enter a statement, and it will be immediately executed. In programming mode, all statement are preceded by a line number. These statements will not execute until you run the program. To try direct mode, type the following:

PRINT 10 + 10

The answer appears immediately on the screen. Now, type the following program on the screen. Each statement is preceded by a line number.

```
10 X = 10
20 PRINT "THE VALUE OF X IS",X
```

Now run the program by typing **RUN** and pressing **Return.** The statement in between the quotation marks is printed on the screen, followed by the value of X. In line 10 we set the variable X equal to 10. You can easily add more statements to this program by inserting them between existing lines or just adding more lines to the end of the program. For instance, type the following line.

```
15 X = X + 25
```

Execute the new program by typing **RUN.** The line tells us that X is now 35. The new line, 15, demonstrates several things. First of all, you were able to insert a line in between lines 10 and 20 by simply picking a number between the two. The reason we increment by 10 initially is so that we can easily add statements to our programs at any time. In line 15, we are adding 25 to the value that has already been assigned to the variable X. List the program by typing LIST:

```
LIST
10 X = 10
20 X = X + 25
30 PRINT "THE VALUE OF X IS EQUAL TO",X
Ok_
```

The three lines above are considered a BASIC program, even though they don't do much of anything. The steps to writing and executing a program are simple. You first load the BASIC interpreter—by loading BASICA instead of BASIC, you will have access to Advanced BASIC, which is a much more powerful version, although it requires a little more memory.

The next step is to begin writing your program, assuming that you have one planned. One of the advantages of BASIC is that you don't have to do a lot of planning when writing a program. Although it is not considered a good programming habit, you can write a simple skeleton of a program and then add finishing touches to it later. This type of programming, however, tends to make your programs less compact and efficient.

After you have written the program, you can run it by typing RUN. Usually, before running a program, you will want to save it to disk, especially if it is a long program. The SAVE command will write the code to the disk. Most programs will require some debugging before they run the way you planned. A program will require debugging if BASIC statements are spelled wrong or the flow of the program is not correct.

The Components of a Program

There are a large number of BASIC statements, commands, and functions which we will not cover here. You can refer to your BASIC manual or a suitable BASIC tutorial for more information. However, all programs perform certain things. Programs can ask for input and print or display output, loop indefinitely or for a specified amount of time, branch to other parts of the program, and make decisions. We will briefly cover each of these here.

The program we wrote earlier outputs data to the screen. The output was defined in the program when we set X to the values in lines 10 and 20. Adding the following line to the program will allow you to assign the value of X when the program is running. Note that by typing line 10 over, you erase the old contents.

10 INPUT X

After typing the above line, list the program by typing **LIST.** Notice that line 10 now contains our new statement. Run the program by typing RUN:

```
RUN
?_
```

The program is waiting for you to input the value of X and displays the question mark as a prompt. Enter a value and press Return. The program will add 25 to the value you gave to X and print the results. You can run the program over and over, supplying different values each time.

Let's create a loop in the program. Add the following line:

40 GOTO 10

Now run the program again. Enter a value and press Return. The value is displayed, and the question mark appears again. The program is running itself over again because the statement we added in line 40 is causing it to loop back to the beginning of the program at line 10. To break out of a loop, press Ctrl-Break.

You can add a statement to the program that will make it stop looping if you enter 0. This provides you with a way to break out of the program without having to resort to Ctrl-Break. Add the following lines to your program. Notice that you still have lines available between lines 10 and 15.

```
12 IF X = 0 THEN 50
50 PRINT "PROGRAM STOPPED BY USER"
```

Now run the program. When you want to stop, enter 0 at the question mark prompt. The statement in line 50 will be displayed. The IF statement in line 12 is known as a conditional jump. In other words, the statement will jump to line 50 only if X is equal to 0.

Let's try a completely different program. First, you must clear the old program from memory. Type **NEW** at the BASIC prompt to clear the program. To prove that it has been erased, you can type **LIST**. Nothing will appear.

Type in the following lines and run the program.

```
10 X = 5
20 PRINT "A LOOP HAS OCCURRED"
30 X = X - 1
40 IF X = 0 THEN 60
50 GOTO 20
60 PRINT "END OF PROGRAM"
RUN
A LOOP HAS OCCURRED
A LOOP HAS OCCURRED
A LOOP HAS OCCURRED
A LOOP HAS OCCURRED
A LOOP HAS OCCURRED
END OF PROGRAM
Ok
```

This program is referred to as a decrementing loop. It executes five times because it subtracts 1 from X every time it goes through the loop and breaks out of the loop when X becomes 0.

You can change the number of times the program loops by changing the value of X. To demonstrate the editing capabilities of BASIC, type the following to change line 10 and the value of X.

```
LIST 10
 10  X  = 5
Ok_
```

Use the Arrow keys to move up to the 5 in line 10 and change it to some other number. After changing the number, you *must* press Return or the change will not become permanent.

You can have the program ask the user for the value of X by replacing line 10 with the following line.

10 INPUT X

We have only brushed the surface. There are so many things you can do with BASIC that we could never cover them here. We hope that you've taken the plunge and are off to a good start. Explore!

Chapter

32

Using BASIC from DOS

You should be somewhat familiar with BASIC before you begin this chapter, but whatever your level, you will find the techniques shown here useful.

Executing a BASIC Program from DOS

To run a BASIC program directly from DOS, enter the name of the program after the BASIC command. First determine what level of BASIC your program requires. The following command will run the SAMPLES program supplied with IBM PC-DOS using BASICA.

BASICA SAMPLES

The next command starts the program if it is on the disk in drive B:

BASICA B:SAMPLES

You can also start BASIC from another drive and have it run a program that resides on the default drive:

B:BASICA SAMPLES

I/O Redirection in BASIC

Statements in BASIC programs that normally request input from the operator may receive their input from outside the program. You can build a file that contains the responses to BASIC statements like INPUT, INPUT$, INKEY$, and LINE INPUT and direct the data from this file into a BASIC program. Directing data into a BASIC program follows the rules of standard input. You can also direct the standard output (responses normally displayed on the screen) to a file. The following format is used to redirect input and output:

BASIC file name [<standard input] [>] [>standard output]

The following examples will help explain how this works. Data read by INPUT, INPUT$, INKEY$, and LINE INPUT in the program COMPUTE in the example below will come from the keyboard. Data written by the PRINT statements in the program COMPUTE will be directed to the file COLLECT.DAT.

BASICA COMPUTE > COLLECT.DAT

In the next example, the standard input statements in the program will receive their responses from the data in the file DATA.TXT.

BASICA COMPUTE < DATA.TXT

The next example illustrates a combination of both input and output. The program COMPUTE gets its input from the file DATA.TXT and sends all output to the file COLLECT.DAT.

BASICA COMPUTE < DATA.TXT > COLLECT.DAT

The last example appends data to the COLLECT.DAT file, assuming that COLLECT.DAT has been used to collect data from a previous run of the program and contains data from that run.

BASICA COMPUTE < DATA.TXT >> COLLECT.DAT

The following example will illustrate how data is input to a BASIC program. Each line in a data file acts as one input response to the program. Create the following data file:

```
COPY CON:DATA.TXT
2943.34
3253.12
<F6> <Return>
```

then create the following BASIC program by entering the keystrokes shown below.

```
BASIC
Ok
10 INPUT X
20 INPUT Y
30 PRINT X + Y
SAVE"COMPUTE
SYSTEM
```

To run the program and direct the input responses from DATA.TXT into the program, type the following:

BASIC COMPUTE < DATA.TXT

As input is read from DATA.TXT, it is displayed on the screen. The resulting addition of the two numbers requested by the program is then displayed:

```
?2943.32
?3253.12
 6196.46
```

To see how the program reacts when you direct the output to a file, enter the following commands. The TYPE command allows you to see the contents of TEMP.FIL after it receives data from the BASIC program.

BASIC COMPUTE < DATA.TXT > TEMP.FIL
TYPE TEMP.FIL

Practical Use of I/O Redirection with Basic

Normally, when a program is being developed in BASIC, it goes through several phases of debugging. A section of the program is built and debugged and then more code is added. While debugging the program, you will occasionally run it to see how it operates. If the program requires a lot of input, you will have to answer the input questions every time you run it unless you use the technique shown here.

Using standard input, you can direct responses from a file into the program. The following example will demonstrate how this is done. The program below asks for a set of variables and then does some calculations with the variable. Assume that you are trying to debug a section of the program that performs the calculation and have already designed the input part of the program. You have placed a set of responses to the program's input statements in the file TEST.DAT.

```
10 'COMPUTE: a program to calculate something.
20 INPUT "Enter your name"; NAME$
30 INPUT "What is your age"; AGE
40 INPUT "What is the current date"; DATE$
50 INPUT "Enter first parameter"; FIRST
60 INPUT "Enter second parameter"; SECOND
70 INPUT "Enter third parameter"; THIRD
   .
   .
   .
THE REST OF THE PROGRAM . . .
```

Here are the contents of TEST.DAT:

```
TEST.DAT
Joe
40
04-14-84
1234
5678
9012
```

The following command will direct the responses in the TEST.DAT file to the input statements in the program:

```
BASIC COMPUTE < TEST.DAT
```

Creating Your Own Filters

Since standard input and output can be directed to and from BASIC programs, you can use this feature to create your own filters. You will recall from previous chapters that a filter takes data and acts on it in some way, producing altered output. For instance, you can input the contents of a file to the SORT filter and direct the sorted output to another file.

All of the filter programs we show here input one character at a time except ADDLINES.BAS, which inputs a line at a time. The reason for inputting one character at a time instead of a line is that commas in lines cause BASIC to see the line as more than one input and to display the message "?Redo from start." In ADDLINES.BAS you can input a line at a time because the input is composed of graphics normally not containing commas.

To run any of the programs, enter its name as a parameter following the BASIC command on the command line. Use the I/O redirection symbols to input your data files into the programs.

The PAGE Filter Program

The PAGE filter program performs a simple but important task. It prints normal text files like those created with EDLIN and COPY CON, one page at a time, with top and bottom margins and page numbers. The program is as follows:

```
05 'PAGE (prints a text file in paged format with page
        numbers)
10 'by TOM SHELDON
20 '-----------------------------------------------------------
30 ON ERROR GOTO 170                    'checks for end of input
40 FOR BLANK = 1 to 6:LPRINT:NEXT               'beginning margin
50 FOR PAGELOOP = 1 to 54                'print 54 lines per page
60 X$ = INPUT$(1)                          'get first character
70 IF X$ = CHR$(13) THEN GOTO 100   'go to 170 at end of line
80 TEXT$ = TEXT$ + X$                'build line to be printed
90 GOTO 60                           'get more characters
100 LPRINT TEXT$;                        'print completed line
110 TEXT$ = ""                                       'erase it
120 NEXT PAGELOOP                             'go get a new line
130 PAGENUM = PAGENUM + 1              'increment page number
140 LPRINT:LPRINT:LPRINT:LPRINT TAB(35) PAGENUM       'print pg #
150 FOR BLANK = 1 TO 8 :LPRINT:NEXT               'advance paper
160 GOTO 50                               'start another page
170 RESUME 180         'hey, there's still a line in the buffer!
180 LPRINT                                         'print it
190 END
```

We leave the task of tracing the contents of the program to you. Basically (no pun intended), the program assumes that a page has 66 lines and prints 54 lines of text, placing 6 blank spaces at the top and bottom of each page, along with a page number.

To use the PAGE program, simply specify the name of the file to be paged on the command line. For instance, type:

BASICA PAGE < MYFILE.TXT

The CAPS Filter Program

CAPS converts any standard ASCII text file of the type that is created by EDLIN and COPY CON to uppercase. More specifically, the characters a through z are converted to uppercase; all others are unaffected. The most important use for the CAPS filter is to convert files to uppercase so they can be searched and sorted more efficiently by the DOS FIND and SORT commands. The following will explain why this is so. Suppose that you wanted to find all instances of the word "the" in a file. Typing the command shown below would only find "the," not "The" or "THE." You would have to run the FIND filter again to locate every occurrence of the word.

To use the CAPS filter, specify it by name on the command line with the BASIC command. Use I/O redirection to specify the file to be capitalized. You should direct the output into another file. In the example below the capitalized output is directed to the file TEMP.DAT.

    BASICA CAPS < TEXT.DAT > TEMP.DAT

The next example uses the piping feature to direct the output from CAPS into the FIND filter.

    BASICA CAPS < TEXT.DAT ¦ FIND "COMPUTER" > TEMP.DAT

The CAPS program is shown below. Line 110 of the program adds 95 to the ASCII value of the specified character, producing the uppercase version of the character.

```
05 ' CAPS (converts standard text files to uppercase)
10 ' by Tom Sheldon
20 ' ------------------------------------------------------------
30 ON ERROR GOTO 190                    'check for end of input
40 X$ = INPUT$(1)          'get a character from standard input
50 IF X$ = CHR$(13) THEN 150            'check for end of line
60 '
70 '        check for characters that don't need to be converted
80 IF ASC(X$) < 97 THEN 120             'check for low ASCII
90 IF ASC(X$) > 123 THEN 120            'check for high ASCII
100 '
110 X$ = CHR$((ASC(X$) AND 95))      'convert a-z to uppercase
120 UPPER$ = UPPER$ + X$                'add character to line
130 GOTO 40                     'go back and get another character
140 '
150 X$ = INPUT$(1)                      'throw out line feed
160 PRINT UPPER$                        'print completed line
170 UPPER$ = ""                         'erase old line
180 GOTO 40                             'go get another
190 END
```

The ADDLINES Filter

In Chap. 16, you created a menu frame by using the graphics characters available on the IBM PC (and on some compatibles). Graphics screens are easily created with EDLIN by using its REPLACE command to replace dummy characters that were entered into a file with the COPY CON command. Creating screen graphics in BASIC, however, is another matter. The line number and the PRINT statement must be entered before the graphics string, which offsets the whole line, sometimes causing it to wrap around to the next line. This can make it hard to actually see what you are creating.

The ADDLINES filter program is an alternative method of creating screen graphics. You can use the full screen features of COPY CON and the editing features of EDLIN to create the graphics screen. Then, using ADDLINES, you can add the line numbers and PRINT statements to each line in the file, making it suitable for merging into a BASIC program.

To use the ADDLINES filter, type it in as a parameter following the BASIC command on the command line as shown below:

BASIC ADDLINES < FRAME.PIC > TEMP

Here is the program listing:

```
05 'ADDLINES  (add BASIC statement numbers and print statements
10 '                           to extended ASCII graphics screens.)
20 'By Tom Sheldon
30 '----------------------------------------------------------------
40 ON ERROR GOTO 100                        'check for end of input
50 NUMBER = 200 'starting statement number (can be any number)
60 PRINT NUMBER; "PRINT ";CHR$(34);      'build statement & line
                                                            number
70 INPUT "", GRAPHICS$                              'erase old line
80 NUMBER = NUMBER + 1          'increase statement line number
90 GOTO 60                               'go get another line
100 END
```

Encrypting and Decrypting files

The next two filters work together. ENCRYPT is used to make a file unreadable and DECRYPT converts the file back to its readable state. The method used to ENCRYPT a file is to add 128 to the ASCII value of each character in the file. This will convert each character to its related character in the extended ASCII set (ASCII 128 through 256). You cannot use any value other than 128 or some characters will be converted to

ASCII control codes, thus corrupting the file. This encryption method is not meant to be completely secure. It is analogous a locked desk drawer that keeps honest people honest.

DECRYPT reverses the effect of ENCRYPT by subtracting 128 from the ASCII code for each character in the file. You can use DECRYPT to read a file or direct the reconverted output back into the original file.

The following example illustrates encryption and decryption of the file FINANCE.DAT. The program files are listed after the example.

BASIC ENCRYPT < FINANCE.DAT > TEMP.DAT

BASIC DECRYPT < TEMP.DAT > FINANCE.DAT

```
05  ' ENCRYPT              (converts text file to unreadable text)
10  '                      (use DECRYPT to reconvert file)
20  ' By Tom Sheldon
30  '-------------------------------------------------------------
40  ON ERROR GOTO 140                  'check for end of input
50  X$  = INPUT$(1)                    'get a character
60  IF X$  = CHR$(13) THEN 100         'check for end of a line
70  X$  = CHR$((ASC(X$) + 128))  'convert character to high ASCII
80  TEXT$ = TEXT$ + X$                      'add to the line
90  GOTO 50                            'go get more characters
100 X$  = INPUT$(1)                    'discard line feed
110 PRINT TEXT$                        'print the line
120 TEXT$  = ""                        'erase it
130 GOTO 50                            'start next line
140 END
```

```
05  ' DECRYPT (converts encrypted files back to readable form)
10  ' By Tom Sheldon
20  '----------------------------------------------------
30  ON ERROR GOTO 130                  'check for end of input
40  X$  = INPUT$(1)                    'get a character
50  IF X$  = CHR$(13) THEN 90          'check for end of a line
60  X$  = CHR$((ASC(X$) - 128))  'convert character to low ASCII
70  TEXT$  = TEXT$ + X$                     'add to the line
80  GOTO 40                            'go get more characters
90  X$  = INPUT$(1)                    'discard line feed
100 PRINT TEXT$                        'print the line
110 TEXT$  = ""                        'erase it
120 GOTO 40                            'start next line
130 END
```

The Mailing List Filter Program

In Chap. 27 under the heading "A Special Technique: Data Coding," you created a special data file that contained names and addresses. The filter below called PRNTLIST.BAT will take sorted or filtered data from this file and print mailing labels. This file assumes that the labels are standard 1- by 3-inch, continuous feed, single-column labels. It also assumes the following line format for the file:

Field	Column
Search code	1 through 10
Name	11 through 30
Address	31 through 55
City,state,zip	56 through 80

The Space Bar and not the Tab key must be pressed between fields. It is also best to create the file in uppercase characters to improve sorting and searching.

To use the filter, type the following on the command line after you have alligned the print head on your printer to the position at which the first line is to be printed:

BASICA PRNTLIST < (maillist file name)

The program listing is:

```
 10 'PRNTLIST (prints mailing labels input from a DOS file)
 20 'by Tom Sheldon
 30 '-------------------------------------------------------
 40 ON ERROR GOTO 160                'check for end of input
 50 X$ = INPUT$(1)                       'get a character
 60 IF X$ = CHR$(13) THEN 90      'check for carriage return
 70 TEXT$ = TEXT$ + X$                  'build text string
 80 GOTO 50                        'go get more characters
 90 LPRINT MID$(TEXT$,11,20)               'print name
100 LPRINT MID$(TEXT$,31,25)              'print address
110 LPRINT MID$(TEXT$,56,25)      'print city, state, zip
120 LPRINT:LPRINT:LPRINT          'advance to next label
130 TEXT$ = ""                         'clear string
140 X$ = INPUT$(1)                'throw out extra line feed
150 GOTO 50                'get next name until end of file
160 END
```

We hope we have inspired you with the filter programs shown above. BASIC provides you with a way to create elaborate filters for text files and other files. For instance, you can create a filter that displays a count of the frequency of each word in a file. Another filter could add numbers in a text file.

33

Structure of DOS

Your operating system may seem like an abstraction at times. It is something you must have but rarely see. An operating system, however, is the most important piece of software you have. The operating system interacts between you and the actual hardware of the computer. With it, you can direct the computer to do what you want and in a language that you understand.

The operating system also provides a link for applications programs. They are able to run on your computer by interacting with it. This makes the whole job of designing software much easier for manufacturers and also provides a standard environment for software developers to work in. The benefit to you is a proliferation of applications software available to run on your PC.

Internally, your computer only knows two states: 1 and 0. Strings of these 1s and 0s are combined in various ways, forming a sort of code that the computer understands. In the early days of computing, systems programmers entered commands into the computer by placing switches on the outside of the computer in either on or off states. This was how computers were coded. Eventually, it was realized that the code being entered would probably be used again or could be used by someone else. So a set of standard coding routines was developed that handled the more common types of input and output to computers, making the job of programming much easier and more reliable.

Operating systems grew from those early routines. Today, operating systems help insulate the programmers from the actual hardware of the machine, allowing them to call on a set of standard routines that handle the components of the computer, such as memory, disk storage, and screen display. In today's world of proliferating microcomputers, operating systems also help insulate the novice or inexperienced computer user from the technical details of computer operation.

DOS consists of several main components. These components are placed in a specific location on the diskette and in the computer's memory when it is running. This chapter explains what each of the DOS components do. Although this information is not essential to the operation of your computer, it is helpful to understand what is going on "behind the scenes."

Tasks of an Operating System

DOS is similar to all other operating systems when you consider its functional components and not its special features, utilities, commands, and enhancements. Most microcomputer operating systems perform the following functions:

- Command and program execution
- Input and output
- Memory management
- File and disk management
- Boot up

Command and Program Execution

After you boot your system, the DOS prompt appears, indicating that DOS is waiting for you to enter a command. When you enter a command at the prompt, the DOS command processor, or "Executive," responds by first locating the command or program in memory or on disk. The Executive loads the program into memory if it is not already there. Control is then passed to the program. All of these functions are performed by COMMAND.COM in DOS.

The Executive has the job of interfacing between you and the rest of the functions in the operating system. It handles the task of interpreting whether the command you entered is correctly typed and whether the command exists. The Executive also looks for parameters you may have entered on the command line, such as switches or batch file parameters.

Input and Output

The I/O functions are remnants from the earliest operating systems. They provide the basic routines for moving information within the system and for receiving and sending information to and from devices. The I/O handler keeps track of the devices attached to the system and coordinates the flow of information among them.

Transferring information between devices is much more complicated than you might think. Programming these functions is very tedious, so the operating system provides a standard set of routines that allow programmers to easily perform I/O routines, cutting down on development time. Input and output are handled in DOS by the physical components MSDOS.SYS (IBMDOS.COM) and IO.SYS (IBMBIO.COM), which are the hidden files stored on the DOS disk.

Memory Management

The memory management capabilities of DOS allocate your system's memory to software and the data that it uses. The location of various DOS routines and command files are logged and protected from being erased if necessary. As memory is freed up, it is allocated to new software. The memory management functions are performed in the system by the physical components of MSDOS.SYS (IBMDOS.COM).

File and Disk Management

Handling diskettes is one of the more sophisticated functions of DOS. The file routines keep track of data and group it for storage on disk into structures called files. The routines also keep track of where files are on diskette and retrieve information from files when requested. The file manager also maintains the disk directory. When files are erased on a disk, it is the job of the file manager to reallocate the open space to new files. The functions of the file manager are contained in MSDOS.SYS (IBMDOS.COM).

Boot Up

The boot loader "kick starts" DOS. It is responsible for loading the rest of the DOS system files into memory. Once the system is loaded, it is no longer used and is discarded from memory. The boot loader is located on the first sector of a bootable disk.

Physical Components

DOS consist of the following physical components. In this section, we will describe each of the following:

- Boot loader
- IO.SYS (IBMBIO.SYS)
- MSDOS.SYS (IBMDOS.SYS)
- COMMAND.COM

The Boot Loader

The boot loader helps get the system up and running. It is located in the first sector of every disk that has been formatted as a bootable disk. When the system is started, the boot loader is placed in the system memory. The boot loader contains information about the format of the disk in the boot drive. It knows where the rest of the boot files are and how to load them. It causes the IO.SYS and MSDOS.SYS files to be loaded from the disk. Control is then passed to IO.SYS and the boot loader is no longer used.

IO.SYS (IBMBIO.SYS)

IO.SYS receives instructions from MSDOS.SYS and interprets those instructions. IO.SYS performs most of the work from there. It issues the specific instructions used by the microprocessor to perform tasks. The instructions issued by IO.SYS include information about what hardware should be used and how the hardware should operate.

IO.SYS is able to translate the more general instructions issued by MSDOS.SYS into specific instructions required by the computer hardware. IO.SYS is hardware dependent. In other words, every version of DOS comes with a special IO.SYS that matches the computer it will run on. In many cases, however, MS-DOS machines will be hardware compatible. Differences in hardware usually crop up in the keyboard and disk drives as well as in the microprocessor itself in some cases.

MSDOS.SYS (IBMDOS.COM)

MSDOS.SYS is considered the director of the system. As described above, it sends commands to IO.SYS so that they may be translated for use on the existing hardware. MSDOS.SYS is considered hardware independent because it performs most of its function without regard for the physical characteristics of the system.

MSDOS.SYS provides a high level interface for programs. Since it provides "calls" that programmers can use to perform certain built-in functions, it eases the task of writing DOS compatible programs.

COMMAND.COM

COMMAND.COM is the Executive controller of the system. It acts as the interface between the user and the rest of the operating system. It is the tip of the iceberg and the only part of the DOS system that the user sees. COMMAND.COM is sometimes referred to as the "command interpreter," the "console command processor," or the "shell." It consists of a resident portion and a transient portion.

The resident portion of COMMAND.COM includes the software that enables the system to load programs and batch files, among other things. It also allows you to interrupt programs using Ctrl-Break. This portion always remains resident in memory, unlike the transient portion. The transient portion of COMMAND.COM contains programs that may be overwritten by other programs. The resident portion contains the routines to reload the transient portion if it has been overwritten.

The transient portion of COMMAND.COM includes the resident DOS commands such as DIR, CLS, PATH, and COPY. The transient portion is loaded high in memory. It contains the internal command processors and the batch file processor. It also displays the system prompt, reads commands from the command line, and causes the commands to be executed by passing them to MSDOS.SYS.

The transient portion resides in a portion of memory that may be overwritten by transient commands such as DISKCOPY.COM. This feature allows large programs to be loaded in systems that only have a small amount of memory. When the transient program ends, the resident portion of COMMAND.COM causes the transient portion to be reloaded. If COMMAND.COM is not on the current disk, the user is prompted to insert a disk containing the file.

Behavior of the System During Boot Up

During the boot process, several steps occur to get the system up and running. These steps are described briefly here:

1. Boot up begins when the user turns the systems on or reboots with Ctrl-Alt-Del.

2. The boot loader is copied to memory. Control is passed to it.

3. The boot loader program loads IO.SYS and MSDOS.SYS into memory and transfers control to IO.SYS.

4. IO.SYS initializes the hardware devices.

5. MSDOS.SYS is initialized. The DOS version number and copyright message is displayed on the screen.

6. The system searches for the CONFIG.SYS file on the disk. If it is found, MSDOS.SYS is modified according to the subcommand in the file.

7. The system searches for COMMAND.COM.

   a. If COMMAND.COM exists in the ROOT directory of the default drive, it is loaded into memory and control is passed to it.

   b. If a different COMMAND.COM was specified in CONFIG.SYS, it is loaded into memory and control is passed to it.

  c. If COMMAND.COM does not exist, the message "Bad or missing command interpreter" appears on the screen.

8. COMMAND.COM looks for the AUTOEXEC.BAT file. If it exists, the commands in the file are executed. If it doesn't exist, DATE and TIME are executed, and the DOS system prompt is displayed.

System Behavior after Boot Up

If the boot up is successful, the DOS prompt appears on the screen indicating that DOS is waiting for a command. The following steps are performed by DOS when a command is executed:

1. The user enters a command at the system prompt.

2. COMMAND.COM receives the command.

3. COMMAND.COM scans the command line and compares it with the resident commands contained within memory such as DIR, COPY, and ERASE.

4. If the command is in memory, it is executed immediately.

5. If the command is not in memory, COMMAND.COM examines the directory of the disk in the default drive or the drive specified in the command line.

   a. If the drive specified contains a single file that matches the command, the program is executed.

   b. If the drive contains several command files with the same name, the file containing the highest priority is executed. Files with the extension of .COM have the highest priority, followed by .EXE files, and then .BAT files.

   c. If the command file is not on the drive, the message "Bad command or file name" appears.

These are the routines and processes that happen behind the scene whenever you are working with your system. As mentioned, you don't really need to know how DOS operates at this level, but it is interesting to know the different levels of control that DOS uses to execute a command. Through this discussion, you probably have a better understanding of the importance of DOS.

Desktop Workstation

Now that you are familiar with DOS, its time to bring all of the lessons, concepts, and utilities together. You can start thinking of your PC as a desktop workstation, with DOS at the center, providing enhancements and convenience. By now you've seen the power that can be obtained from DOS when all of its features are combined. The database routines, the batch files, the DOS commands, the menus, and the key assignments all work together to make DOS the most important piece of software you can own.

Putting It All Together

Let's review some of the major utilities, tips, and techniques we covered in the book and see how they can be combined to make your PC a desktop workstation. The idea is to create a DOS boot/utility disk that you use to start your system every day. When you turn your computer on in the morning, messages stored previously are displayed. After reading the messages, you can review notes and memos or an appointment file. As you need to look up phone numbers, you can refer to your phone number file. When you need important information, you can quickly refer to your database.

To start, format a new disk and place the most-used DOS command files on it. Since you will be saving other files to this disk, you should keep excess files to a minimum. Next, create a subdirectory for the phone management system discussed in Chaps. 12 and 26. You can also create a subdirectory for a database system like the one discussed in Chap. 27.

If you have a RAM drive and are working with a data management system similar to the ones discussed in Chap. 27, you may want to consider adding a line to your AUTOEXEC.BAT file that copies the data files to the RAM drive. This way, you will have the data at your fingertips all day in an area in which it can be quickly accessed.

To create an automatic message center, refer to "Log-on Messages" and "Sending and Receiving Mail" in Chap. 26. Using these utilities, you can write messages to yourself (or other users) that will be displayed on any given date.

The DOS menu system created in Chaps. 22 and 23 is a great way to organize your system if you like menus. Keep in mind that a menu system may be slow on floppy-disk systems. You can operate with the menus until you get used to your system and then delete them. The utility batch files discussed under "Some Handy Utilities" in Chap. 22 are helpful on any system. The DOS command and syntax menus created in Chap. 13 and App. E are also very helpful.

Now that you know that so much can be done with DOS, we hope you will explore further—and enjoy your system even more.

ASCII Codes

Characters typed into the computer, displayed on the screen, sent over phone lines, or stored on disk are all coded. This coding follows a standard established by the American National Standards Institute (ANSI) and is known as ASCII, an acronym for American Standard Code for Information Interchange. Almost all American and some foreign computer manufacturers support the ASCII code set.

Seven bits are used in the ASCII scheme to code 96 printable characters and 32 control characters. This gives us a total of 128 standard codes. IBM has added an extra set of codes to their personal computer that is known as the extended ASCII set. These character codes represent various graphics, Greek, and mathematical symbols. In total, the PC has 256 distinct codes.

Figure A-1 lists the ASCII codes and characters that are available on the IBM PC and most compatable units. The column headed "Control Character" lists the standard interpretations of ASCII codes 0 to 31, which are used for control and communications purposes.

Each of these characters may be entered from the keyboard by pressing and holding the Alt key down while keying in the ASCII code for the character on the numeric keypad. Some of the codes have special meaning and will not display a character on the screen.

ASCII value	Character	Control character	ASCII value	Character
000	(null)	NUL	032	(space)
001	☺	SOH	033	!
002	●	STX	034	''
003	♥	ETX	035	#
004	♦	EOT	036	$
005	♣	ENQ	037	%
006	♠	ACK	038	&
007	(beep)	BEL	039	'
008	◘	BS	040	(
009	(tab)	HT	041	)
010	(line feed)	LF	042	*
011	(home)	VT	043	+
012	(form feed)	FF	044	,
013	(carriage return)	CR	045	-
014	♫	SO	046	.
015	☼	SI	047	/
016	►	DLE	048	0
017	◄	DC1	049	1
018	↕	DC2	050	2
019	!!	DC3	051	3
020	¶	DC4	052	4
021	§	NAK	053	5
022	▬	SYN	054	6
023	↨	ETB	055	7
024	↑	CAN	056	8
025	↓	EM	057	9
026	→	SUB	058	:
027	←	ESC	059	;
028	(cursor right)	FS	060	<
029	(cursor left)	GS	061	=
030	(cursor up)	RS	062	>
031	(cursor down)	US	063	?

Figure A-1

ASCII value	Character	ASCII value	Character	ASCII value	Character
064	@	096	`	128	Ç
065	A	097	a	129	ü
066	B	098	b	130	é
067	C	099	c	131	â
068	D	100	d	132	ä
069	E	101	e	133	à
070	F	102	f	134	å
071	G	103	g	135	ç
072	H	104	h	136	ê
073	I	105	i	137	ë
074	J	106	j	138	è
075	K	107	k	139	ï
076	L	108	l	140	î
077	M	109	m	141	ì
078	N	110	n	142	Ä
079	O	111	o	143	Å
080	P	112	p	144	É
081	Q	113	q	145	æ
082	R	114	r	146	Æ
083	S	115	s	147	ô
084	T	116	t	148	ö
085	U	117	u	149	ò
086	V	118	v	150	û
087	W	119	w	151	ù
088	X	120	x	152	ÿ
089	Y	121	y	153	Ö
090	Z	122	z	154	Ü
091	[	123	{	155	¢
092	\	124	|	156	£
093	]	125	}	157	¥
094	∧	126	~	158	Pt
095	—	127	△	159	ƒ

Figure A-1 *(Continued)*

ASCII value	Character	ASCII value	Character	ASCII value	Character
160	á	192	∟	224	α
161	í	193	⊥	225	β
162	ó	194	⊤	226	Γ
163	ú	195	├	227	π
164	ñ	196	—	228	Σ
165	Ñ	197	+	229	σ
166	ª	198	╞	230	μ
167	º	199	╟	231	τ
168	¿	200	╚	232	Φ̄
169	⌐	201	╔	233	⊖
170	¬	202	╩	234	Ω
171	½	203	╦	235	δ
172	¼	204	╠	236	∞
173	¡	205	═	237	Ø
174	⟨⟨	206	╬	238	ε
175	⟩⟩	207	╧	239	∩
176	░	208	╨	240	≡
177	▒	209	╤	241	±
178	▓	210	╥	242	≥
179	│	211	╙	243	≤
180	┤	212	╘	244	⌠
181	╡	213	╒	245	⌡
182	╢	214	╓	246	÷
183	╖	215	╫	247	≈
184	╕	216	╪	248	°
185	╣	217	┘	249	•
186	║	218	┌	250	·
187	╗	219	█	251	√
188	╝	220	▄	252	ⁿ
189	╜	221	▌	253	²
190	╛	222	▐	254	■
191	┐	223	▀	255	(blank 'FF')

Figure A-1 *(Continued)*

B

IBM Graphics Set

╔ 201	╦ 203	╗ 187	┌ 218	┬ 194	┐ 191
╠ 204	╬ 206	╣ 185	├ 195	┼ 197	┤ 180
╚ 200	╩ 202	╝ 188	└ 192	┴ 193	┘ 217
	║ 186	═ 205	│ 179	─ 196	

╒ 213	╤ 209	╕ 184	╓ 214	╥ 210	╖ 183
╞ 198	╪ 216	╡ 181	╟ 199	╫ 215	╢ 182
╘ 212	╧ 207	╛ 190	╙ 211	╨ 208	╜ 189

176	177	178	219	220	221	222	223

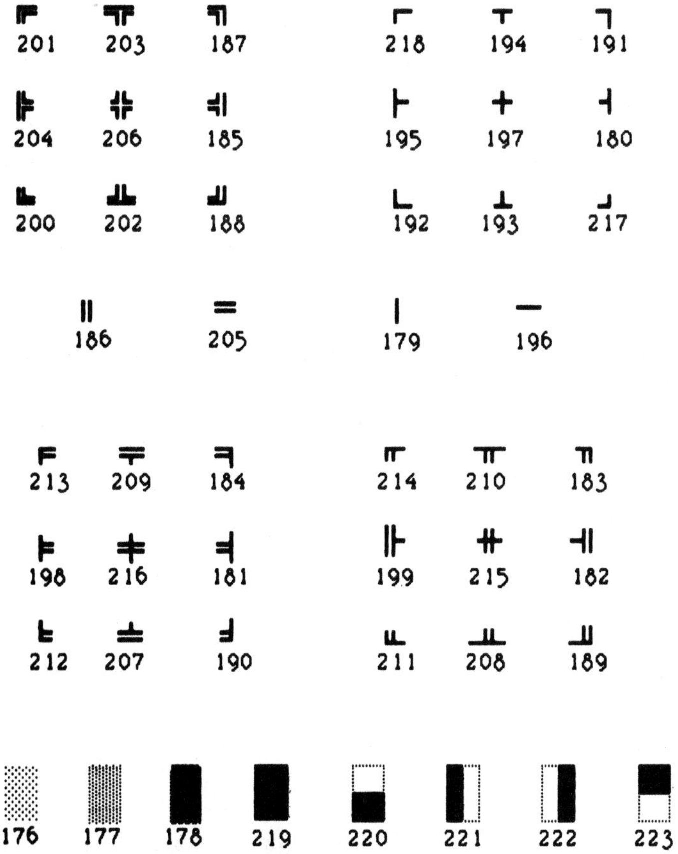

Figure B-1 Extended ASCII code.

Graphics Key Reassignment

The key assignments shown in Fig. C-1 can be assigned by creating the following file. A full description of key assignments is given in Chap. 21. Briefly, the simplest way to build the file is to type the first line and then make 10 more copies of it, using the EDLIN COPY command. Once you have 10 identical lines, you can edit each line, adding the code shown below.

To create the first line, type **Ctrl-V** and [to get the Escape code, followed by **[0;** and the rest of the string as shown below. To obtain the graphics characters shown on the keys in Fig. C-1, hold down the **Alt** key while entering the number shown between the brackets.

After creating the file, display it on the screen using the TYPE command to set the key assignments. The ANSI.SYS driver must be installed for the key reassignments to take effect, as covered in Chap. 21.

```
EDLIN GRAPHIC.KYS
 1:^[[0;104;"<Alt-201>"p
 2:^[[0;110;"<Alt-203>"p
 3:^[[0;105;"<Alt-187>"p
 4:^[[0;111;"<Alt-205>"p
 5:^[[0;108;"<Alt-204>"p
 6:^[[0;93;"<Alt-206>"p
 7:^[[0;109;"<Alt-185>"p
 8:^[[0;113;"<Alt-186>"p
 9:^[[0;106;"<Alt-200>"p
10:^[[0;112;"<Alt-202>"p
11:^[[0;107;"<Alt-188>"p
```

The next file is used to deassign the keys assigned by GRAPHIC.KYS. To create this file, make a copy of GRAPHIC.KYS, renaming it ERASE.KYS in the process. Edit each line, removing the character that

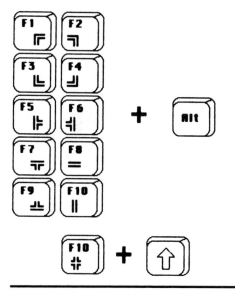

Figure C-1

appears between the quotes. To erase key assignments created by GRAPHIC.KYS, use the TYPE command to display ERASE.KYS on the screen. This will cause the key assigned by the previous file to be deassigned.

EDLIN ERASE.KYS

```
1:^[[0;104;""p
2:^[[0;110;""p
3:^[[0;105;""p
5:^[[0;108;""p
6:^[[0;93;""p
7:^[[0;109;""p
8:^[[0;113;""p
9:^[[0;106;""p
10:^[[0;112;""p
11:^[[0;107;""p
```

Appendix

Examples of Using the Editing Keys

Various way of using the DOS editing keys are listed below. For a complete description of these keys, refer to Chap. 3.

Example 1

There is a file called MYFILE.TXT on the disk in drive B that you want to copy to drive A. You type in the command COPY MYFILE.TXT but realize that you forgot the drive specifier before the file name. To correct this mistake, you can backspace and retype, or you can press the following key sequence:

1. Press F5 to copy the text, as it is, into the template. The template now holds COPY MYFILE.TXT.
2. Press F2 and M to copy the template out to the position at which B: needs to be inserted.
3. Type B: and press the F3 key to copy the rest of the template. Then press Return to execute the command.

Example 2

The previous example fixed a command with only a few characters. It might have been easier to backspace and retype. But consider the following command, which copies files from one directory to another:

COPY A:\MYGAMES\ZAP1 B:\ZAP1GAME

This command involves a lot of typing. It copies a game called ZAP1, which resides in the subdirectory A:\MYGAMES, to a subdirectory called B:\ZAP1GAME. Assume that you have issued the command and now need to copy another game file in the MYGAME directory called ZAP2 to a subdirectory on B called \ZAP2GAME. Since only two characters need to be changed in the existing template, you should edit it to create the new command.

Assume the following command is in the template:

```
COPY A:\MYGAMES\ZAP1 B:\ZAP1GAME
```

You would then:

1. Press F2 and 1 to copy the template out to the first 1. Type in a 2 to replace the 1.
3. Press F2 again and press 1 to copy out to the next 1 in the template. Replace this with a 2.
4. Press the F3 key to copy out the rest of the template and press Return.

Using the editing keys, you were able to reissue the command with only 7 keystrokes instead of 30.

Example 3

Here's another example. You are racing along, typing a command that will copy a file from the disk in drive A to the disk in drive B. You are about to press Return when you realize you forgot to check the other disk and see if a file already exists with the same file name. To correct, press the Esc key to cancel the command you were typing and enter your next command.

Example 4

In this example, you are copying individual files to a backup disk and then erasing the originals. You can use the editing keys to change the command COPY to DEL on the command line and avoid retyping the file name. Suppose you enter the following command to copy the first file:

```
COPY MYFILE.TXT B:
```

The COPY command is now in the template and the original file has been copied to the disk in drive B. It may now be erased on the original.

DEL is another name for ERASE. The two can be used interchangeably. In this example we will use DEL.

1. Type DEL at the DOS prompt.

2. Press the Del key (don't confuse DEL with the Del key) to remove the fourth character in the template, which is the Y in COPY.

3. Now press the F3 key to copy the rest of the template.

The DEL command will ignore the B: at the end of the line since it only recognizes one parameter. This example demonstrates a quick way to copy and then erase files with minimum of typing. If the file names are also similar, other parts of the template may be copied.

A Help Screen for Command Syntax

The following help screen can be created with COPY CON or EDLIN. You can then display it any time when you need help in issuing a DOS command. To display the screen type:

TYPE SYNTAX.MNU

To enter the menu, type the following:

```
A:\>COPY CON:SYNTAX.MNU
ASSIGN [x=y]    (y is the substitute drive)
BACKUP d:[path][file name[.ext]] d:[/S][/M][A][D:mm-dd-yy]
BREAK [ON][OFF]
CHDIR [[d:]path]    (or, CD [[d:]path])
CHKDSK [d:][file name[.ext]][/F][/V]
COMP [d:][path][file name[.ext]] [d:]path][file name[.ext]]
CTTY device-name
DIR [d:][path][file name][.ext][/P][/W]
DISKCOMP [d:][d:][/1][/8]
DISKCOPY [d:][d:][/1]
ERASE [d:][path][file name[.ext]]    (or, DEL)
FIND [/V][/C][/N] string [[d:][path]file name[.ext]...]
FORMAT [d:][/S][/1][/8][/V][/B]
MKDIR [d:]path    (or, MD [d:]path)
PATH [[d:]path[[; [d:]path]...]]
PRINT [[d:][file name[.ext]][/T][/C][/P]...]
RECOVER [d:][path]file name[.ext]    (or, RECOVER d:)
REN[AME] [d:][path]filename[.ext] file name[.ext]
RESTORE d: [d:][path][filename[.ext]][/S][/P]
RMDIR [d:]path    (or, RD [d:]path)
SET [name = [parameter]]
SORT [/R][/+n]
TREE [d:][/F]
TYPE [d:][path]file name[.ext]
```

You can use the FIND command to locate specific items in the file. For instance, to locate information on the FORMAT command, you can type:

```
A : \>FIND "FORMAT" SYNTAX.MNU
```

To save yourself a lot of typing, you can create a batch file that will make the task easier:

```
A : \>COPY CON:SYNTAX.BAT
FIND "%1" SYNTAX.MNU

A : \>_
```

Now all you have to type to see the syntax of the FORMAT command is:

```
A : \>SYNTAX FORMAT
```

The keyword FORMAT will be placed in the position of parameter %1 and the command will display the line containing the keyword FORMAT.

Refer to Chap. 22 for information on using this menu with a system of menus that is used to organize a filing system.

DOS Extended Keyboard and Screen Controls

The following list of special character sequences can be used from within a program to control screen cursor positioning, screen attributes, and the meaning of any key on the keyboard. To use any of the Escape codes, the ANSI.SYS device driver must be loaded. The American National Standards Institute (ANSI) has specified a set of standard Escape sequences that a program can use to control the screen and keyboard (the standard input and output). Having a standard set of these sequences allows programmers to create programs that can be used on any machine that follows the ANSI standard. The Escape sequences shown below are part of that standard set. Many are meant to be used by programmers, although you may find them useful while working with DOS. For instance, if you have a color monitor, you can change the foreground and background colors of your screen.

Cursor Positioning

CUP, Cursor Position

ESC[#;#H   Sets the horizontal and vertical (x/y coordinates) positions of the cursor. The first variable can have a value of 1 to 25, which corresponds to the number of horizontal lines on the screen, and the second variable can have a value of 1 to 80, which corresponds to the number of characters that can be displayed across the screen (1 to 40 if in 40 by 25 display mode). The default value for both variables is 1. If no value or 0 (nul) is specified, the cursor returns to its home position at the top left corner of the screen.

CUU, Cursor Up

ESC[#A   Moves the cursor up by the number of lines specified. The variable can have a value of 1 to 24; the default is 1.

CUD, Cursor Down

ESC[#B   Moves the cursor down by the number of lines specified. The variable can have a value of 1 to 24; the default is 1.

CUF, Cursor Forward

ESC[#C   Moves the cursor to the right by the number of columns specified. The variable can have a value of 1 to 79 (or 1 to 39); the default is 1.

CUB, Cursor Backward

ESC[#D   Moves the cursor to the left by the number of columns specified. The variable can have a value of 1 to 79 (or 1 to 39); the default is 1.

HVP, Horizontal/Vertical Position

ESC[#;#f   Changes the horizontal and vertical position of the cursor. The first variable can have a value of 1 to 25; the second, a variable of 1 to 80 (or 1 to 40); the default for both is 1.

DSR, Device Status Report

ESC[6n   Requests a cursor position status report. The computer replies with the following: ESC[#;#R. The first variable gives the horizontal position of the cursor, and the second variable gives the vertical position.

SCP, Save Cursor Position

ESC[s   Saves the cursor position for later recall.

RCP, Restore Cursor Position

ESC[u   Restores the cursor to the position saved by SCP.

ED, Erase Display

ESC[2J   Erases the entire display and positions the cursor at the home position.

EL, Erase Line

ESC[k   Erases a line from the cursor position forward (to the right).

Screen Display Options

SGR, Set Graphics Rendition

ESC[#;...;#m   Sets various screen modes (display, background, and foreground characteristics) for displaying graphics. The variables can be replaced with any combination of values from the following list:

0	All attributes off
1	High intensity (boldface) on
4	Underscore (underline) on
5	Blinking on
7	Inverse video on
8	Invisible display
30	Foreground black
31	Foreground red
32	Foreground green
33	Foreground yellow
34	Foreground blue
35	Foreground magenta
37	Foreground white
40	Background black
41	Background red
42	Background green
43	Background yellow
44	Background blue
45	Background magenta
46	Background cyan
47	Background white

SM, Set Mode

ESC [= #h. Variances: ESC [= h, ESC [= Oh, and ESC [?7h   Sets the screen width or type specified by the parameter:

0   40 × 25 black and white
1   40 × 25 color
2   80 × 25 black and white
3   80 × 25 color
4   320 × 200 color
5   320 × 200 black and white
6   640 × 200 black and white
7   Wrap at end of line

RM, Reset Mode

ESC [= #1. Variances: ESC [= 1, ESC [= 01, and ESC [?71   The parameters are the same as those listed above under SM except that parameter 7 causes characters past the end of line to be discarded.

Some examples of how to use these features are shown below. First, make sure ANSI.SYS is installed by including the command DEVICE = ANSI.SYS in the CONFIG.SYS file. The following prompt will set a yellow foreground with a blue background on a color graphics monitor:

PROMPT $e[33;44m

The next example sets the 640 × 200 black and white graphics mode on a color graphics display:

PROMPT $e[= 6h

Other Software

The following disk is available from the author:

PUBLIC DOMAIN DOS UTILITIES
$7—Covers shipping, handling, and disk cost. It includes a screen save program,
IBM's RAM drives, Scroll Lock programs, subdirectory file search program, file
cleaning utility (converts WordStar files to ASCII), and more.

Tom Sheldon/DOS Utilities
P.O. Box 902
Santa Barbara, CA 93102

Index